Intelligent Management Support Systems

Intelligent Management
Support Systems

Hossein Bidgoli

Q

QUORUM BOOKS
Westport, Connecticut • London

Library of Congress Cataloging-in-Publication Data

Bidgoli, Hossein.
 Intelligent management support systems / Hossein Bidgoli.
  p.   cm.
 Includes bibliographical references and index.
 ISBN 1–56720–176–8 (alk. paper)
 1. Management information systems.   2. Decision support systems.
 I. Title.
 HD30.213.B53   1998
 658.4'038—dc21   97–13411

British Library Cataloguing in Publication Data is available.

Library of Congress Catalog Card Number: 97–13411
ISBN: 1–56720–176–8

First published in 1998

Quorum Books, 88 Post Road West, Westport, CT 06881
An imprint of Greenwood Publishing Group, Inc.

Printed in the United States of America

The paper used in this book complies with the
Permanent Paper Standard issued by the National
Information Standards Organization (Z39.48–1984).

10   9   8   7   6   5   4   3   2   1

*To so many fine memories of
my brother Mohsen
for his uncompromising belief
in the power of education*

Contents

Illustrations

FIGURES

TABLES

Acknowledgments

Several colleagues reviewed different versions of this manuscript and made constructive suggestions. Without their assistance the text could not have reached in its present shape. Their help and comments are greatly appreciated.

Many different groups assisted me in completing this project. I am grateful to students in my undergraduate and graduate classes who have provided feedback. Also, executives who attended my seminars on information systems provided me with insights regarding the practicality of the materials. They helped me fine tune the manuscript during its various stages. My friend and colleague Andrew Prestage assisted me with some of the art presented in the text. As always his support is appreciated.

A group of professionals from the Greenwood Publishing Group assisted me in various stages in completing this text. Eric Valentine, publisher, had faith in this project since its inception, and Alan Sturmer, my acquisitions editor, assisted me in putting finishing touches on it. John Beck and his colleagues provided editorial and publishing assistance. I appreciate their help.

Last, but not least, I want to thank my wonderful wife Nooshin and my two lovely children Mohsen and Morvareed for being so patient during this venture. Also, my two sisters Azam and Akram provided moral support as always. I am grateful to all for their support.

CHAPTER 1

Intelligent Management Support Systems at a Glance

This chapter reviews decision support systems, elaborating on their unique characteristics as compared with electronic data processing and management information systems. It defines expert systems and discusses the costs and benefits of decision support systems and expert systems. Products readily available on the market have improved the design and implementation of these systems. This chapter also provides a sample of these packages (products) for future reference and introduces other management support systems, including executive information systems, group support systems, geographic information systems, neural networks, fuzzy logic, and genetic algorithms. As you will see in the forthcoming chapters, all of these technologies have potential for assisting decision makers in implementing organizational decisions. This chapter concludes with an examination of the past and provides an outlook for management support systems. Chapters 2 through 10 discuss the material in this chapter in greater detail.

INTELLIGENT MANAGEMENT SUPPORT SYSTEMS: A SURVEY

For the past fifty years, various applications of computer technology have assisted decision makers in making diverse decisions in a broad range of business activities. Although these systems have a lot in common and utilize more or less the same kind of technologies, each system is designed with a unique goal. In this book we call these systems collectively management support systems (MSS). Among these systems, decision support systems (DSS) and expert systems (ES) have been the most successful types of applications. DSS and ES, as you will learn in this book, share many common features and complement one another.

In recent years, a number of integrated or hybrid systems have been introduced. These systems try to utilize the strong features of various management support systems, such as neural networks, fuzzy logic, and expert systems, in order to present a unified solution to a number of business needs. The integration of DSS, ES, fuzzy logic, and neural computing is an example of a hybrid system. Figure 1.1 presents these various applications.

Figure 1.1
Intelligent Management Support Systems

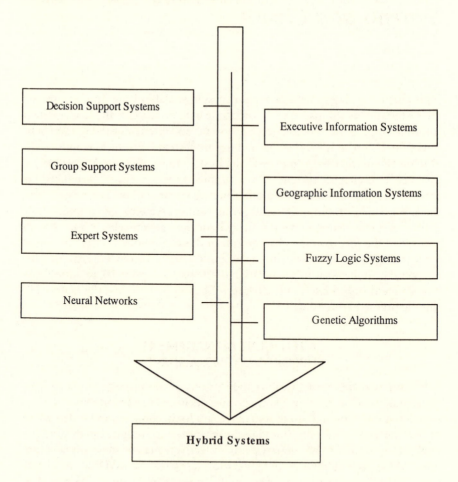

BACKGROUND FOR DSS

In recent years, several interesting applications of decision support and information technology in general have been successfully implemented in real-life situations. We refer to these systems as intelligent management support systems (IMSS). A careful examination of these systems reveals that they perform well beyond traditional record keeping, data storage, and retrieval systems. Each provides unique decision-making support [3].

When a United Parcel Service (UPS) package got lost, finding out who signed for it used to mean an extensive search through paper receipts. Now UPS customers sign on a hand-held computer. Once a day, UPS drivers transmit the signatures to Mahwah, New Jersey, where they can easily be viewed the next day.

To overcome cost advantages in purchasing and distribution that a larger competitor, K-Mart, had in the early 1980s, Wal-Mart started using computer networks to establish tight links among suppliers, warehouses, and stores. Using this process, Wal-Mart reduces inventories and keeps costs down.

To improve service and shorten check-in lines, the Hyatt Hotel chain allows guests to check in by phone. To do this, Hyatt established a toll-free telephone center, with a data link to every hotel in the chain. This procedure gives each hotel operator access to hotel and customer information from the other hotels in the chain.

For the past fifty years, electronic data processing has been applied to structured tasks. These systems are primarily suitable for record keeping, simple clerical operations, and inventory control. Payroll, for example, was one of the first applications to be automated. The emphasis in these systems has been in data collection and data processing. To perform such tasks, there is always a well-defined standard operating procedure. For example, in the payroll calculations the number of hours is multiplied by the pay rate and deductions are subtracted to calculate the net pay.

MIS, since their inception in the mid-1960s, have been utilized for information processing. The objective of these systems has been the production of timely, accurate, and useful information for middle management on a scheduled basis. MIS, though it supplies more information, lacks flexibility and is not suitable for "ad hoc" applications. However, the majority of MIS are becoming more flexible and more suitable for "ad hoc" applications. This is due to the sophistication in hardware and software technologies and users' requirements. An inventory system that produces weekly, biweekly, and monthly reports regarding the various inventory statuses is a good example of a MIS. These reports are generated on a regular basis, regardless of what the inventory status is.

Although much has been written over the past few years about DSS, there is no common or accepted definition for them; they have been defined in many different ways. Most experts define a DSS as any computer-based information system that helps decision makers with semistructured and unstructured tasks.

Decision support systems have been applied to many different disciplines, including manufacturing, marketing, human resource management, strategic planning, accounting, small business, and so forth. The power of these systems has been demonstrated in the business world, leading many to conclude that DSS is the way of the future. The decreasing cost and the increasing sophistication of both hardware and software have made these systems available not only to large organizations, but small businesses as well.

WHAT IS A DSS?

Keen and Scott-Morton offer this comprehensive description of a DSS [9]: "A DSS is a coherent system of computer-based technology (hardware, software and supporting documentation) used by managers as an aid to their decision-making in semi-structured decision tasks." For our purpose, we define DSS as a computer-based information system consisting of hardware, software, and the human element designed to assist any decision maker at any organizational level. However, the emphasis is on semistructured and unstructured tasks. This simple definition underscores several requirements for a DSS:

- DSS requires hardware;
- DSS requires software;
- DSS requires human elements (designers, programmers, and users);
- DSS is designed to support decision making;
- DSS should help decision makers at all organizational levels;
- DSS emphasizes semistructured and unstructured tasks.

DSS differs from traditional EDP and MIS in many ways. For example, Keen and Scott-Morton [9] address the distinction between EDP/MIS and DSS. They describe DSS as the use of computers to

- assist the manager in the decision making process for semistructured tasks;
- support, rather than replace, managerial judgment;
- improve the effectiveness of decision making rather than its efficiency.

They describe the characteristics of MIS somewhat differently:

- Efficiency through cost reduction is the key point.
- The emphasis is on structured tasks.
- Data storage, access, and report generation are the major processing tasks.

Comparing EDP, MIS, and DSS, one can set up a normative approach regarding design and utilization of DSS. The following are some of the key factors that differentiate DSS from the other systems:

- emphasis on semistructured and unstructured decisions versus structured decisions
- emphasis on the present and future versus past
- emphasis on planning versus control
- emphasis on ease of use
- emphasis on active involvement of the users in all phases of design and utilization
- emphasis on internal and external data usage versus internal data usage
- emphasis on the overall efficiency and effectiveness versus on efficiency only

However, you should remember that DSS is not a disjointed technology. It shares a number of common technologies. One can also say that DSS is a natural progression or expansion of EDP and MIS.

DSS APPROACHES

Decision support systems were initially developed from a synthesis of ideas originating from two major engineering institutions. The theoretical studies of organizational decision making were completed at the Carnegie Institute of Technology during the late 1950s and early 1960s, while the technical work on different aspects of computer systems was carried out at the Massachusetts Institute of Technology (MIT) in the early 1960s.

Steven L. Alter [1] surveyed fifty-six systems with DSS characteristics and divided them into a seven-category taxonomy according to their generic operations:

1. file drawer systems
2. data analysis systems
3. analysis information systems
4. accounting models
5. representational models
6. optimization models
7. suggestion models

He further divided them into two groups: data-oriented systems (the first three) and model-oriented (the last four) systems. As you will see later in this chapter, DSS products or generators offer capabilities suited for this taxonomy.

A file drawer system is basically the automated version of a simple file cabinet. The major difference between these systems and file cabinet type systems is improved accuracy and speed.

Data analysis systems perform simple data analysis. An online budgeting system is a good example. The present results of operations can be compared with the past or with a target budget, and variation can be reported.

Analysis information systems utilize a series of decision-oriented databases and small models in order to provide management information. Regional analysis and sales force analysis are two examples of this type of system. These systems can analyze the present situation by using the internal data. They can also generate a forecast for the next period based on the past performance.

Accounting models use definitional relationships and formulas in order to calculate the consequences of a particular action. Any "what-if"analysis-type model can be classified within this group. Sources and uses of funds is one example; break-even analysis is another.

Representational models include simulation models that do not use definitional relationships available in accounting models. A Monte Carlo simulation-type model is one example of this type. The outcome of this type of system is usually the estimation of consequences of a particular action over the entire system. For example, using Monte Carlo simulation one can see the effects of varying the number of operators assigned to a service station.

Optimization models, the most commonly used models, are designed to either maximize the profit or minimize the cost. Any type of allocation model can be classified within this group. Linear programming technique is a good example of this type. We will talk about various mathematical and statistical models in Chapter 3.

Suggestion models are more structured than optimization systems. The output of these systems is the answer to a problem. A good example is a manufacturing control system. Based on a series of constraints and the existing situation, the system will calculate the production mix. This type of system can utilize any kind of model or formula in order to come up with the solution.

The major distinction dividing data-oriented systems and model-oriented systems is that the latter uses modeling analysis and the former uses pure data analysis. To illustrate the differences, consider Tely-Tak, a manufacturer of electronic devices. Tely-Tak has collected the sales data for the past eighteen months from corporate headquarters. Using data-oriented analysis, we can organize these data based on sales regions (e.g., which region has generated the highest sales, which region has generated the lowest sales), or we can organize it based on the performance of different products (e.g., which product has generated the highest total sales, which product has generated the lowest total sales). Up to this point all we have done is the pure manipulation of data. By looking at these data as is, you cannot say anything about the future, nor can you establish any possible relationship among these data items.

Now, let us say we create a regression model using the past eighteen months' sales in order to generate a sales forecast for the next period. In this case we can say we have performed a modeling analysis. By looking at the outcome of this regression model, with relative confidence you can plan for the next budget based on the results of the forecasting model. For example, you may have to hire new salespeople, or you may have to order more raw materials based on this modeling analysis.

Regardless of the type of analysis performed, the objective is providing managerial support for decision making. Throughout this book, we will provide other examples of these types of analyses.

The findings from this fifty-six-system study show that applications are being developed and used to support the decision maker making, justifying, and implementing decisions, rather than to replace the decision maker. In other words, people in a growing number of organizations are using DSS to improve their managerial effectiveness.

DSS CAPABILITIES

In recent years, DSS have appeared in a variety of disciplines. These applications can be categorized under the following major functions [5]:

1. *What-if analysis*: Many analyses can be performed using this approach. The effect of a change in one variable over the entire system can be easily illustrated. If, for example, labor costs increase by 4 percent, what is going to happen to the final cost of a chair? Or if the advertising budget increases by 2 percent, what is the impact on total sales?

2. *Goal-seeking*: This capability is the reverse of what-if analysis. As an example, you may ask, How much should I charge for a particular unit in order to generate $200,000 profit? Or, how much should I advertise in order to generate $50 million total sales?

3. *Sensitivity analysis*: Using this feature will enable you to perform analysis applying different variables. For example, what is the maximum price that you should pay for raw material and still make a profit, or how much overtime can you pay and still be cost effective?

4. *Exception reporting analysis*: This feature will monitor the performance of variables that are outside a predefined range. It would key in on the region that generated the highest total sales or the production center that spent more than the predefined budget.

These are only some of the capabilities of a typical DSS. There are many more analyses and capabilities available, such as graphical analysis, forecasting, simulation, statistical analysis, modeling analysis, and so forth.

DSS PRODUCTS: WHAT IS AVAILABLE?

The available DSS software, or generators, can be classified into two main categories: modeling products and data-management products. Although there is some overlap between these products, each group is still identified by one capability or the other. These products can also be classified as either mainframe-based or micro-based. Recently, the majority of mainframe vendors have been offering micro-based versions of mainframe-based DSS products. Although the micro versions are less powerful than their mainframe counterparts, the gap is narrowing. The following are some of the most popular DSS products on the market.

Mainframe-Based Modeling Products

Accent R by National Information Systems, Inc.

CSP by IBM

Express by Information Resource, Inc.

Focus by Information Builders, Inc.

IFPS by Comshare

Nomad by Must Software, Intl.

Ramis II by On-Line Software

SAS by SAS Institute, Inc.

SPSS by SPSS, Inc.

Micro-Based Modeling Products

Excel by Microsoft Corp.

Lotus 1-2-3 by Lotus Development Corp.

Quattro Pro by Borland Intl.

SAS/PC by SAS Institute, Inc.

SPSS/PC by SPSS, Inc.

Mainframe-Based Data Management Products

DB2 by IBM

IMS, DMS by IBM

Ingres by Ingress Corp.

Oracle by Oracle Corp.

Procol by Procol, Inc.

Progress by Progress Software, Inc.

SQL/DDS by IBM

Micro-Based Data Management Products

DBASE by Borland Intl.

Focus/PC by Information Builder, Inc.

Fox Pro and Access by Microsoft Corp.

Oracle by Oracle Corporation

Paradox by Borland Intl.

EXPERT SYSTEMS: AN OVERVIEW

Expert systems (ES) mimic human expertise in a particular discipline in order to solve a specific problem in a well-defined area. If a problem is not specific, and if it has not been solved previously by an expert or a series of experts,
that problem is not suitable for ES implementation.

While traditional computer-based information systems generate information by using data, models, and well-defined algorithms, ES work with heuristics. Heuristics are sometimes referred to as "rules of thumb," or general knowledge available in a discipline. Heuristic reasoning does not imply formal knowledge but rather considers binding a solution to a problem without following a rigorous algorithm. For example, if I tell you that a canary is a bird, you know that a canary knows how to fly because it is a bird. Or, if I tell you that John owns a horse, you quickly include this animal with other horses and separate it from thousands of other animals.

ES have been around since the 1960s and have been continually improved during the past thirty years. There is a variety of ES on the market. News about ES is kept somewhat secret. Developers of these systems do not reveal detailed information regarding technical capabilities of these systems until their final release. Practitioners and companies who are using these systems are also reluctant to reveal all the successes achieved by these systems due to the competitive advantages that may be gained by the systems' other users. Even with all the secrecy, significant cost savings and successes are reported in the literature [6].

ES, by providing the explanation capabilities and an easy-to-use interface, provide a strong compliment to DSS. By applying the expertise of a human expert, ES can almost duplicate a human expert in situations where human experts are rare, retiring, or dying. PC-based shells (programs that simplify ES construction) have made ES more affordable to even small- and medium-sized organizations. ES have been successfully utilized in many disciplines. The following are some of the popular ES shells on the market. These shells expedite the ES development time and reduce the cost by not programming the entire system from scratch.

- ACQUIRE by Acquire Intelligence, Inc.
- ANGOSS KNOWLEDGE SEEKER by Angoss Software International Ltd.
- BUSINESS INSIGHT by Business Resource Software, Inc.
- DCLASS by CAM Software
- DPL by Applied Decision Analysis
- EZ-EXPERT by Trimmer Software Company
- FORECASTPRO by Business Resource Software, Inc.
- HELPDESK EXPERT AUTOMATION TOOL (HEAT) by Bendata Management Systems
- PENSION PLANNER by Foundation Technologies, Inc.
- ROCKY by Expert Edge Corporation

SURVEY OF ES SUCCESSFUL APPLICATIONS

There are numerous applications of ES that have proven to be successful. ES software began to emerge in 1965. Edward Feigenbaum developed DENDRAL for determining the chemical structure of molecules. In 1969, Martin and Moses at MIT developed MACSYMA, a math ES. The development and application of ES expanded in the 1970s with MYCIN for medical diagnosis of blood infections. Today, various companies are engaged in the research and development of ES. The following is a survey of some of the popular applications of ES [17]:

- aerospace technology: When NASA launched the space shuttle Discovery in 1988, mission control used ES to make flight control decisions.
- airline industry: American Airlines has developed an ES to manage frequent flier transactions.
- banking and finance: Manufacturers Hanover Trust Company developed a foreign currency trades ES to assess historical trends, new events, and buying and selling factors.
- criminology: The FBI has developed several ES to create personality profiles of violent criminals.
- education: Arizona State University has developed an ES to teach and evaluate children's math skills.
- food industry: Campbell's Soup Company has developed an ES to capture the knowledge of a highly specialized, long-time employee who possessed all knowledge of plant operations and sterilizing techniques.
- healthcare management: The British National Health Service has developed an ES to evaluate the performance of national healthcare providers. This system has more than 11,000 rules, which qualifies it as one of the largest ES applications in the world.
- manufacturing design and assembly: Northrop Corporation has developed an ES to assist in the planning process of manufacturing jet fighters, reducing the planning and assembly stages by a factor of 12 to 18.
- oil exploration: Texaco has developed an ES to help drilling engineers diagnose and manage drilling-fluid problems.
- personnel management: IBM has developed its own ES to assist in the training of technicians, which has reduced training time from fourteen to sixteen months to three to five months.
- security: Canadian Trust Bank has developed an ES to track their credit card holders' purchasing trends, and report deviations like unusual activity on the card. The system has saved more than $1.2 million since it was installed.
- tax planning: Coopers & Lybrand developed an ES to assist in tax planning analysis.
- U.S. government: ES have been developed to monitor nuclear powerplants and assist such departments as the Internal Revenue Service, Immigration and Naturalization Service, U.S. Postal Service, Department of Transportation, Department of Energy, and Department of Defense in decision-making processes.

Other interesting applications of ES have been developed and utilized in such recognizable companies as Hewlett-Packard, DuPont, General Dynamics, Nippon Steel, Dun & Bradstreet, the Swiss Bank, and many more.

To understand the true impact that an ES may have on an organization, let us take a closer look at specific case applications in the areas of criminology, education, oil exploration, and tax planning.

The U.S. Federal Bureau of Investigations (FBI) has developed more than twenty ES. The Behavioral Science Unit of the FBI has developed an ES to create personality profiles of violent criminals by consolidating information from reports acquired from crime scene investigators, victim data, the media, crime research statistical data, pattern analysis, and activity analysis. The ES then processes the database on its programming in expert criminology reasoning and knowledge, and develops its own hypothesis about the psychological type of person who committed the crime as well as his profile. Another ES developed by the FBI is in the area of arson investigation. The Arson Information Management System (AIMS), designed similarly to the violent crime ES, is used to analyze an arsonist's psychological profile and activity to help forecast the possible locations the arsonist may strike next.

At the local law enforcement level, burglary detectives in Baltimore County, Maryland, were the first to get a look at an ES prototype developed to analyze information about burglary sites and a possible list of suspects. Information about 300 burglary cases that had been solved and 3,000 records about unsolved cases and known burglars were loaded into the system. Eighteen detectives were interviewed for their insight into local burglaries and came up with 397 ES input statements, including categorical information such as characteristics of the residence, its environment, the type of entry used, behavior, types of property stolen, and possible means of transportation to or from the scene. The residential burglary prototype system was successful, and it is now used in other police departments around the United States [13].

In the field of education, Arizona State University has developed and implemented a three-part interactive, multimedia ES to teach and evaluate children's math skills. The user interface aspect of the ES was programmed using IBM's Info Windows and M-Motion video platforms. The system also incorporates laserdisk and touch screen technologies. The ES tracks and interprets students' mathematical progress from kindergarten to twelfth grade. The system predicts, diagnoses, plans, and monitors the work of the students and instructs them through off-site learning center nodes placed in various local schools. It can quiz a student and analyze why he or she missed a particular question or set of questions, as well as identify strengths and weaknesses to develop customized learning plans. Students may select English or Spanish audio on-screen instructions. This project, named the Hispanic Math Project, is funded by the National Science Foundation and is equipped with all IBM hardware [10].

In the field of oil exploration, Texaco originally set out to build a "Question and Answer" ES to help engineers detect drilling-fluid problems and make recommendations. However, Texaco has now expanded its ES, named Exsys system. The user has a choice of two screens, either a question-driven screen or a word and/or numeric input screen. After a ten-minute question-and-answer session, the ES reaches a conclusion and makes recommendations to the engineers on possible solutions to drilling problems. The system has proved to be an invaluable training tool, and has helped to uncover weaknesses in Texaco's well-drilling operations [10].

In the field of tax planning, Coopers & Lybrand, a world-renowned accounting firm, has developed an ES called ExperTax that assists auditors with tax planning. ExperTax's purpose is to provide junior auditors with senior-level tax expertise and replace a 200-page tax-planning questionnaire previously used. The system analyzes income, assets, liabilities, and so on, and makes recommendations to the auditor about the best approach to improve the client's tax liability position. ExperTax contains more than 3,000 rules developed by the senior-level partners and runs on IBM-compatible hardware. It has proven invaluable to Coopers & Lybrand by improving the completeness, accuracy, and consistency of its customer service, as well as providing increased production and training for their lower-level auditors [11].

In the previous examples of companies who have incorporated ES technology in their day-to-day business activities, it is clear that ES can play an important role related to training and education, data analysis and interpretation, planning, forecasting, and identification of strengths and weaknesses. When utilized properly, an ES can help an organization attain a competitive advantage in its particular field, whether it be criminology, oil exploration, tax planning, or some other discipline.

COSTS AND BENEFITS OF MSS

The costs and benefits of MSS are difficult to assess, because these systems are aimed at effectiveness rather than efficiency and because they are said to facilitate, but not directly cause, improvements. How does one assign monetary values to facilitating interpersonal communication, or expediting and improving problem-solving activities, or receiving information in fifteen minutes as opposed to two hours [15]?

Peter G. Keen [8] conducted an interesting study of a number of organizations regarding their DSS use. He concluded that the decision to build a DSS is based on value, rather than cost. He outlined the benefits of a DSS:

- increase in the number of alternatives examined
- better understanding of the business
- fast response to unexpected situations
- ability to carry out ad hoc analysis
- new insights and learning
- improved communication
- improved control

- cost savings
- better decisions
- more effective teamwork
- time savings
- making better use of data resources

As this study indicates, few of the benefits generated by a DSS are tangible ones. The majority of these benefits are intangible and difficult to assess.

The so-called intangible benefits generated by a DSS can be quantified. However, this quantification may be subjective, and different individuals may come up with different figures. For example, the opportunity cost of wasting two hours of a manager's time can be measured and transferred into monetary values—the two hours spent by a manager looking for information that could have been made readily available by a DSS. A decision maker could have spent this time in a more productive session making more effective decisions. A less frustrated manager can also be generally easier to work for and more productive.

The fact that DSS are increasing communication and interaction between clients and organizations, between organizations and employees, and among employees is also a benefit worth mentioning [1]. DSS can, and are, facilitating the way in which decision makers view themselves and their jobs, and the way they spend time. In fact, improving communication and expediting learning are among the objectives of creating a DSS.

A DSS is said to have achieved its goals if employees find it useful in doing their jobs. Some DSS have had definite clerical savings, while others have caused significant improvements in the decision-making process.

Overall, it seems that the majority of DSS can be developed from the existing resources already available in the organization. One may assume that the cost of developing a DSS compared to its benefits is minimal.

ES and other MSS include most of the benefits outlined for DSS. In addition, ES are able to duplicate and replicate the rare expertise in the organization and provide explanation capabilities. The explanation capabilities can further assist decision makers in better understanding the problems under investigation. Some ES can be developed using the existing resources; others need specialized shells or languages. Overall, the literature reports significant savings and payoffs for MSS, and their benefits outweigh their costs.

EXECUTIVE INFORMATION SYSTEMS

In recent years, some new buzzwords have been introduced to the field of information systems. These are executive information systems (EIS), executive support systems (ESS), and executive management systems (EMS). Although their definitions and place among EDP, MIS, and DSS are still evolving, we consider these systems to be a branch of DSS. At the center of these systems, there is always a microcomputer (or a workstation) that serves as an intelligent terminal. The microcomputer can serve as a stand-alone system or be used as a workstation to connect the executive decision maker to a wealth of information from both internal and external databases.

EIS attempt to deliver only information critical to a decision maker and are user or business-problem driven. There is a heavy emphasis on providing an easily understood format for the executives who use the information. One of the primary objectives of these systems is to reduce the vast amount of information that bombards executives. This is achieved by exception-type reports and by reporting only the critical information. An EIS combines the decision maker's imagination and judgment with the computer's ability to store, retrieve, manipulate, compute, and report internal and external data.

EIS utilize integrated office technologies for planning, forecasting, and controlling managerial tasks. They may use any of the following:

- graphical user interface (GUI)
- touch screens versus traditional keyboards
- voice input
- mouse
- menu-driven interfaces
- color screens
- key commands that are close to user verbs such as SOLVE, DISPLAY, DRAW, PLOT, and PRINT
- local area network (LAN)
- wide area network (WAN)
- metropolitan area network (MAN)
- electronic mail (e-mail)
- facsimile equipment
- voice mail
- electronic message distribution
- teleconferencing (audio, video, and computer)
- graphics
- spreadsheets
- lap-top, notebook, and palm-top computers
- scanners
- integration of voice, data, and images through ISDN (Integrated Services Digital Network)
- image-transmission systems through facsimile

Comparing EIS with DSS, some specific advantages can be highlighted. An EIS provides

- easier user-system interface
- more timely delivery of information
- more understandable format for the information provided
- increased executive productivity by reporting on key items
- a better understanding of the information and its interrelationships

We will discuss EIS in detail in Chapter 5. For now, remember that through communications systems an organization can share the same data among many decision makers in an efficient way. Also, by using a communications system, an executive can be connected to a wealth of information through public and private databases.

COMPARATIVE ANALYSIS OF EDP, MIS, DSS, AND EIS

EDP, MIS, DSS, and EIS are not unique technologies. In fact, they share many common features. Each technology addresses a particular user group. Table 1.1 provides a comparative summary of these four technologies.

EDP, MIS, DSS, and EIS can be developed from a series of design tools. Design tools are software technologies used to design any of these technologies. They can be either high-level programming languages such as BASIC, FORTRAN, C, and so forth, or computer packages, 4GL, or DSS generators.

Table 1.1
EDP, MIS, DSS, and EIS Comparison

Key Factor	EDP	MIS	DSS	EIS
Problem Addressed	Structured	Structured	Structured/ Semistructured	Structured/ Semistructured
User	Lower Management	Middle Management	All Management	Top Management
Design Team	Mostly Data Processing Professional	Data Processing Professional and the User	The User and Data Processing Professional	Top Management and Data Processing Professional
Design Tools	Mostly High Level Language	High Level Language and Packages	Mostly Packages	Mostly Packages
Data Used	Internal	Internal	Internal and Mostly External	Internal and External
Interface Mode	Mostly Batch	Batch and Interactive	Mostly Interactive	Interactive

The 4GLs (fourth-level computer languages) or DSS generators such as FOCUS, ORACLE, IFPS, NOMAD, and so forth are more user-friendly and powerful than traditional programming languages—much easier to use and learn.

GROUP SUPPORT SYSTEMS

As you will see in Chapter 6, group support systems (GSS) make collaborative decision making or group computing a reality. These systems carry the traditional DSS one step forward. Within this collaborative environment, there has been an increase in the use of computer-aided group support technologies. Electronic Meeting Systems (EMS) and GroupWare have found their way into the corporate environment.

There are several types of GSS, but all have one common goal. The goal is the implementation of decisions where multiple decision makers are involved. These decision makers can be in one office or scattered throughout the world.

Corporate decisions are complex and multifaceted. By bringing multiple perspectives into decision making, the chances of success improve, and the risks of decision implementation decrease. GSS technologies make this a reality [4].

GEOGRAPHIC INFORMATION SYSTEMS

As you will learn in Chapter 7, geographic information systems (GIS) can provide unique decision-making capabilities by utilizing spatial and nonspatial data and specialized techniques for storing the coordinates of complex geographic objects, including networks of lines (e.g., roads, rivers, streets, highways), and by reporting zone (e.g., zip codes, census tracts, cities, or counties). A properly designed GIS can assist executives in a number of organizations to answer the following questions [2]:

Where should a new airport be located to minimize its environmental impact?

What route should our delivery truck follow between stops to minimize driving time?

Where should we locate a new store?

Where should we locate a new plant?

Based on centralized areas, where should we locate a fire station?

Based on the population growth, where should we locate a new public school?

Where should we locate a new fast-food restaurant?

NEURAL NETWORKS

Neural computing, or neural networks, is one of the new multidisciplinary research fields that has grown because of the study of the brain and its potential for solving poorly structured business problems. Neural networks are capable of performing tasks that conventional computers find difficult. Neural computing technology is also known as connectionism and parallel-distributed processing. The computers that we come in contact with in our daily lives are based on the architecture laid down by John Von Neuman.

Similar to ES, neural computing is used for poorly structured problems. Unlike ES, neural computing is not able to explain its solution, because neural computing uses "patterns" versus "rules" used by ES. A neural network uses a large amount of linked microprocessors and software that tackle a problem in a unified, rather than a sequential manner. A neural network learns by doing various tasks. Neural networks achieve the learning process by creating a model based on its input and output.

For example, in a loan application problem the input data are income, assets, number of dependents, job history, and residential status. The acceptance or rejection are the output data. By using many of these loan applications, the neural network establishes a pattern for an application to be approved or rejected [14]. Other applications for neural computing are characteristics of potential oil fields, diagnosing automobile engine problems, and analysis of price and volume patterns in stock trading. Generally speaking, neural computing is suitable in applications where data are fuzzy and uncertainty is involved. We will talk about neural computing in detail in Chapter 10.

FUZZY LOGIC SYSTEMS

As you will learn in Chapter 9, fuzzy logic theory tries to define the gray areas that do not have clear-cut answers. For example, if I ask you the question, "Do you like going to school?" your response could be "sometimes," "usually," "it depends," "only if . . ." or "most often." Fuzzy logic addresses these kinds of situations.

Fuzzy logic creates a membership function and assigns a number between 0 and 1 to each member in this set. For example, a 6'8" tall person may receive a .9 score in the membership function of all the tall people. Professor Zadeh, the founder of fuzzy logic theory, explains how, in conventional computers, everything is crisp—such as 0 or 1, black or white, pass or fail—but fuzzy logic can deal with items that are between 0 and 1 [18].

Fuzzy logic has been extremely successful in commercial products such as washing machines, camcorders, and toasters. The real power of fuzzy logic for decision making has been its use in hybrid systems where fuzzy logic, neural networks and ES are combined to solve problems that none of them can solve separately [16, 18].

GENETIC ALGORITHMS

Although not as widely accepted, genetic algorithms (GAs) are becoming more recognized as a form of artificial language that lets machine thought processes evolve. As with natural selection and evolution, GAs reproduce in various recombination, each time hoping to find a new recombinant which will be better adapted than its predecessors. GAs are emerging as a new way to look at problems in their entirety or in large chunks instead of one piece at a time [12].

John Holland originated the concept of GAs in the 1940s while he was working at MIT [7]. The term genetic algorithms applies adaptive procedures to a set of bit string used in a computer system that are based on Darwin's theory of natural selection and survival of the fittest. It can put complicated items of information into a simple bit string that represents a solution to the current problem. The GAs then refine the solution through an evolutionary process until an acceptable solution is found. The original bit strings are just a "guess at a solution," and the evolutionary process imitates the processes of reproduction and natural selection. We will talk more about GAs in Chapter 9.

A LOOK AT THE PAST

To better understand the future of MSS, a review of the past would be helpful. If we consider the three main components of a MSS to be user, software, and hardware, these three components have gone through major changes.

The highly trained computer personnel are not the only users of computer technology throughout the organization. Computer education and computer awareness among all levels of the management team is a reality. Computers are easier to use, more widespread, and more accessible to a typical user than in the past. A majority of business organizations either provide computer training inside the organization or send their employees to college classes, seminars, and vendor training in order to make them computer-trained employees. Also, the availability of graphical user interfaces such as Windows and OS/2 and the mouse, touch screen, multimedia, voice input, and menu-driven systems have made it easier to train an employee with a minimum computer background.

The software technology has improved significantly. When the first computers were introduced in the early 1940s, the only language understood by these computers was the machine language. Machine language consists of a series of 0s and 1s, and it is difficult to program a computer using such language. At that time the only users of computers were highly trained data processing personnel. The second generation of computer language was called assembly language, and it consisted of a series of short codes or mnemonics. One can say, in general, that assembly language is easier to use than machine language. But still, rigorous training is needed to become a proficient user of a computer using this language. The third generation of computer languages called high-level languages or higher-level languages are more English and user oriented. A language like COBOL is self-documentary. Users can basically get a general idea when they read a program written in COBOL. These languages are easier than the first two to learn and use; however, they are very specific in nature, and each one is more suitable for one type of application. The fourth-level computer languages, or 4GLs, are a lot more forgiving than the first three. They are by far the easiest to learn and use. Much less time is needed to perform a task using these languages compared to their predecessors. To use even these languages, the user has to have some basic computer training, and the user should be familiar with the keyboard. The fifth generation of computer languages, natural language processing (NLP), promises a great deal of flexibility and power. If these languages ever become a reality, computers will become much easier to use, friendlier, and more flexible. The following highlight the software trends:

- first generation: machine language
- second generation: assembly language
- third generation: high-level language
- fourth generation: fourth-generation language (4GL)
- fifth generation: natural language processing (NLP)

Computer hardware has also gone through major improvements. The first generations of computers were working with vacuum tubes. They were bulky and unreliable. The second generation, the transistor era, added power, speed, and reliability to the computer industry. These computers were much smaller and much more powerful than their ancestors. The third generation of computer technology is associated with chip technology. An integrated circuit is the building block of the third-generation computer. Computer technology in the third generation was improved in all dimensions. In the early 1970s, the fourth generation of computer technology was introduced. It is basically the miniaturization era, in which computers became smaller and more powerful than the earlier generations. The widespread uses of microcomputers and desktop computing are the main features of this generation.

The fifth generation features the artificial language computers, the computers that are more "intelligent" than those in earlier generations. Widespread uses of parallel processing and gallium arsonide are some of the other attributes of this generation. The following highlight the hardware trends:

- first generation: vacuum tubes
- second generation: transistors
- third generation: integrated circuits
- fourth generation: VLSI (very large scale integration) and ULSI (ultra large scale integration)
- fifth generation: gallium arsonide, parallel processing, and artificial intelligence computer

OUTLOOK FOR MSS

In order to provide an outlook for the quickly growing field of MSS, we can examine one of the major subfields of MSS—that is, DSS. Basically, the outlook is the same for all MSS.

We have suggested that DSS is a new part of the MIS concept but will in no way replace MIS. It is called "decision support systems" because its purpose is to support decision makers in making and implementing decisions. DSS is characterized by active use in all aspects of management activities and is used at all organizational levels to facilitate communication, interaction, and learning among a myriad of users, not necessarily all of whom are managers. Successful implementation is assured when there is interaction between users and designers. The emphasis of DSS is on increased individual and organizational effectiveness. The philosophy of DSS is to improve or expedite the processes by which people make decisions. Because DSS are both flexible and evolutionary, their effectiveness should steadily increase as they are applied. ES, on the other hand, complement DSS by adding explanation capabilities and duplicating and replicating expertise of a human expert(s).

To address the future of DSS, we choose to stay within the confines of the short range rather than the long range. Only recently have DSS begun to take hold in the business world. For some time, research (as well as technology) has been ahead of the practical application of DSS. Users have only recently picked up on the concept of DSS and have begun using their creativity and the resources of their organizations to make DSS applications a reality. People in positions to use DSS are continuing to gain knowledge about what can be done and will be able to use these systems more effectively.

Although DSS will probably continue to grow, decision makers must *first* accept the idea that computers can be used to support rather than replace a human decision maker. *Second* the interpersonal and technical relationships between decision makers and designers must be developed. DSS will become more prevalent in the future if these two conditions are met and if the users continue to take an active part in the development of DSS. The ability of DSS to meet the decision makers' needs with ever-increasing effectiveness will ensure their continued existence. In the ultimate sense, we regard DSS as the most significant, current frontier in the organizational application of computers.

We cannot end this discussion without remarking on the almost unlimited possibilities of the future. Artificial intelligence and its supporting technologies, such as natural language processing, will undoubtedly play an important part in the future of DSS because artificial intelligence is concerned with "humanlike" reasoning. Potential integration exists between artificial intelligence products and DSS. Generally speaking, artificial intelligence computers are more powerful than traditional computers (the Von Neuman computers).

The future of MSS will be influenced by three factors:

1. *Computer hardware*: Computers are becoming more powerful, faster, less expensive, and more manageable. Microcomputers will continue to play an important role in information storage, retrieval, and analysis. Telecommunications and networking will be improved. A mainframe micro (high-powered desktop computer) will become a reality. The information superhighway concept should make the information transfer a more feasible and economical task.

2. *Computer software*: We will see further improvements and cost reduction in all areas of MSS software. Micro-based MSS software will become more powerful and will perform more of the standard MSS-type analyses. The notions of "user-friendly," graphical-based, and menu-driven software will become a reality. Artificial intelligence and ES applications will become more common and more business-oriented. Also, we should see more integration among all MSS applications.

3. *Users of computers*: The users and managers of the future will be computer sophisticates and have higher expectations. The notion of computer support will be more acceptable and less threatening. The users of computers will be anybody, not just hardcore computer scientists.

SUMMARY

DSS, ES, and other MSS have been around for several years. The power of these systems has been demonstrated in many applications. Through comparative analysis we have demonstrated the unique characteristics of DSS, ES, and other MSS. A historic progression from EDP to MIS to DSS showed the natural progression that is continuing today. The future seems very promising. Further development in artificial intelligence and ES should enhance the power and utilization of DSS. This chapter briefly introduced EIS, GSS, neural computing, GAs, and fuzzy logic as other technologies for improving the decision making process.

So what does all this mean to MSS? The trend for hardware, software, and users indicates an increasing utilization of MSS. The design and utilization of MSS should become much easier, and MSS will become more powerful and "user-friendly." It is hard to imagine a significant corporate enterprise in the near future *without* a management support system.

REFERENCES

1. Alter, Steven L. *Decision Support Systems: Current Practice and Continuing Challenges*. Reading, Mass.: Addison-Wesley Publishing, 1980.
2. Bidgoli, Hossein. "Geographic Information Systems: A New Strategic Tool for the 90s and Beyond." *Journal of Systems Management* (May/June 1995): 25.
3. Coy, Peter. "The New Realism in Office Systems." *Business Week*, June 15, 1992, 128–133.
4. Desanctis, Geraldine, and Brent Gallup. "Group Decision Support Systems: A New Frontier." *Data Base* (Winter 1985): 3–9.
5. Eom, Hyun B., and M. Lee Sang. "A Survey of Decision Support System Applications (1971–April, 1988)." *Interfaces* (May/June 1990): 65–79.

6. Gill, Grandon T. "Early Expert Systems: Where Are They Now?" *MIS Quarterly* (March 1995): 51–69.

7. Holland, John H. "Genetic Algorithms." *Scientific American* (July 1992): 66–72.

8. Keen, Peter G. W. "Value Analysis: Justifying Decision Support Systems." *MIS Quarterly* 5 (March 1981): 1–15.

9. Keen, Peter G. W., and Michael S. Scott-Morton. *Decision Support Systems: An Organizational Perspective*. Reading, Mass.: Addison-Wesley Publishing, 1978.

10. Kestelyn, Justin. "Application Watch." *AI Expert* (May 1991): 71.

11. Kneale, Dennis. "How Coopers & Lybrand put Expertise into its Computers." *Wall Street Journal*, November 1986, 33.

12. Lane, Alex. "Programming With Genes." *AI Expert* (December 1993): 23–27.

13. Newquist III, Harvey P. "In Practice: Bloodhounds and Expert Systems." *AI Expert* (March 1990): 67–69.

14. Rochester, Jack B. "New Business Uses for Neuro Computing." *I/S Analyzer* (February 1990): 1–12.

15. Semich, William J. "Here's How to Quantify IT Investment Benefits." *Datamation* (January 1994): 45–48.

16. Shandle, Jack. "Fuzzy Logic is Shedding Its Half Baked Image; Easy to Use Tools and a Symbolic Relationship With Neural Networks Will Make the Difference." *Electronic Design* (March 21, 1994): 75.

17. Sviokla, John J. "An Examination of the Impact of Expert Systems on the Firm: The Case of XCON." *MIS Quarterly* (June 1990): 127–140.

18. Zadeh, Lotfi A. "Yes, No and Relativity, Part 1." *Chemtech* (June 1987): 340–344.

CHAPTER 2

Tools and Techniques for Building an Effective Management Support System

This chapter reviews the principles of systems analysis and design. First, the chapter will discuss the classic life-cycle approach. Different phases in this life cycle will be explained. Then the chapter will discuss the product life cycle as it relates to the development of a MSS. The chapter reviews various new methodologies for designing a MSS, including a brief discussion of computer-assisted systems engineering (CASE) tools. By synthesizing these approaches, the chapter will introduce an "integrated approach," which is more suitable for developing a MSS. The chapter concludes with a brief discussion on traditional approach, outsourcing, and end-user computing as three approaches for building a MSS.

CLASSIC LIFE-CYCLE APPROACH

This approach, which has been utilized for many years [15] in traditional EDP and MIS design and implementation, is a series of well-defined steps. Understanding this approach should help the user to better understand MSS design and implementation, which employs a special version of this approach. The following are the phases involved in the classic life-cycle approach:

- problem definition
- feasibility study
- systems analysis
- systems design
- systems implementation
- post-implementation audit

Problem Definition

During this stage, the user and the designer of the system try to define and understand the problem faced by the organization. This very important step must be undertaken with great care. It is possible to mistakenly identify the symptoms of the problem instead of the problem itself. The resulting system may alleviate the symptoms of the problem without resolving the problem.

The problem may have been identified internally or brought to the attention of the organization by the customers, suppliers, employees, external agencies, and so forth. The following are some examples of problems in a typical business organization:

Problem #1: Improper allocation of resources

Problem #2: Inaccurate billing system

Problem #3: Inefficient inventory system

Problem #4: Inaccurate budgeting system

Problem #5: Customer complaints regarding the timeliness of services

Problem #6: Inaccurate sales forecasts

In a MSS environment, the problem may not be as well defined as these problems. For example, the problem may be how to improve competitiveness in the marketplace or employment of a new technology to analyze the environment of the organization more thoroughly. Problems in the MSS environment are usually novel, nonrecurring, and unstructured.

Feasibility Study

A feasibility study is conducted to determine the level of desirability of a MSS project considering several factors. Before starting this phase, the objective of the new system must be defined.

During this stage of the life cycle, the systems analyst or a team of systems analysts tries to investigate the feasibility of a proposed solution, which may resolve the problem. The feasibility study may include different dimensions as follows: economic, technical, social, and time.

Economic feasibility is concerned with the costs and benefits of the system. For example, if the net gain of the implementation of an inventory system is $350,000 and the system would cost $500,000 to implement, this system is not economically feasible. To conduct an economic feasibility study, the systems analyst team must identify all the costs and benefits of the proposed system. The costs and benefits may be either tangible or intangible. The tangible costs may include equipment, training, new employees, and so forth. The intangible costs may include the social issues related to automation, such as privacy, security, and employee turnover.

The real challenge for the systems analyst team is to accurately assess the intangible costs. The team should attempt to estimate and attach a realistic monetary value to the intangible costs and then conduct an economic feasibility study.

When it comes to the benefits or potential benefits of a new system, the systems analyst is again faced with the same issue. The assessment of the tangible benefits is usually straightforward: They usually include all the cost savings generated by the new system. The assessment of the intangible benefits is a challenging task. However, the systems analyst team should attempt to estimate and attach a monetary value to these intangible benefits and then conduct an economic feasibility study.

To make the assessment of intangible benefits more clear, let us give you an example. Let us say one of the intangible benefits of a new system is improved customer service. How do you assign a monetary value to this? One way to look at this issue is by quantifying the intangible benefit. Customer service means maintaining the present total sales and possibly increasing the total sales by a certain percentage. If improved customer service means 10 percent growth, it means 10 percent of $15 million for ABC Company. This means a $1.5 million increase in sales. If the ABC Company has a 20 percent net margin, this means an additional $300,000 of net profit just by increasing the customer service. The same type of analysis can be performed for the assessment of intangible costs.

Technical feasibility is concerned with the technical aspects of the new system. One way to investigate the technical feasibility would be to study the state of technology. A proposed solution may not be technically feasible for implementation. For example, the technology may not exist for the implementation of the new system. As an example, a full-featured, voice-activated monitoring system at this point is not technically feasible. However, given today's computer technology, this is not a major problem; and for many proposed solutions, the technical support is available.

Lack of technical feasibility may also stem from an organizational deficiency. A specific system may not be feasible because the organization lacks the expertise, time, or personnel required to implement the new system. This has been referred to as a lack of organizational readiness. If this is the case, the organization must first take the appropriate steps to prepare its employees, and then consider the new MSS. This may be achieved by extensive training and ongoing education for the key personnel in all of the affected functional areas.

Social feasibility investigates the proposed system within the context of social issues. This dimension is generally concerned with the social issues of automation, which may include employee replacement, privacy issues, turnover, employee dissatisfaction, and so forth. An organization may choose not to implement a new system because of the social problems a new system may cause. Some of the social issues can be overcome by a series of design measures performed by the systems analyst team. These may include ongoing training and heavy user involvement in all phases of the systems analysis and design.

However, some of these issues are an inherent part of any change, and there is no way to completely eliminate such problems.

Finally, a feasibility study may be concerned with the time factor. Let us say a system is feasible economically, technically, and socially; however, it may not be ready within the time frame needed by an organization. For example, an organization may critically need an automated payroll processing application to reduce the overtime required to maintain the existing manual system. However, if the new system cannot be delivered in time, the drain on the organization's resources created by the excess overtime may force the organization out of business. If this is the case, you may say the proposed system is not feasible from the time-factor viewpoint. The issue of overtime and overbudget is a common problem in the information systems field. The designer(s) of MSS, by employing appropriate project management and project control tools and techniques, can minimize this issue.

Systems Analysis

The third step in the life-cycle approach is systems analysis. In this phase, the systems analyst or a team of analysts specifically define the problem and generate alternatives for solving it. A variety of tools may be utilized during this phase. These may include the following: interviews, questionnaires, observation, work measurement, form investigation and control, flowcharts, and data-flow diagrams (DFD).

The output of this phase, as mentioned earlier, will be a clear problem definition, one or several alternatives, and some initial documentation relating to the operation of the new system.

Interview, questionnaire, and observation techniques are used to build better understanding of the problem area. Graphical tools such as the flowchart and DFD are used for highlighting the problem area, gaining a clear understanding of the input/process/output cycle and the bottlenecks encountered throughout the entire system operation. Flowcharts usually show the *logic* involved in the system and highlight the detail by using special symbols. DFDs, by using bubbles and arrows, show the *process* in the system and highlight the overall procedure and operations of the system. Again, these tools are very useful when the prespecifications can be done. These tools may not be suitable if the problem under investigation is unstructured. Figure 2.1 illustrates a typical flowchart, and Figure 2.2 depicts a DFD.

Systems Design

During this phase the team of analysts tries to choose the alternative which is the most realistic and presents the highest payoff to the organization. At this point, the details of the proposed solution will be outlined. The output produced by the team would be a document very similar to a blueprint for implementation. This blueprint will include specifications for file and database design, form

Figure 2.1
Example of a Flowchart

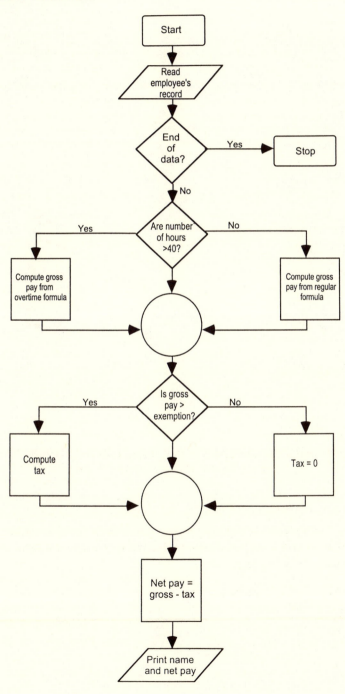

Figure 2.2
Example of a DFD

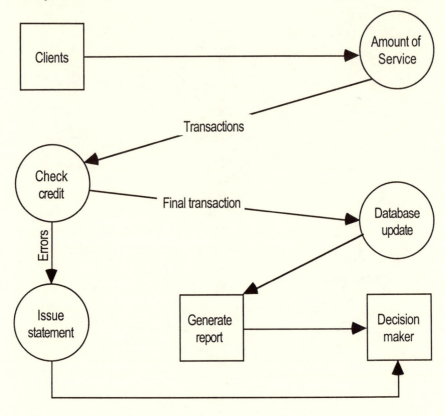

and report design, documentation design, procedure design, hardware and software specifications, and general system specifications.

Systems Implementation

During this phase, the solution is transferred from paper to action. A variety of tasks will take place while the implementation phase is underway. These may include the following:

- acquisition of new equipment
- hiring new employees
- training new employees
- physical planning and layout design
- coding

- testing
- security design
- disaster recovery specification
- conversion planning and documentation
- communications requirements

When a system is ready to be converted, there are several options available to the designer, including parallel conversion; phased-in–phased-out conversion; direct (crash) conversion; and pilot conversion.

Using the parallel conversion approach, the old and the new system are run simultaneously for a short time, in order to ensure that the new system will operate properly. However, this approach is costly and will only work if an operational system is already in place.

Using the phased-in–phased-out approach, depending on the suitability of the system for such conversion, as each module of the new system is converted, the corresponding part of the old system is retired. This process continues until the entire system is converted. This approach is not suitable for all applications; however, in accounting and finance areas, this approach may be very effective.

Using the direct (crash) conversion approach, the old system is stopped and the new system is implemented. This approach is risky; however, the organization may save a lot of money by not running the old and new systems concurrently.

Finally, using a pilot conversion approach, the analyst develops the system and introduces it only to a limited area of the organization, such as a division or a department. If the system is working properly, it is made available to the rest of the organization.

Post-Implementation Audit

This last phase in the life-cycle approach attempts to verify the suitability of the system after the implementation. The team of analysts tries to collect data and talk with the users, customers, and other people affected by the new system to make sure that the system is doing what it was designed to do. If the objectives of the system have not been met, then the team of analysts must take corrective actions.

PRODUCT LIFE-CYCLE APPROACH

Design and implementation of computer-based information systems, particularly EDP, MIS, and to some degree, MSS, follow the product life cycle [3, 5]. This means that these systems follow the four stages of the life cycle: introduction, growth, maturity, and decline. Understanding this life cycle is important and should help the designer of a MSS with a series of tools that can be used to design a more successful MSS.

Traditionally, life cycle has been discussed with respect to product obsoles-cence due to change in consumer preference, technological change, and so on. Increasingly, the life-cycle concept is being more broadly defined. It has been applied to various professionals, including engineers and physicians [13], as well as to such unusual areas as organizational rules [7] and even plant open-ings and closings [11]. Thus, it is not unusual to consider the life-cycle concept in the design, implementation, and continuous evaluation of MSS. As each of us has experienced, entropic processes (this may include change in customer taste, technological breakthroughs, change in market, etc.) adversely affect the life cycle of products, systems, and people. To manage these processes, we need to (1) understand what affects the life cycle of these products, systems, and people; (2) determine what stage of the life cycle they are currently in; and (3) decide what interventions, if any, are appropriate for that particular stage. These interventions should be built into the MSS framework.

In order to meet these objectives or needs, the concept of a management support systems life cycle (MSSLC) must be defined. The MSSLC consists of the four specific stages of introduction, growth, maturity, and decline. These are similar to other life-cycle concepts, but are different in their application. More specifically, the transformation of the MSSLC from infancy or intro-duction to decline and abandonment is effected mainly by technological ad-vancements in hardware and software, rapidly changing environments, and continuous change in the information needs of the organization in general and the decision makers in particular. In addition, one could suggest that MSS actually experience a half-life. This is the amount of time in which the effi-ciency, effectiveness, and even relevance of these systems has been reduced to half its original full value. The MSS can, however, be modified to extend its full life. Despite this extended period, complete replacement of the existing sys-tem is inevitable and must be planned for a particular time frame.

As discussed later in this chapter, appropriate design tools in the MSS environ-ment such as prototyping and iterative and adaptive design help the MSS designer to carefully evaluate each stage of MSS life cycle and determine its effectiveness. These appropriate measures may prevent a MSS from experiencing a half-life.

The most important features of a MSSLC are their characteristics, which are unique or indigenous to different stages of the cycle. By understanding these characteristics or determinants, the MSS user and designer will be able to identify not only the stage the MSS is in (macro), but where it is within that stage (micro). This will help the designer take whatever action is appropriate at that particular time. The following are stages of the MSSLC and how they might be characterized.

Introduction

The introduction phase is characterized by a series of technical problems, unrealistic demand by users, lack of interest and familiarity, and so forth. There may even be adverse feelings or attitudes toward the introduction of this new technology due to individual, group, or organizational habit structures.

Growth

The growth phase is characterized by an increase in awareness and interest, multiplying usage, new applications suggested and incorporated, and so forth.

Maturity

The maturity phase is characterized by a high degree of efficiency and effectiveness, a low cost/benefit ratio, widespread satisfaction with "our" systems, and so forth.

Decline

Though a MSS designer would want to anticipate the decline stage, many do not understand the human, as well as technical, responses to this process. Characteristics in this phase include lack of interest, slow response time to requests, technological obsolescence, and the inevitable bypassing of the MSS by using "personal" micros and individually contrived or procured databases. These characteristics will help MSS designers identify what stage the system is in and what action must be taken to resolve any possible problems.

The classic phases involved in building a MSS as mentioned earlier include problem definition, feasibility study, analysis, design, implementation, and a post-implementation audit. A careful examination of the variables involved in each phase should significantly improve the life cycle of the MSS in the various stages of its life. This may result in a shorter introduction phase and a longer maturity phase, as well as a high quality of life for the system throughout the entire cycle. The use of appropriate tools, techniques, and methodologies for each phase or step should bring about a successful MSS introduction. When these phases of the product life cycle are applied to a MSS they should include the following:

1. *Analysis phase*: This should include economic, technical, operational, time, and human concerns. The user(s) of the system must be identified, and style, status, and preferences of these users must be considered. Both quantitative as well as qualitative benefits must be evaluated in this phase. Also, a combination of top-down, bottom-up, and middle-out methodologies should be utilized (discussed later in this chapter).

2. *Design phase*: This should include more flexible methodologies such as iterative design, task force design, and/or modular design in order to reflect user information needs. This phase should also consider potential technological advancements and changing user needs.

3. *Implementation phase*: This provides the first impression of the MSS to the users. Fortunately or unfortunately, user acceptance is based to a great extent on the user's first impressions, and is akin to a job interview for the system. In order to smooth the implementation process and minimize human resistance, the parallel conversion (if appropriate) may be considered the best conversion method. Parallel conversion provides the users with advantages, including more on-the-job training than the other conversion methods and a safety net (physically and psychologically) in case of system failure. In the particular case of MSS, online prototyping may achieve the same goal as parallel conversion. Online prototyping provides the user with an idea regarding the operation of the MSS and makes it possible to integrate the views of the user into the system during the final stages of completion. This allows the user to suggest design changes and specifications and encourages user acceptance through increased participation and "buy in."

4. *Post-implementation audit phase*: This should continuously monitor the system. Implementation of a MSS is no different than any other organizational change that requires evaluation of operations as an absolute necessity. The behavior of the system and the users will indicate the stage in the MSSLC. The designer must make appropriate decisions in each situation.

PRODUCT LIFE CYCLE AND MSS DESIGN CONSIDERATIONS

As will be discussed in Chapter 4, the conceptual model of a MSS includes three components: database, model base, and dialog management. The major players involved in MSS design and implementation include the user, the intermediary, and the managerial and technical designers. Considering these issues, the life-cycle approach identifies the following major elements in construction of a successful MSS: the user, technology, top management, and environment.

User

The user and the user's information needs are two of the most important elements that could expand or reduce the life expectancy of a MSS. These needs may have been generated either by company requirements or industry pressure. Also, a variety of attributes related to the user such as style, acceptance, convenience, and status are important for an expanded and productive MSS life. A MSS that is not responsive to these factors will have a shorter life expectancy or reduced effectiveness.

Technology

Hardware and software technologies and their proper augmentation into the conceptual model for a MSS are another important factor for an expanded and effective MSS life. In many cases, MSS have failed to respond to user needs because of improper employment of either software and/or hardware technologies. Production of timely, integrated, and useful information, which is the prime objective of any MSS, could have a significant impact on the proper employment of these technologies. A MSS can be built by using either MSS tools or MSS generators. The proper selection of these technologies has a direct impact on the effective life of a MSS.

Top Management

Heavy involvement of top management in all phases of analysis, design, and implementation could facilitate the introduction of a more viable MSS. This involvement could speed up the introduction phase and improve the cost/benefit ratio of the system during the growth and maturity phases. This involvement could also accelerate the planned abandonment of the MSS and consequently shorten the MSSLC.

Environment

There are many elements outside the boundary of the MSS that could have a very significant impact on the life expectancy of such a system. Increasing business volume is one element that could shorten the life expectancy of a MSS. There are several other factors within the environment that have a direct or indirect impact on the life expectancy of a MSS. These factors could involve changes in present and future competition, customer preferences, government action, suppliers, union activity, the labor market, tax structure, and economic conditions.

MONITORING MECHANISMS FOR MSS IMPLEMENTATION

When considering the design and implementation of a MSS, it is essential to establish monitoring mechanisms that gather information and evaluate the status of the internal and external determinants of the MSS life cycle, including change in volume, significant changes in hardware and software, or major changes in the user information needs. If significant variance or change occurs in these determinants, the MSS designer may need to take action to minimize any adverse impact of the change. This would be analogous to political risk analysis as a monitoring mechanism for the investment decision process with respect to a project in a foreign country. The investment process (or life cycle) could be abandoned or redesigned if the value of the investment project has changed significantly. This variance has, in effect, changed the potential or useful life of the project.

An example of external determinants would be a drastic breakthrough in hardware technology. Microcomputer capacity has increased so significantly in the past few years that many companies that were using minicomputers are now able to use microcomputers for the same, and even expanded, service capability. Some individual or individuals must be responsible for providing this continuous evaluation of the status of hardware and software technologies, such that the abandonment of current technology can be anticipated prior to the actual decline phase of the MSS life cycle.

With these monitoring mechanisms in place, the MSS designer can both enhance the design and implementation of the MSS, as well as manage its movement through its useful life cycle. These monitoring mechanisms should also tell the MSS designer where he or she is in the life cycle at any moment in time.

Some examples of monitoring mechanisms and how they might be used include the following:

IF the user need is not satisfied, THEN the MSS designer should change the data collection strategy in order to reflect the quality and quantity of collected data.

IF the information provided does not match the user's personal and organizational style and status, THEN the MSS designer should vary the format of provided information.

IF the user has problems with the acceptance of the MSS, THEN the introduction phase should provide for ongoing education, OR the MSS should hide the MSS's complexity (i.e., through use of a user-friendly system interface). In other phases, the redesign or planned abandonment should be considered.

IF the user is not comfortable in using the MSS, THEN the MSS designer should provide easy access to the system.

IF the MSS is not responsive to volume increase, THEN the MSS designer should upgrade the database, OR improve the data input/output channels.

IF the user is bombarded by the information provided, THEN the MSS designer should use intelligent filtering and exception reports.

IF the views of top management or user have not been considered in any phases of MSS design and implementation, THEN the MSS designer should use task force design AND/OR interactive design.

IF hardware/software components of the MSS are not responsive to various needs of the user or environment, THEN the MSS designer should employ more suitable hardware/software OR upgrade these components OR plan abandonment.

IF the MSS does not provide information related to the changing environment, THEN the MSS designer should modify the data collection strategy AND/OR redesign the database.

Numerous other examples that are related to the conceptual model of the MSS can be generated.

NEW DESIGN METHODOLOGIES IN MSS ENVIRONMENT

As mentioned earlier, understanding the life-cycle approach is necessary, but it is not sufficient to design a MSS. Life-cycle approach and traditional design methodologies may not be appropriate in a MSS environment. The major reasons for this unsuitability are the following:

1. Lack of prespecification in MSS environment: The problem under investigation is not always well defined. The input–output process cannot be fully identified, and the problem itself is usually poorly defined. The problems addressed by MSS are mostly "ad hoc," nonrecurring, and one-of-a-kind.

2. Changing needs of the user: The user's needs in the MSS environment are continually changing; therefore, a system may have to undergo several changes until it satisfies the unique user needs. Even this system may be suitable for the short range, but in the medium and long range, the system may not be suitable.

Because of these issues, traditional methodologies are not suitable in a MSS environment, and the designer of the MSS must utilize other methodologies. Let us briefly explain some of these methodologies.

Computer-Assisted Systems Engineering

Computer-assisted systems engineering, or computer-assisted software engineering (CASE), refers to the tools used by systems analysts to automate parts of the application development process. CASE tools are a collection of computer programs similar to computer-aided design, which has been used by drafters and engineers for years. The capabilities of CASE tools vary from product to product, but some of the general capabilities offered by a typical CASE tool include the following:

- graphic tools such as DFDs, flowcharts, and structure charts to depict the entire system's operation graphically
- dictionary tools designed to record the operation of the system in detail
- prototyping tools for designing input and output format, forms, and screens
- code generators to minimize or eliminate the programming efforts
- project management tools to help control the time and budget of the project

Several CASE tools are currently available. Some of the most popular ones are Excelerator (Index Technology), Analyst/Designer Toolkit (Yourdon), System Developer's Prokit (McDonnell Douglas), and Information Engineering Facility (Texas Instruments).

CASE offers several advantages for systems analysis and design: Design errors can be spotted graphically; an analyst can design several alternatives, and addition and deletion are more manageable (there is no need to redraw the entire design after each change); because the tools perform some of the repetitive tasks, the analyst is free to concentrate on more important issues; users can participate actively in the design process and express their opinions; and CASE expedites prototyping.

Prototyping

The prototyping methodology has been around for many years in physical science. It is easier and cheaper to build a "prototype" of a system first than to build the entire system. Throughout the information systems history, we have learned that by building small models or prototypes and testing them, the problems, as well as the solutions, become more understandable. The knowledge gained by building, using, and modifying a prototype enables the designers to better understand the problems, information related to the problems, and alternative solutions, and perhaps to choose the "best" solution for a given situation.

Prototyping as a methodology for MSS construction has gained popularity in recent years [8,10,14]. This popularity is mainly due to the changing information needs of decision makers and lack of prespecification in the majority of problems encountered by MSS. Because the construction of a complete system is time consuming, difficult, and expensive, a prototype of the system is developed first. The small-scale system is significant enough to highlight the value of the MSS to the user. Prototyping makes it possible for the user to express his or her views regarding the final MSS, and it is the fastest way to put the MSS into operation.

A comprehensive survey of emerging prototyping methodologies defines the prototyping process in four steps [4]:

1. define initial requirements;
2. develop initial prototype;
3. review and evaluate the prototype;
4. revise the prototype.

To define the initial requirements, the user and the team of designers must agree that a prototyping approach is the most suitable approach for solving the problem at hand. After agreeing on the approach, the user and the designer team work together to gather information about the components of the prototype and how those components relate to one another. The team may decide on one of the following three approaches for the construction of the prototype: using an external vendor to construct the prototype; using application packages; or developing the prototype from scratch using high-level languages or MSS tools.

It is extremely important to include the users of the MSS and top management in the construction phase of the prototype, because problems may arise that only they will be able to resolve. The construction phase increases the organization's knowledge about the problem(s) that the MSS will resolve. The team of users and analysts will learn a lot about the decision-making process of a given situation during the construction phase.

When the prototype is completed, the user begins to use it to make decisions. With each use of the prototype, the user and the analyst team evaluates the prototype. This evaluation process may result in the team (1) revising the prototype; (2) canceling the MSS project; (3) developing an entirely new prototype; or (4) building a complete system based on the prototype.

Regardless of the decision made, the prototype has provided useful information to the user/analyst team. At this point, the problem is better defined, and the system's operations are more understandable.

There are four major types of prototyping methodologies reported in the literature [4]: illustrative (or throwaway), simulated, functional, and evolutionary.

The throwaway, or illustrative, prototype is designed to illustrate and provide feedback. If the user does not like the prototype, it can be thrown away and a new prototype designed. This may also result in the abandonment of the MSS project. If the user is happy with the prototype, this may either evolve to the final system, or it may be used until a separate full-featured MSS is constructed. In this methodology, sample screens and reports for user reviews are generated. It is usually a noniterative process that is used to enhance communication between the user and designer during the requirements definition and design phase. This is probably the most commonly used type of prototyping methodology.

The simulated prototyping methodology provides models that behave as if they were parts of the desired MSS. Simulated models appear to function as parts of the desired MSS, but simulate the interaction with other components of the final MSS, such as the database and dialog management. This model is interactive, because the model can be refined and enhanced.

The functional prototyping methodology is similar to the simulated methodology, with one difference. It provides models that represent a more complete set of system functions. In other words, a functional prototype is a more realistic version of the actual MSS.

The evolving prototype starts from a small-scale system and evolves into the final system by continuously adding new features and upgrading the existing features. The model (or models) developed in this methodology is nondisposable and will be used in the final MSS. Evolutionary methodology is more suitable for systems whose requirements are poorly defined.

Prototyping Development Tools.   To construct a prototype of a system, numerous tools can be utilized. Some of the most popular tools include spreadsheet packages such as Lotus 1-2-3 and Excel, and database management packages such as Access and Paradox. In recent years, tools have been developed to provide "rapid" prototyping. Rapid prototyping is an approach to system development that uses prototypes to help both the designer and users visualize the prototype system and depict its operations and properties in an interactive process [12].

Rapid prototyping makes use of CASE tools to develop prototypes quickly. However, any of the fourth-generation languages and MSS generators, or even third-generation languages or MSS tools, can be used to construct a prototype.

Some of the popular examples of prototype generators are Computer-Aided Prototyping Systems (CAPS), Prototype System Description Language (PSDL),

Rapid prototyping makes use of CASE tools to develop prototypes quickly. However, any of the fourth-generation languages and MSS generators, or even third-generation languages or MSS tools, can be used to construct a prototype.

Some of the popular examples of prototype generators are Computer-Aided Prototyping Systems (CAPS), Prototype System Description Language (PSDL), Knowledge-Based Rapid Prototyping Systems (KBRPS), and Framed-based Software Requirements Specialization System (FSRSS).

Advantages and Disadvantages of Prototyping.   As mentioned earlier, because of the lack of prespecifications and changing needs of decision makers, prototyping offers several unique advantages, as follows: Prototyping provides a method to investigate an environment in which the problem is poorly defined and information is difficult to gather; reduces the need for training the MSS users, because they are involved in development of the system; results in cost saving because it is cheaper to build a model of the system than to build the complete system, and may result in the abandonment of the system (resulting in major savings); increases the chances of success by promoting the user's involvement; is easier to modify and maintain than the actual system; enhances the documentation process of the system by walking through some versions of the system; and improves communications among users, top management, and information systems personnel.

With all these advantages, prototyping has some disadvantages as well: Uncontrolled use of the selected data for developing the prototype may result in incorrect decisions; developing prototypes may require more user and top management support and assistance than they are willing to provide; and prototypes may not reflect the actual operation of the final system.

Middle-Out Methodology.   To understand the middle-out methodology, we should first explain top-down and bottom-up methodologies. In top-down design, a global view of a problem is identified first. Then the problem under investigation is divided into a series of subproblems or modules. Each module is designed separately. At the end, these different pieces will be put together. This methodology has gained popularity for designing traditional computer-based information systems. According to its advocates, this methodology makes designing, modifying, and maintaining a system easier.

However, this methodology may not be suitable for MSS design. The major reason for its unsuitability to MSS environment is its long development process. It takes months, or even years, until a user sees the final product. By that time, the requirements already may have been changed. Also, top-down methodology assumes prespecification, which is not always possible in the MSS environment.

Bottom-up methodology starts in a piecemeal fashion, and may suffer from lack of direction. The solution it offers to a subproblem may not be entirely suitable for a particular situation; or it may not keep in touch with the organizational needs of a particular setting.

The middle-out methodology begins close to the level of the problem at hand [6], and it develops a process of generalizing (bottom-up) and specifying (top-down) at each stage of the problem-solving process. Middle-out methodology begins with a much less global view of the problem, unlike top-down methodology. This approach is justified because of the lack of understanding of all the dimensions (lack of structure in the problem) of the problem under investigation.

Middle-out methodology advocates the utilization of a prototype. The prototype provides quick feedback on the suitability of a solution to a particular problem. The feedback to the prototype may either support the final construction of the system or its complete abandonment. In middle-out methodology, the prototype usually addresses a part of a problem under investigation. Later, several prototypes may be linked together to solve the entire problem. Although the prototype is a small-scale version of the system, it should be able to illustrate the value of a MSS and recommend its final construction.

Iterative Design.   This design methodology concentrates on a small but significant part of a problem and, by going through repetitive steps, tries to improve the system until the user's requirements and design specifications are satisfied, similar to evolutionary prototyping. However, this is different from illustrative prototyping, which may not lead to the final system. The initial system is real, usable, and live, and the user and designer have already agreed on the subproblem under investigation.

Adaptive Design.   This methodology advocates an evolving process in building MSS [1, 9]. In the short range, a MSS may respond to the immediate needs of the user. In the medium range, a MSS may have to improve its capabilities by incorporating new features into its architecture to respond to the changing needs of the user. However, in the long range the MSS may have to utilize a totally new technology to respond to the changing information needs of the user. The entire computer field is a good example of such an adaptive design process.

Computers have evolved from the first through the fourth generation. Each generation introduces brand new technology that is more advanced than the previous. Fifth-generation computers are going to be different from the fourth generation in many radical directions. MSS generators have been improving continuously. A specific MSS that is designed by using a MSS generator has the potential to grow in parallel with the MSS generator. In other words, this process may provide an adaptive environment for the specific MSS.

UNIQUE FEATURES IN MSS SYSTEMS
ANALYSIS AND DESIGN

As discussed in Chapter 1, MSS are different from traditional EDP and MIS. These systems are designed to assist decision makers in making and implementing organizational decisions that are more user and application oriented and more futuristic. These differences in operations and objectives require a different approach when it comes to the analysis and design phases of these systems. We can summarize these unique features under three major categories: decision objectives, design issues, and evaluation criteria.

Decision Objectives

- MSS are designed to address structured, semistructured, and unstructured problems (focus on semistructured and unstructured problems)
- MSS are designed to address current decisions and primarily future decisions
- MSS are designed to address simple and complex decisions
- MSS are designed for control and primarily for planning decisions
- MSS are designed to provide flexibility in decision making and decision implementation.

Design Issues

- In MSS design and implementation, the user is the core.
- In MSS design and utilization, special tools are used, such as prototypes, iterative design, and MSS generators.
- In MSS design and utilization, internal and external data are used.
- MSS provide output that is flexible and tailor-made to the users' needs.
- MSS address both modeling and data analysis applications.
- MSS address ad hoc decisions.
- In most cases, MSS are interactive.
- In MSS, the implementation is never final.

Evaluation Criteria

- In MSS design and utilization, effectiveness and efficiency of the system (mostly effectiveness) are both important.
- In MSS, decision-making and decision-implementation improvement are the ways that decisions are improved and are important.
- In MSS, user satisfaction is very crucial.
- In MSS, iterative and continuous design process are important in order to reflect changing needs.
- In MSS design and utilization, responsiveness of the system to changing needs is very important.

In the systems analysis and design phases, the analyst or team of analysts must consider these issues and, by integration of the classic life-cycle approach, product life-cycle approach, and new design methodology, follow a new methodology which we call an "integrated" approach.

SYSTEMS ANALYSIS AND DESIGN FOR MSS:
AN INTEGRATED APPROACH

Because MSSs are designed to be used by key decision makers, their involvement plays a major role in determining the systems' success. The classic life-cycle approach changes direction in the MSS environment. Differences can be traced by examining the following steps: problem definition, formation of the task force, construction of an online prototype, and evaluation.

Problem Definition

In this step, the objective of the system must be defined. The user must be informed and in agreement with the following four Ws:

Why is the system going to be designed? What decision(s) will be effected? How will the organization use this system?

Who is going to use the system? Is it going to be used by one decision maker or a group of decision makers?

When will the system be operational? From now until the final implementation, how will decisions affected by the MSS be made?

What kind of capabilities will the MSS provide? Is it a modeling type, a database management system (DBMS) type, or a combination? How will these different capabilities be used, and how will the system provide these capabilities?

Formation of the Task Force

For the continued success of the MSS, different users must have input in the design and maintenance of the system. Their views must be highly regarded. This issue will be of considerable significance, particularly if the system is going to be used by more than one user.

The task force should include representatives from different user departments, top management, and technical staff. Preferably, the task force should include the individuals presented in Figure 2.3. The task force members should work to define the user's needs as precisely as possible.

Construction of an Online Prototype

A simple prototype shows the user how the system will work and greatly improves the chances of success. The "online" prototype gives the user a chance to see a small-scale version of the system in action, while allowing the designer to find out the possible problems associated with the system. As discussed earlier, there are four kinds of prototypes. A prototype may even be developed into the final system.

The process of prototype design and modification should continue until the user is satisfied with the prototype. Then the construction of the final system can be started.

Figure 2.3
MSS Task Force

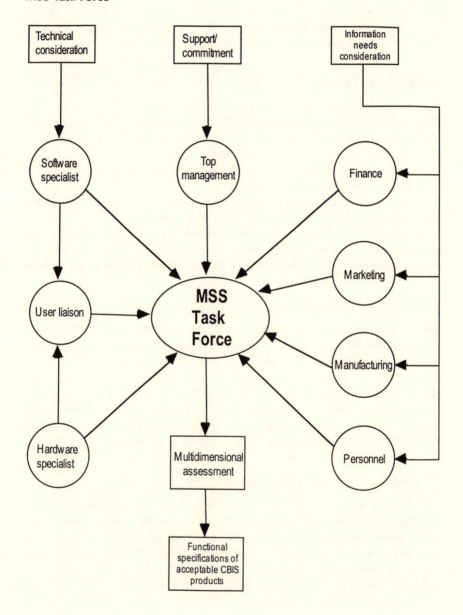

Evaluation

As will be discussed in Chapter 4, the evaluation of a MSS is not based only on the monetary benefits generated by the system. The impacts of the system on decision making, decision implementation, and learning and the overall effectiveness of the system are equally important.

Based on the results of the evaluation, the process of modification may continue or be halted temporarily until the user uses new features of the system or adds new features to the system (Figure 2.4). As this figure shows, all the phases of the classic life-cycle approach are combined into one phase, and this phase continues in an iterative manner until the system is constructed. After construction of the system, the monitoring mechanism improves the quality of life for the system and suggests any corrective action(s) that must be taken to guarantee the user's satisfaction.

THREE APPROACHES FOR BUILDING A MSS

There are three approaches for building a MSS: traditional, outsourcing, and end-user computing (EUC). In the traditional approach, the data processing department mainly constructs the MSS with some input from the user group. This approach has its own advantages and disadvantages. The advantages are that these systems are usually technically sound; include appropriate security measures; and meet the information systems standards.

Among the most serious disadvantages of this approach are that the systems are not tailored to the specific needs of the users and they are not constructed in a timely fashion.

Using the outsourcing approach, an organization may hire an external vendor or consultant(s) who specializes in providing construction services. This approach has its own advantages and disadvantages. Among the advantages are cost-effectiveness, timeliness, and flexibility (which may allow the organization to concentrate on other projects).

Some of the disadvantages of outsourcing include loss of control, dependency, and vulnerability of strategic information. The organization may lose control over its information systems functions, so the final system may not reflect the specific information requirements of the organization. Also, the organization becomes dependent on the outsourcing company. A significant change in the financial or management status of the outsourcing company may reduce the quality of the provided information system. Also, using outsourcing may jeopardize important information and may leak information to competitors.

For these reasons, a number of users and organizations consider EUC an attractive approach for MSS construction with little or no formal assistance from the information systems group. These users occupy various positions such as accountants, bankers, lawyers, or other professionals and may not

Figure 2.4
Iterative Process of MSS Design

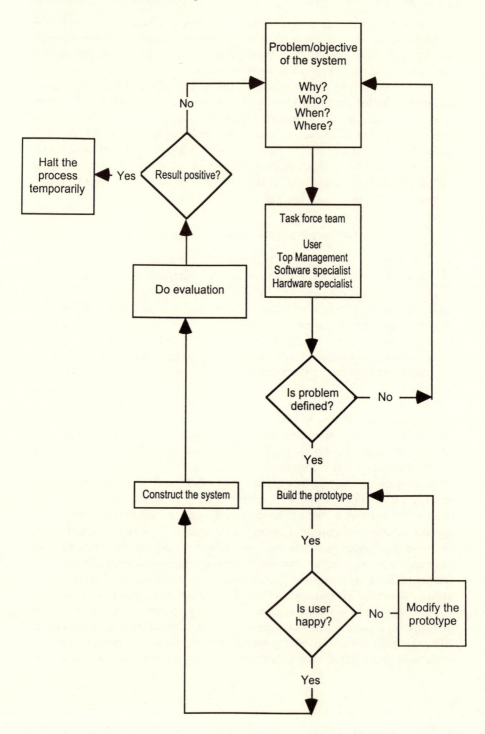

know how to write programming codes but are eager and skilled enough to take off-the-shelf PC software such as spreadsheets and databases and produce custom-built applications [2].

EUC is a development resulting from lengthy system backlogs, the availability of affordable hardware and software, and the increasing dependence of business organizations on timely and relevant information. With the help of EUC tools such as query languages, report generators, and fourth-generation languages, EUC has become an active partner in sharing information systems functions and resources. EUC has positive effects, such as reducing application backlog, supporting user-defined systems analysis and development, and providing the flexibility in responding to users' unique information needs. In the meantime, EUC also brings challenges to managers who are concerned with the lack of adequate system analysis and design background, loosening systems standards, and the proliferation of uncontrolled "private" data and applications.

SUMMARY

In this chapter, we discussed tools and techniques for building a MSS. By explaining the classic life-cycle approach, the product life-cycle approach, and the new design methodologies, we have combined and integrated these approaches and proposed an "integrated approach" that is more suitable for MSS design.

REFERENCES

1. Alavi, Maryann, and H. Albert Napier. "An Experiment in Applying the Adoptive Design Approach to DSS Development." *Information & Management* 7 (July 1984): 21–28.
2. Benson, David H. "A Field Study of End User Computing: Findings and Issues." *MIS Quarterly* (December 1983): 35–40.
3. Bidgoli, Hossein, and Howard Rudd. "Information Systems Life Cycle as a Tool for Design and Implementation of Computer Based Management Information Systems." *Proceedings S.E. AIDS* (February/March 1985): 316–318.
4. Doke, Reed E. "An Industry Survey of Emerging Prototyping Methodologies." *Information & Management* 18 (1990): 169–176.
5. Gaydesch, Alexander, Jr. *Principles of EDP Management*. Reston, Va.: Reston Publishing Company, 1982: 79–90.
6. Hurst, E. Gerald Jr., David N. Ness, Thomas J. Gambino, and Thomas H. Johnson. "Growing DSS: A Flexible Evolutionary Approach." In *Building Decision Support Systems*, edited by John L. Bennett, pp. 111–132. Reading, Mass.: Addison-Wesley Publishing, 1983.
7. Jackson, John F., and Susan W. Adams. "The Life Cycle of Rules." *Academy of Management Review* (October 1979): 269–273.
8. Janson, Marius A., and L. Douglas Smith. "Prototyping for Systems Development: A Critical Appraisal." *MIS Quarterly* (December 1985): 305–316.
9. Keen, Peter G. W. "Adaptive Design for Decision Support Systems." *Data Base* 12 (Fall 1980): 15–25.

10. Lantz, Kenneth. "The Prototyping Methodology: Designing Right the First Time." *ComputerWorld* (April 7, 1986): 69–72.
11. "Plant Shutdowns: States Take a New Tack." *Business Week* (October 24, 1983): 73, 76.
12. Seigerwald, R., R. Lupi, and J. McDowell. "CASE Tool for Reusable Software Component Storage and Retrieval in Rapid Prototyping." *Information and Software Technology* 33 (November 1991): 698–706.
13. Smith, E. Paul. "Measuring Professional Obsolescence: A Half-Life Model for the Physician." *Academy of Management Review* (October 1978): 914–917.
14. Sroka, John M., and Martha H. Rader. "Prototyping Increases Chance of Systems Acceptance." *Data Management* (March 1986): 12–19.
15. Whitten, Jeffery L., and Lonnie D. Bently. *Systems Analysis & Design Methods*, 4th ed. Burr Ridge, Ill.: Irwin, 1998.

CHAPTER 3

Modeling in Management Support Systems

In this chapter, the model and modeling analysis in the MSS environment will be discussed. For MSS to be able to support all phases of decision making (intelligence, design, and choice), a model base, a database, and dialog management are needed. This chapter provides a background for models and modeling analysis and types of models with some examples. The chapter also highlights problems associated with traditional modeling techniques. As you will learn, the majority of these problems will be solved when models are used in the MSS environment. The chapter then presents applications of modeling techniques within functional areas of business, and ends with guidelines for implementing modeling techniques in a MSS environment. The capabilities of Microsoft Excel and the Interactive Financial Planning System (IFPS) as two popular MSS modeling products will be introduced. These two products are chosen because of their popularity both in the academic and business worlds. The chapter also highlights the important capabilities of SPSS and SAS, two of the strong modeling tools available for both academic and business use, and introduces other modeling software.

WHAT IS A MODEL?

A model is a representation of a real-life situation. Because studying a real-life situation is usually difficult, costly, and, in many cases, not practical, we build a model of the real-life situation and then conduct a study of the model.

A model is made up of a series of elements and relationships. In modeling terms, the elements are called variables, and the relationships are the constraints imposed, either internally or externally. There are many types of models. An organizational chart is a model representing a particular organization and the relationships existing among individuals in the organization. For MSS purposes, we are interested primarily in mathematical and statistical models. These models are constructed using a series of variables and possibly a series of constraints. A simple example of a model would be a balance sheet:

$$\text{Total Assets} = \text{Fixed Assets} + \text{Current Assets}$$

$$\text{or } TA = FA + CA$$

If two of the variables were defined, the third would be automatically defined. Another example of a model is a break-even analysis formula:

$$\text{Break-Even Point} = \text{Fixed Cost}/(\text{Sales price} - \text{Variable Cost})$$

$$\text{or } BEP = FC/(SP - VC)$$

If the fixed cost is \$500, the sales price is \$15, and the variable cost is \$10, the break-even point is 100 units. Assuming all the units that are produced can be sold, the company is neither losing money nor gaining any profit. Above this point (100 units) the company is making a profit, and below this point the company is losing money.

The models used in the MSS environment are more complicated and involve many more variables and constraints; however, the principle is the same.

MODEL BUILDING PROCESS

To build a model in a MSS environment, the following steps are usually followed.

1. Problem definition
2. Construction of the model
3. Solving the model
4. Analyzing the solution
5. Testing and Validation

Problem Definition.   Because this is the most important step, you have to make sure to define the problem under investigation as precisely as possible. A comprehensive problem definition makes the task of model building an easier one. The following are some examples of problems to be addressed by a MSS:

An online sales forecast for a department store: This model provides decision makers with a tool to avoid the over or underforecast. Either forecast error can be costly.

Effective advertising media selection for a service agency: This model assists decision makers in spending the advertising budget effectively. A company can choose any medium or combination of media. Which combination is the best? Which combination will reach the highest number of potential customers?

An online budgeting model for city hall for the next five years: An online budgeting model may save time and frustration for the budget specialist in the organization. This model, if properly designed, can provide sophisticated features, such as what-if analysis, goal seeking, sensitivity analysis, and so forth. This powerful tool can help an organization meet its financial goals in a comprehensive manner.

Construction of the Model.   After careful definition of the problem, the model is constructed. This means all variables, constraints, and assumptions are stated in mathematical terms. In a forecasting assignment, the most appropriate forecasting model is selected. This may be a time series or regression model, or a combination of these.

Solving the Model.   The constructed model must be solved in order to determine the numerical value of each variable. This is usually done with a computer.

Analyzing the Solution.   The solution must be analyzed and conclusions drawn. It may require some corrective action, but models in a MSS environment go through continuous updating procedures. It is a natural process because the information needs of decision makers and the environmental factors are continuously changing.

Testing and Validation.   Discussion of model building and computerized models should not lead you to the conclusion that computerized models in MSS solve all the problems. Also, you should not have the impression that a decision maker directly uses and relies on the modeling analyses. This is far from the truth. Computerized models can be misleading. Only expert statisticians and operations researchers are aware of all the assumptions underlying these models. The decision maker must use his or her judgment and utilize the advice of intermediaries, which in this case are usually experts from operations research departments. That is why large organizations have operations research departments. Therefore, the "amateur" use of computerized models must be avoided, and the output of these models must be thoroughly interpreted before their actual use. A good example of amateur use of a model would be multiple linear regression (MLR) analyses. In MLR, the value of R^2 usually indicates the strength of correlation between dependent and independent variables. At the same time, a large R^2 may have been generated by severe multicollinearity problems or a gross failure of the model's normality assumptions.

The issue of misuse of modeling techniques is more serious than ever, because of the availability of inexpensive modeling software. Constructing models using these readily available microcomputer's modeling software is relatively an easy task. The main challenge is to understand all the assumptions that a model is based on and the interpretation of the result [4]. For a detailed discussion of MLR and its assumptions, see *Methods and Applications of Linear Models* by Hocking [5] and *Introduction to Linear Regression* by Montgomery [8].

MODELING ANALYSIS VERSUS DATA ANALYSIS

Database, model base, and dialog management are integral components of most MSS. If the MSS is designed to support all phases of decision making (intelligence, design, and choice), all three components are necessary. The database component supports the intelligence phase of decision making. The modeling component is required for the design and choice phases of decision making [9].

All information provided by a typical MSS is generated by data analysis, modeling analysis, or a combination of both. To make this distinction clearer, consider the following example: The data presented in Table 3.1 have been extracted from the corporate database of Online Automated, a wholesaler of electronic devices. By manipulating these data, some valuable questions can be generated:

• Who has generated the highest total sales?
• Who has generated the lowest total sales?
• Which city has generated the highest total sales?
• Which city has generated the lowest total sales?
• What are the total sales of the company?

Can anything be said about the future by examining these data? Can any statistical conclusion be drawn, either for the salespersons or the sales regions? Using such simple data analysis, the answer to these questions is no.

Using modeling analysis, however, we can provide answers to these questions and more. Using a simple forecasting model, we can generate a forecast for total sales for any city or salesperson. We can use statistical models to compare the performance of cities or salespersons to spot significant differences. Here the key point is that modeling analysis is attempting to look into the future and investigate any possible relationship among the various data points. By analyzing different alternatives and choosing the most desirable alternative,

Table 3.1
Online Automated Corporate Database

Salespersons	L.A.	Denver	Portland	St. Paul	Detroit
Jack	150	510	750	500	980
Bob	180	580	900	480	640
Robin	200	610	830	900	720
Mary	600	920	650	600	690
Becky	250	630	490	400	950
Sylvia	350	640	500	600	250
John	750	510	610	720	700
Melanie	550	650	450	950	900

Note: Figures in thousands.

modeling analysis provides support for the design and choice phases of decision making.

Modeling analysis utilizes data available in the database and, by using mathematical and statistical models, generates some insight into what might happen in the future. For example, we can apply a simple regression model to the data presented in Table 3.1 and predict Melanie's performance in the next period based on her past performance. As you will see later in this chapter, there are many models that have been successfully utilized in the MSS environment.

LIMITATIONS OF TRADITIONAL MODELING TECHNIQUES

Traditional modeling techniques have been criticized for the following reasons [2, 9]:

1. The typical model user has not easily understood their output.
2. They are unable to cope with discontinuities, especially in model input data.
3. They are unable to evaluate model validity based on its output.
4. They are unable to guide the user through possible analyses beyond the output of the model.
5. They are unable to explain why the model acted the way it did.
6. All necessary input data have not always been available for models to analyze.
7. Models have not always included all necessary variables.
8. Interaction between the model and the user has been minimal.
9. Certain variables and relationships are not easily quantifiable, or are not mathematically traceable.

In a MSS environment, the majority of these problems will be either resolved or significantly reduced.

Output of a MSS can be in a variety of formats: graphic, tabular, detailed, or summary. These options are provided to suit the different styles and needs of decision makers. In a MSS environment, there are different types of intermediaries trained to obtain and explain MSS output to the MSS user. Of course, these intermediaries are used if they are needed. They will go over the model output, explain its meaning, and interpret the assumptions employed in the modeling process.

MSS are designed to utilize different types of models. By their nature, these models are supposed to utilize both continuous and discrete data input. Through the screening process, MSS utilize the most relevant data for further analysis.

Through feedback control, the validity of MSS models can be continuously evaluated. By using some of the output generated by the model as input to the model in the next round, models in the MSS environment are controlled and updated continuously. By using the most current data, the parameters of the model can be modified, the structure of the model can be modified, or both.

The parameters refer to the constant values or coefficients in the model, and structure refers either to the number and types of variables included in the model or replacing a model with another model in the same group.

When models are used in the MSS environment, diverse analyses can be performed and more insight can be gained. This feature is possible either with the help of an intermediary or some of the built-in features, such as what-if, goal seeking, and sensitivity analyses, available in the MSS modeling component.

Because models in the MSS environment are using the most relevant, accurate, and recent data, the user knows why the model acts the way it does. Database management systems (DBMS) continually modify, update, and integrate all data available in the database component of the MSS. These functions maintain the most relevant data in the database for a more accurate modeling analysis.

The database component of the MSS provides all data needed by the modeling component. The quality and quantity of data is guaranteed by virtue of an extensive information pool.

Because all relevant data needed for modeling analysis are included in the database and because the user or designer of the MSS has complete control regarding the type and quantity of data to be entered into the model, it is possible to decide which variables will be included in the model. A good example of this type of modeling is the step-wise MLR for forecasting. This technique, by including some of the most relevant data, can tell the user which variable should be included or excluded from the model. The user can include all variables in the model and later eliminate those that prove to be insignificant.

Another example would be moving average or exponential smoothing models used for forecasting. These techniques utilize some of the most relevant data in the model or assign the heaviest weight to the most recent data. When new data become available, the older data are automatically eliminated. This process generates the best possible forecast.

Finally, flexible user interface and intermediaries should produce maximum interaction between the MSS and the user. As discussed in Chapter 2, using flexible and progressive design methodologies such as prototyping, task force, and iterative design should encourage the use of MSS, and the majority of earlier problems should be resolved.

MODELING IN THE MSS ENVIRONMENT

To be able to support all the phases of decision making (intelligence, design, and choice), the following capabilities are needed[9]:

1. The modeling component of the MSS should be able to *analyze* the data in the database component. This should include different types of analyses, such as arithmetic operations, statistical analysis, trend analysis, and so forth.

2. The modeling component of MSS should be able to *generate alternatives* for solving a problem. Using alternative data sets or alternative models in the same family can generate these alternatives.

3. The modeling component of MSS should be able to *compare alternatives* and choose the best or make suggestions regarding each alternative. This feature could be built into the MSS modeling component. For example, comparing the error generated by each forecasting technique and then choosing the one that generates the smallest error helps the decision maker select the best forecast.

4. The modeling component of a MSS should also perform *simulation, optimization,* and *forecasting*. These techniques can be included in the model base component of the MSS.

The most challenging task in model building and modeling analysis in a MSS environment is the inclusion of the most appropriate data and variables in the model. The data included in the database component of MSS are both internal and external. The challenge is to identify and include all the relevant external data. Figure 3.1 highlights the factors in the environment of a MSS that might be relevant and should be included in modeling analysis. Naturally, these factors are not suitable for all MSS. Depending on the situation, the relevant external factors must be carefully identified, then, if possible, integrated in the model base component of a MSS.

Finally, models in MSS should include what-if, goal seeking, and sensitivity analyses. As we will see later in this chapter, these features can be either built into the modeling component of a MSS or purchased as part of the commercial MSS products available on the market.

TYPES OF MODELS

There are several methods by which models can be classified: They can be classified by their functions, by the techniques they use, or by their mathematical structure. For MSS purposes, we choose to classify models by the functions they perform: optimization models and nonoptimization models.

Optimization models are designed to generate the best possible solution to a particular problem. Linear programming is an excellent example of this type. We will provide a detailed explanation of this model later in this chapter.

Nonoptimization models are designed to provide a "good enough" solution to a problem using different techniques: These models "satisfy" as opposed to "optimize." However, this solution does not presume to be the best possible solution. Actually, the problems solved by these techniques are not suitable for optimization-type analysis.

Optimization Models

Optimization models are designed to either maximize profit or minimize cost. They are summarized as follows:

- linear optimization models (allocation models, assignment models, transportation models, network models) (program evaluation review technique [PERT], critical path method [CPM], management operation system technique [MOST], and line of balance [LOB])

- inventory optimization models (EOQ and EMQ)
- portfolio optimization models
- dynamic programming optimization models
- nonlinear optimization models

Figure 3.1
External Factors Relevant to the Model Base Component of a MSS

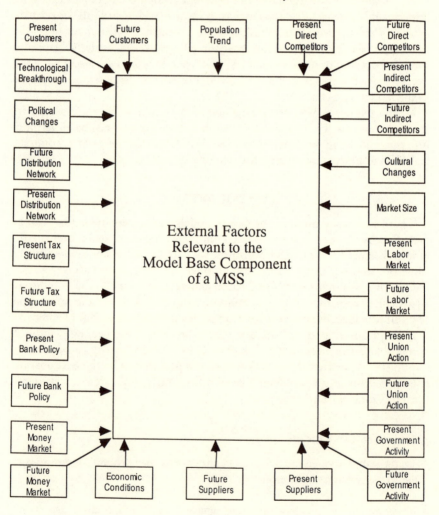

Linear Optimization Models.   Allocation models include linear programming models and are used to allocate limited resources among competing demands for these resources.

Example #1: Allocation of 100 hours of labor and 200 units of leather to either making shoes or bags to maximize the profit.

Example #2: Allocation of 400 hours of labor and 300 hours of assembly-line time to manufacturing either color or black and white televisions to maximize profit.

Assignment models are special applications of linear programming models and are used to assign activities to individuals, machines to operators, and so forth.

Example #1: Assignment of five machines to five operators to minimize the total cost or total time of operation.

Example #2: Assignment of four runners to four races to minimize total running time.

Transportation models are also applications of linear programming models. They are designed to establish the best possible link between sources (origin) and sinks (destination) in a transportation-type problem.

Example #1: There are five warehouses and ten shopping centers. Which warehouses should ship to which shopping centers to minimize shipping costs?

Example #2: There are twelve tankers and six oil rigs. Which tanker should be assigned to which oil rig to minimize traveling distance and total cost?

Network models use PERT or CPM methods to determine the critical path for the completion of a series of interrelated activities. Network models are also used to establish a telecommunications network system to minimize distance and wiring cost.

Example #1: Site preparation for a computer center. How must all activities be organized to minimize the total construction time? Which activity or activities can be delayed and still be able to complete the project on time?

Example #2: To establish a LAN in a ten-story building that includes thirty-six offices on each floor. How should all these nodes (offices) be connected to minimize the wiring cost?

There are two other models used in this group: MOST is used to improve some features of PERT. It is mostly used in production-oriented organizations. LOB was developed by the U.S. Navy as a graphic method for industrial programming; it is useful in a production setting. PERT, MOST, and LOB can be combined to provide a more effective scheduling tool for decision-making purposes. For more information on these three techniques, consult Iannone [6] and Mittra [7].

Inventory Optimization Models. Inventory models are used to minimize the cost of inventory. These models assist the decision maker in solving problems regarding the amount of products ordered and the timing of the order. Economic order quantity (EOQ) and economic manufacturing quantity (EMQ) are two good examples of this type. For example, a shoe company sells 48,000 pairs of shoes. When and how many pairs of shoes should be ordered to minimize the total inventory cost?

Portfolio Optimization Models. A combination of capital budgeting, such as present value, future value, internal rate of return, and mathematical models, is used to determine the best possible combination of securities in an investment setting problem. For example, a newly established high-tech company decides to establish a sound portfolio policy that minimizes the risk to capital. What is the best combination of common stocks, preferred stocks, bonds, and real estate?

Dynamic Programming Optimization Models. These models are suitable for interrelated decisions and can be either deterministic or probabilistic. Usually, in these types of models, the next outcome is related, directly or indirectly, to the previous outcome. They emphasize the overall effectiveness of the entire system and deconstruct one large problem into a series of subproblems that are easier to solve. Therefore, these techniques are very suitable for multistage problems (e.g., a 12-month decision that can be broken down into three separate decisions in each quarter). Dynamic programming models may utilize different techniques such as linear programming, network techniques, or inventory models, depending on the nature of the problem. For example, regarding the replacement of machinery in a manufacturing operation, when should a particular machine be replaced? Should a machine be replaced or repaired?

Nonlinear Optimization Models. In these models, the relationships among variables are not linear, meaning, in mathematical terms, that the variables are of the second degree or higher. For example, X, Y, Z are linear, but X^2 or XY or XYZ are nonlinear. An example of this type is the quadratic model: $Y = A + BX + CX^2$. An example is a linear model that includes all linear constraints, but the objective function is quadratic in decision variables. For example, when you sell more, the price of items will decrease in a nonlinear fashion. This means the subsequent units will generate profit at a different rate than previous units. In a linear programming problem, all units must generate the same amount of profit and all the units will consume the same amount of raw material(s) and labor.

Example of an Optimization Model. To show the steps involved in model building and model formulation, let us examine a simple problem faced by a local manufacturer of leather products.

1. *Problem definition*: A manufacturer of leather products is planning to allocate its two limited resources, 120 units of raw materials and 90 hours of labor, between two competing products, shoes and bags. The following data have been collected from the past operation's database:

each pair of shoes requires 2 units of leather

each pair of shoes requires 3 hours of labor

each leather bag requires 4 units of leather

each leather bag requires 1 hour of labor

each pair of shoes generates $100 profit

each leather bag generates $80 profit

All assumptions of a classic linear programming model are present, so all units of the same products will be sold at the stated prices, and different units of both products will consume the specified amount of resources.

2. *Construction of the model.* Formulate the problem as follows:

X_1 = the number of pairs of shoes

X_2 = the number of leather bags

Z = the objective function to be maximized

$2X_1 + 4X_2 \leq 120$	Constraint #1
$3X_1 + X_2 \leq 90$	Constraint #2
$Z = 100X_1 + 80X_2$	Objective function
$X_1, X_2 \geq 0$	This assumption indicates that the production cannot be negative.

Constraint #1 indicates that there are at most 120 units of raw materials that can be allocated, and constraint #2 indicates that there are at most 90 hours of labor that can be allocated between the two competing activities.

3. *Solving the model.* This problem, though simple, shows how modeling works. The problem can be solved either graphically or by using the simplex method, or one of the commercial packages. In any event, the numerical values are:

$$X_1 = 24$$
$$X_2 = 18$$
$$Z = \$3,840.00$$

This is the best possible solution to this problem. No other combination can generate a profit as high as $3,840.

4. *Analyzing the Solution.* Now the decision maker may want to perform some sensitivity analysis. If the profit generated by each pair of shoes is decreased by 15 percent, what will happen to the product mix? If manufacturing each leather bag requires 4

units of leather instead of 3 units, what will the product mix be? Other important and interesting questions can be put to the model, and the model will answer them. Actually, in linear programming models, these questions can be answered using a technique called shadow pricing. For more information, consult Anderson [1].

5. *Testing and Validation.* As discussed earlier, model testing is an important phase in modeling analysis. In this phase, the decision maker, with the help of an intermediary, should make sure the underlying assumptions of a particular model are well understood. The decision maker must use his or her judgment to make sure the provided answers make sense and are consistent with the overall goals and objectives of the organization. After careful analysis, the provided solution can be put into action.

Nonoptimization Models

Nonoptimization models provide a good enough solution to many problems. These models include forecasting, regression, trend analysis, and simulation and decision tree. They are summarized as follows:

- forecasting models (quantitative [moving average and exponential smoothing] and qualitative [delphi and analogy])
- regression models (simple linear regression [SLR] and multiple linear regression [MLR])
- decision-tree models
- simulation models

Forecasting Models. There are two types of forecasting models: statistical (quantitative) and technological (qualitative). In a MSS environment, we are interested primarily in statistical forecasting models. There are a variety of forecasting models that can be used for short-, medium-, and long-range forecasting problems. For example, exponential smoothing, moving average, and mean are used for short- to medium-range forecasting. In this group, we can also include trend analysis (linear and nonlinear models). In a trend analysis model, one of the variables is always time. Using the past data available in the database, these models can generate the best possible forecast.

Regression Models. There are two types of regression models: SLR and MLR. In a simple linear regression, the relationship between two variables is established and a forecast is generated. For example, considering the advertising budget, you may be interested in predicting the company's total sales for the next period. You may want to first find out how strong such a relationship is and then generate a forecast. The SLR model can be a valuable tool in a situation like this.

In MLR, the performance of one variable, called the dependent variable, is predicted by a series of other independent variables. For example, you may want to predict the sales performance of a salesperson based on his or her education, years of experience, and sales territory. In this example, the sales performance is dependent, and the other three variables are independent.

Decision-Tree Models. Decision-tree models are used when a decision maker must deal with several alternatives, each with a different outcome. Usually there are some probabilities associated with each alternative. A decision tree can help you graphically depict the entire tree and evaluate the expected value of each branch (or each alternative) of the tree. The alternative with the highest expected profit or the lowest expected cost will be selected. For example, Tri-Teck, an oil company, is dealing with four alternatives in its newest oil field: drilling, drilling with condition, leasing, and leasing with condition. Also, there are three states of nature related to each alternative: hitting water, hitting low-quality oil, and hitting high-quality oil. There is a probability associated with each state of nature. The probabilities are based on historical data stored in the database. The question is, Which alternative must be chosen in order to minimize the risk or maximize the profit? A decision-tree model can demonstrate this process and help the decision maker calculate the expected value of each alternative (outcome multiplied by its probability is the expected value). Table 3.2 presents the payoff table for the oil company, and Figure 3.2 illustrates the decision tree generated based on data in Table 3.2.

Expected values for the four alternatives are as follows:

Expected value of alternative a1 = $(12 \times .25) + (13 \times .40) + (17 \times .35) = 14.15$
Expected value of alternative a2 = $(14 \times .25) + (15 \times .40) + (16 \times .35) = 15.10$
Expected value of alternative a3 = $(11 \times .25) + (12 \times .40) + (18 \times .35) = 13.85$
Expected value of alternative a4 = $(16 \times .25) + (11 \times .40) + (14 \times .35) = 13.30$

Table 3.2
Payoff Table for Tri-Teck

	State of Nature		
Alternative	Hitting Water S1	Hitting Low-Quality Oil S2	Hitting High-Quality Oil S3
a1 Drilling	12	13	17
a2 Drilling with condition	14	15	16
a3 Leasing	11	12	18
a4 Leasing with condition	16	11	14
Probability	.25	.40	.35

Figure 3.2
Decision Tree for Tri-Teck

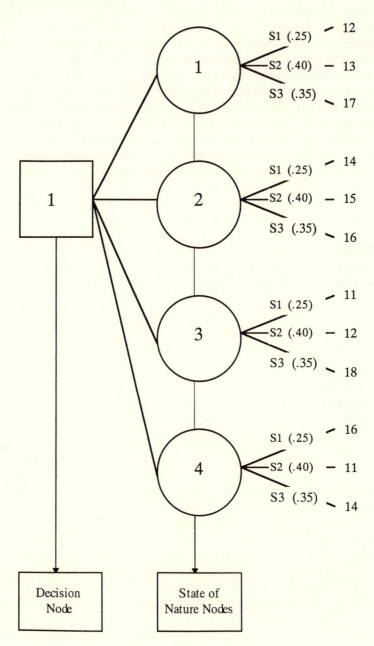

According to this calculation, alternative #2, drilling with condition, has the highest expected value; therefore, regardless of the state of nature, this alternative must be chosen.

Simulation Models. Simulation models are used to evaluate alternative courses of action based on variables and constraints built into the model. For example, a newly established service center is deciding on the number of operators to be assigned to run the service center. If there are too many operators, the company may lose a lot of money. At the same time, if too few operators are assigned, the company may lose customers because of long waiting lines. A simulation model can help in a situation like this. The pattern of customer arrival can be simulated by a computer program, and, based on this pattern, the waiting time, the length of the queue, and the service time can be calculated.

Example of a Nonoptimization Model. An example of a nonoptimization model uses data extracted from the corporate database of Tasty Cool, a soft-drink distributor, presented in Table 3.3. The marketing vice president is planning to spend $500,000 on advertising, and she would like answers to two questions: How strong is the relationship between the advertising expenses and the total sales? And if she spends $500,000 on advertising, assuming other factors are constant, how much would the estimated total sales be?

Table 3.3
Tasty Cool Database

Year	Advertising Expenses (in thousands)	Total Sales (in thousands)
1990	60	670
1991	70	660
1992	75	710
1993	92	715
1994	108	770
1995	116	800
1996	157	790
1997	169	820

Using an SLR should provide an answer to both questions. We used Lotus 1-2-3 for Windows, which came up with the following equation:

$$Y = 594,668 + 1,390X$$

$$\text{and } R^2 = .82$$

This means that, first of all, there is a very high correlation between advertising expenses and total sales. Second, if the company does not spend any money on advertising, the estimated total sales would be $594,668; and if the company spends $500,000, the estimated total sales would be as follows:

$$594,668 + 1,390 \times 500,000 = \$695,784,955.64$$

Remember, this is just an example to show how this technique works. In reality, this may not be the final conclusion because there may be other variables having direct impact on the total sales. Also in this analysis, we have presumed that the assumptions of regression analysis are valid.

Types of Decisions and Organizational Levels

MSS are designed to support a decision maker at any level of the organization. However, the emphasis is on the middle and upper levels of the organization and on semistructured and unstructured tasks. Decision makers in different levels of the organization have different information needs and personal and organizational styles. Designers of MSS, therefore, should consider these differences. Because of the unique characteristics of each level and the specific information needs, different models can be used in different levels.

Modeling Applications, Business Functions, and Modeling Techniques Used in MSS

The number of modeling applications in various areas, particularly in business discipline, is well documented throughout the literature. A study conducted by Eom and Lee [3] clearly illustrates these applications in disciplines such as accounting, auditing, finance, human resources management, marketing, and so forth.

A MSS can be designed to assist decision makers in all functional areas of a business. Some areas may benefit more from MSS than others because of the availability of data and models for each specific function. However, a MSS, if properly designed, should be a valuable tool in all business functions. Table 3.4 highlights areas within each business function that may benefit directly from MSS and models used by these systems.

Table 3.4
MSS in Different Business Functions

Business Functions	Particular Area	Model Used by MSS
Accounting	Cost Accounting	Inventory Models
Corporate Planning	Budgeting	Allocation Models
Distribution	Effective Distribution	Linear Programming/ Transportation
Engineering	Product Design	Simulation, Capital Budgeting
Finance	Cashflow Analysis	Simulation
Inventory/Warehousing	Inventory Problems	EOQ, EMQ
Investment	Investment Structure	Portfolio Models
Manufacturing	Waiting-Line Problems	Queuing
Marketing	Advertising Problems	Simulation, Allocation Models
Purchasing	Vendor Performance	Combined Models
Personnel	Skill Evaluation/Promotion	Statistical Models
Sales	Sales Forecast	Forecasting Models

Implementation of Modeling Techniques in the MSS Environment

Modeling techniques can be implemented in several ways. Using subroutines or prepackaged programs are probably two of the most commonly used methods. A subroutine can either be developed in-house or purchased commercially. If the subroutine approach is used, then each model is written as one subroutine. Each subroutine can be retrieved with a CALL statement, and a RETURN statement marks the end of a subroutine where control will be transferred back to the main program. The model base component of a MSS has a close analogy to the database component. This means that a general-purpose program equivalent to DBMS can retrieve the model base component of a MSS. This general-purpose program, model base management system (MBMS), has a built-in facility for access to and manipulation and updating of these subroutines.

Statistical package for social sciences (SPSS) is a good example of a subroutine-oriented package. A variety of statistical, forecasting, and optimization problems can be solved with this package. If the user is interested in a particular analysis not included in the package, that analysis can be developed in-house. The following are the important features of SPSS and SPSS/PC.

- data entry and editing procedures
- direct interface between SPSS and SPSS/PC with popular PC packages such as Lotus 1-2-3, dBASE, Quattro Pro, and Excel
- file-handling routines
- descriptive statistics, including correlation, regression, and analysis of variance
- report writing and plotting functions
- advanced statistical techniques, including factor, cluster, log linear, discriminant analyses, and multivariate analysis of variance
- time series analysis
- forecasting, including smoothing, regression, and Box-Jenkins
- full-color "snapshot" graphics
- tabulation analysis
- direct interface with other graphics programs

Statistical analysis system (SAS) is a powerful modeling software used for numerous applications. The important features of SAS and SAS/PC are summarized as follows:

- information storage and retrieval
- full-screen editing
- data modification and interactive programming
- report writing
- diverse statistical analysis, including regression, multivariate, discriminant, and cluster analyses
- survival analysis
- scoring procedures
- tabulation analysis
- different color graphics and plotting
- analysis of variance
- forecasting and time series analysis
- software interface with graphic and OR packages
- financial analysis and planning
- optimization models

There are a number of commercial packages on the market known as MSS products or MSS generators able to perform a variety of modeling analyses. Table 3.5 provides a listing of some of the popular MSS modeling packages.

Table 3.5
Popular MSS Modeling Products

Product	Vendor
Compete	Computer Associates
Commander Prism	Comshare, Inc.
One-Up	Comshare, Inc.
Improve for Windows	Lotus Development Corporation
Accent R	National Information Systems, Inc.
Express	Information Resources, Inc.
Focus	Information Builders, Inc.
Nomad	Must Software International
Ramis II	Computer Associates
Simplan	Simplan Systems, Inc.

The following are basic capabilities of interactive financial planning system (IFPS) as a popular modeling MSS product.

- information storage and retrieval
- full-screen editing
- data modification and interactive programming
- report writing
- diverse statistical analysis, including regression, multivariate, discriminant, and cluster analyses
- matrix operations
- what-if and goal-seeking features
- tabulation analysis
- different color graphics and plotting
- analysis of variance
- forecasting and time series analysis
- software interface with graphic and OR packages
- financial analysis and planning
- optimization models

In the microcomputer environment, Microsoft Excel has attracted a great deal of attention as a modeling tool in recent years. The following is a brief description of the modeling capabilities of Excel.

Microsoft Excel for Windows includes built-in "what-if" features, more than 300 built-in functions, a goal-seeking option, a scenario manager, and a solver option.

Using the Data Table option, you can monitor the effect of a change of one or two variables over the entire system and can construct sophisticated models and then perform various analyses using one or two variables.

The built-in functions include several categories such as financial, statistical, mathematical, logical, and table search. Even if the desired function is not available among the built-in list, you can simply develop it yourself. Also, the macro capabilities of Excel provide an easy-to-use and comprehensive programming environment. Programming or macro programming in spreadsheet programs is much easier than using high-level languages. The major reason is that by using macro programming you can complete the same task as you would using a high-level language but with much less code.

The Goal Seek option allows you to build a model, then adjust the value in a specified cell until a formula dependent on that cell reaches the value you specify. For example, you may develop a sales-forecasting model based on the advertising budget. If you establish a goal for the sales level, you can manipulate the advertising amount to achieve the preestablished sales goal.

The Scenario Manager feature allows you to create and save different sets of data as separate scenarios, and then use these scenarios to view multiple outcomes based on different assumptions. You can also create a separate summary report that shows the changing cell values and the resulting cell values for each scenario.

The Solver option allows you to define the problem you want to solve by creating a model with multiple adjustable cells. You can impose constraints on your problem that must be satisfied before a solution is reached. The Solver feature allows you to solve optimization-type problems (e.g., maximizing the profit or minimizing the cost). For a detailed discussion about these various features, consult the User Manual published by Microsoft Corporation.

The following are the minimum capabilities that a package must have in order to be effective as a MSS product:

- database capabilities
- spreadsheet capabilities
- general modeling capabilities
- graphic capabilities
- statistical capabilities
- forecasting capabilities
- micro-mainframe linkage

- what-if capabilities
- goal-seeking capabilities
- sensitivity analysis capabilities

INTERACTION AMONG THE THREE COMPONENTS OF A MSS

Figure 3.3 illustrates the relationships among the three main components of a MSS. There is a two-way relationship between the model base and database components of a MSS. Models receive their input data from the database, and this input generates integrity among information generated by the MSS, since all of the models are using the same database. At the same time, the models can input information generated by their analysis back to the database, making this new information available to all models for future analysis.

Returning the data generated by the modeling analysis to the database is one advantage of modeling analysis in a MSS environment as opposed to traditional modeling analyses. In traditional modeling analysis, each model has access only to its own data set, creating a possible inconsistency in the final results. The major reason for this inconsistency is that separate and independent data sets may be created and updated differently. In a MSS environment, all data are stored, manipulated, and updated by a DBMS, nullifying the issue of inconsistency.

The interaction between the dialog management and model base is also a two-way relationship. A user may request an analysis using a specific model, and the model base may query the database for the necessary data. The necessary data is sent to the model, and the model base performs the analysis and then sends the result back to the user. This can be an iterative and continuous process. This interaction will continue until the user stops the process or exits that routine.

SUMMARY

This chapter discussed in detail modes and model building in a MSS environment. For most MSS applications, modeling is essential for a successful MSS design. The chapter introduced types of modeling techniques used in MSS environment, highlighted some of the problems associated with traditional modeling techniques, and how these problems may be resolved in a MSS environment. The chapter also discussed methods used for implementation of model base in a MSS environment and basic capabilities of Microsoft Excel and IFPS as two popular MSS modeling products. General capabilities of SPSS and SAS as two popular modeling tools were introduced. The chapter introduced several other modeling products for both micro- and mainframe computers.

Figure 3.3
Relationships among the Three Components of a MSS

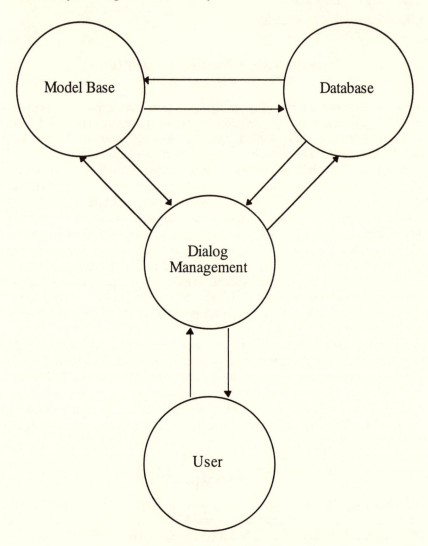

REFERENCES

1. Anderson, David, Dennis J. Sweeny, and Thomas A. Williams. *An Introduction to Management Science*, 8th ed. St. Paul, Minn.: West Publishing Company, 1997.
2. Brennan, T. J., and Jon Elam. "Enhanced Capabilities for Model-Based Decision Support Systems." In *Decision Support Systems Putting Theory into Practice*, edited by Ralph H. Sprague, Jr. and Hugh J. Watson, 130–137. Englewood Cliffs, N.J.: Prentice-Hall, 1986.

3. Eom, Hyun B., and Sang M. Lee. "A Survey of Decision Support System Applications." *Interfaces* (May/June 1990): 65–79.

4. Gass, Saul I. "Model World: Danger, Beware the User as Modeler." *Interfaces* (May/June 1990): 60–64.

5. Hocking, Ronald R. *Methods and Applications of Linear Models.* New York: John Wiley & Sons, 1996.

6. Iannone, A. L. *Management Program Planning With PERT, MOST and LOB.* Engelwood Cliffs, N.J.: Prentice-Hall, 1971.

7. Mittra, Sitansu S. "PERT, LOB and MOST: United for More Efficient Project Scheduling." *Supervisory Management* (November 1976): 30–35.

8. Montgomery, Douglas C. *Introduction to Linear Regression.* New York: John Wiley & Sons, 1992.

9. Sprague, Ralph H. Jr., and Eric D. Carlson. *Building Effective Decision Support Systems.* Englewood Cliffs, N.J.: Prentice-Hall, 1982.

CHAPTER 4

Unique Features of Decision Support and Expert Systems

Because DSS and ES are two of the most popular types of MSS in practice, this chapter explores the unique features of these two systems. It examines the three technologies of DSS and ES, which include specific DSS, DSS generators, and DSS tools and specific ES, ES tools, and ES shells. Other packages for building a DSS will be highlighted. This chapter also introduces different players in DSS and ES design, implementation, and use and emphasizes the equal importance of the technical designer and the managerial designer in this process. The chapter provides a brief discussion on the components of a DSS and ES and the advantages of these systems. The material discussed in this chapter should provide you with a better appreciation and understanding of DSS and ES operations that provide strong decision-making capabilities in all levels of an organization.

UNIQUE CHARACTERISTICS OF DSS

As highlighted in Chapter 1, DSS, compared with EDP and MIS, present a series of unique characteristics that make the design and utilization of these systems somewhat different from the earlier applications. Understanding these features in detail will help the designer and user of these systems to design a more successful DSS.

Central Focus

EDP and some MIS have been utilized to automate routine, programmable, and repetitive functions. Once these tasks are automated, human intervention required for the execution of such tasks is very limited or nonexistent. In the EDP environment, a payroll processing system is a good example. In MIS, an inventory system would be an appropriate example.

Conversely, a DSS tries to aid decision making and decision implementation for nonroutine and nonrepetitive tasks. These systems always work in conjunction with a decision maker. One may further state that the focus of EDP is on data, the focus of MIS is on information, and the focus of DSS is on decisions. A sales-forecasting system that provides an accurate sales forecast for every quarter of a department store is an example of a DSS that helps a marketing manager perform accurate planning on a quarterly basis.

Mode of Usage

EDP and MIS are primarily utilized in a passive mode, which means that these systems usually work based on a series of well-defined standard operating procedures. They generate a series of scheduled reports on a regular basis (e.g., an accounting information system).

DSS are primarily utilized in an active mode. This means the designer and user of the system initiate each instance of the system's use (e.g., an automated cash-flow analysis system).

Type of Activities

Clerical personnel and supervisory staff usually use EDP and MIS. DSS are designed for line managers and key decision makers. Wherever in the organization a decision is being made, a DSS has potential for implementation.

Orientation

There are two issues of paramount importance in any decision: efficiency (doing the things right) and effectiveness (doing the right things). Whereas EDP and MIS are mostly concerned with the efficiency of a decision, DSS are concerned with both the efficiency and the effectiveness of a decision. In other words, DSS are not only concerned with financial savings, but with other aspects of implementation such as improved communication, learning, and ease of decision making as well.

Time Horizon

EDP and MIS are mostly concerned with the past. Sometimes these systems are referred to as the "blaming information systems." Good examples are a balance sheet and an income statement generated by an accounting information system. When the fiscal year is over, a report is generated that highlights "what we did wrong last year." Since the past is already gone, a decision maker cannot do anything about it, but must learn from it.

DSS focus on the present and, to a large degree, the future. These systems usually tell the decision maker what is happening now and what may happen in the future. These systems naturally use past data as well as projected data in conjunction with analytical models to project and predict the present and future status of an organization.

Design Emphasis

EDP and MIS are designed to generate periodic reports with minimum flexibility. Again, a good example is an accounting information system that generates periodic financial reports.

Conversely, DSS place a heavy emphasis on flexibility and "ad hoc" and exception-type reporting. The ability to manipulate information is essential if a DSS is going to be utilized effectively for semistructured and unstructured, nonrecurring, one-of-a-kind decisions.

Key Concepts in DSS

Throughout the computer literature, EDP and MIS are associated with a series of key concepts such as replacement, automation, and computerization [1, 3]. This issue is probably the most important factor causing resistance to change, as employees are concerned about losing their jobs and being replaced by computers. Some systems are designed to replace humans, which happens quite often in record keeping, simple inventory, and a majority of clerical tasks.

The key concepts associated with DSS are usually interaction, support, learning, and coexistence [1, 3]. DSS are not intended to replace a decision maker, but to improve the quality of decision making and decision implementation by assisting the decision maker and improving his or her effectiveness.

System Evaluation

To evaluate EDP and MIS, usually a cost-and-benefit analysis is performed; the system is then evaluated based on these potential economic gains and losses. DSS place equal emphasis on noneconomic gains such as user satisfaction, decision-making improvement, and the overall performance of the decision maker after the implementation of a DSS. In other words, a DSS may not generate any tangible economic gain yet may still be considered a successful venture by its user(s) and designer(s).

Computation Focus

EDP and MIS usually perform basic and simple analyses. These analyses address a well-defined problem where the parameters and variables under investigation are clearly delineated. DSS, on the other hand, utilize a variety of models for numerous computational tasks. These models and computations cover a broad range of analyses from the very basic to the very complex. As an example, a DSS can be used for simple price analysis using a break-even model. At the same time, a comprehensive econometric model that involves more than 200 variables can be used by a DSS in order to predict a realistic price for gasoline in the year 2010.

Output Orientation

As mentioned earlier, the output of EDP and MIS is usually used for operational control. Like accounting systems, the output of the system tells the user whether he or she has operated within an acceptable range. The output of DSS is also used for control, but for the most part it is used for planning. The system's output will tell the user, based on past performance, what he or she should do in the next round of operations. The extensive employment of forecasting, statistical, and simulation models is a good indication of the orientation of the output of these systems.

Problems Addressed

EDP and MIS have been utilized for quantitative analysis. Although DSS have been used for the same purpose, the integration of ES and artificial intelligence products should assist DSS in performing qualitative as well as quantitative analysis in the near future. We have already witnessed some limited applications of these types of analyses by using "rule data models" and "knowledge-based systems" in the database component of DSS. This feature of DSS would be a clear departure of these systems from the domain of traditional EDP and MIS.

Output Format Options

The format of the output generated by EDP and MIS has been limited. As mentioned earlier, scheduled reports have been the dominant output format generated by these systems.

In the DSS environment, the format for the output provided is quite varied. As much as these systems are designed to help a variety of decision makers with assorted decision-making styles, a different output format is essential for such operations. These output formats may include graphic, tabular, detail, and summary reports and exception reporting.

Tailoring to the Personality and Status of the User

With EDP and MIS, the user may not be actively involved in the design and implementation phases of the systems. Usually data-processing personnel design these systems. This means that in the process of building a system the personality, status, and information needs of different decision makers are largely ignored. However, this is changing.

Such is not the case in the DSS environment, where the user is actively involved in all phases of analysis, design, and implementation of the system. In many cases, the user initiates the design of the system. This all means that a DSS is usually tailored to the individual status and styles of different decision makers. This custom fit may be the key factor for the relative success of these systems in recent years.

Mode of User/System Interaction

Once again in EDP and MIS the scheduled report, or "subscription" mode [1], is the dominant type of user/system interface. Obviously the flexibility is minimal when this type of user/system interface is employed. On the other hand, in DSS the user can interact with the system in a variety of modes. These include question and answer, command language, menu, and GUI. Because the majority of users of a DSS are not computer-trained personnel, the user/system interface is highly regarded in the DSS environment. The interface should be straightforward and easy to use.

Design Tools

In EDP and MIS, as discussed in Chapter 2, the traditional life-cycle approach is the dominant design tool. The designers of these systems follow the classic life-cycle approach of problem definition, feasibility study, systems analysis, systems design, systems implementation, and postimplementation audit procedures.

DSS, with intensive user involvement, combines all the phases of the life-cycle approach into one phase and, by using a prototype, performs an iterative design. The design process in a DSS environment is never final: The system is continuously improved to incorporate the varying needs of the decision maker. Other tools used in DSS design such as adaptive design, middle-out approach, and so on, which are not commonly used in traditional EDP and MIS, are discussed in Chapter 2. The main objective of these new tools is to consider the user as the focal point and design systems that are tailor-made to the specific needs of a decision maker.

Flexibility of the Operation

EDP and MIS are not usually flexible. Flexibility may include input and output formats, types of reporting, the user/system interface, and so on. In EDP and MIS, the input/output of the system is defined in advance, and changes usually cannot be made without a major redesign of the system. DSS, on the other hand, are quite flexible and are very responsive to the changing environment of the user. Flexibility is built into the architecture of any DSS by providing several types of user/system interfaces that fit a diverse group of users with different styles and statuses as well as different computer backgrounds.

Organizational Target Group

EDP and MIS are chiefly concerned with the operational and sometimes the tactical level in the organization. DSS are designed to assist decision makers in all levels of the organization, including operational, tactical, and especially strategic management. Use of internal and external data and diverse modeling techniques provides DSS with a good opportunity for success at all levels of management, particularly at the strategic level. This is another departure of these systems from traditional EDP and MIS.

Data Used

EDP and MIS usually use internal data that include transaction data and data collected internally from other departments within the organization. DSS utilize both internal as well as external data. These data may be collected from a variety of sources. Utilization of both internal and external data and analytical models is another departure of these systems from traditional EDP and MIS.

Implementation

EDP and MIS are usually designed by using tools available in the computer field. For example, COBOL, a high-level language, is an example of a tool used to develop a computer-based information system. If this is the case, the development time is long and the system may go through several revisions before it is finalized.

On the other hand, DSS are developed by using both DSS tools and DSS generators. More recently, the availability of highly sophisticated DSS generators has fostered the development of many DSS. These generators include nonprocedural languages, which are easier than high-level languages such as FORTRAN and COBOL. They are more forgiving and provide more flexibility. The user can enter the codes in any order with which he or she is most familiar, and there is no rigorous programming involved. A few hours of training enable a user to write simple programs using these languages. In this process, the development time is usually short. A workable system (operational prototype) is designed and later improved in the next round of the operation. Several of these popular DSS generators were introduced in Chapter 1.

Interactiveness

EDP and MIS are mostly used in batch mode (but this is changing). In batch mode, data and information are sent to the computer periodically. On the other hand, DSS are highly interactive. Interactiveness may expedite decision making by providing online and what-if facilities for DSS users.

Types of Analyses

As mentioned in Chapter 1, there are two types of analyses, which can be performed by any computer-based information system. EDP and MIS usually perform data analysis and, to some degree, may perform limited modeling analysis.

DSS perform data analysis as well as modeling analysis by incorporating a database as well as a model base as integral parts of the DSS architecture.

THREE TECHNOLOGIES OF DSS

In the DSS environment there are three areas of technology that must be understood by both DSS users and designers. These include specific DSS (SDSS), DSS generators, and DSS tools [8]. The following is a brief explanation of each technology.

Specific DSS

A specific DSS is a combination of hardware and software that is used to assist a decision maker with a specific task. This capability may be utilized for any task at any level of the organization. There are many of these systems that have been successfully utilized for many years to support decision makers in a variety of settings. BRANDAID, a marketing-mix model [6] developed by John Little, and an analytical information management system (AIMS) [5] that performs forecasting, planning, and financial analysis at American Airlines are examples of such systems. In a typical business organization, these systems may be designed in different functional areas. For example, a SDSS for a manufacturing department assists in manufacturing decisions. This system may provide timely information on different aspects of a manufacturing environment such as production and distribution decisions. A SDSS may provide online sales forecast for a marketing department. A SDSS for a finance department may assist the portfolio analyst with information to minimize the risk of investment by monitoring and providing timely information on stocks, bonds, and different financial activities.

DSS Generators

DSS generators are a combination of hardware and software used as a package to develop specific DSS. These generators already include most of the capabilities needed by a specific DSS. A typical DSS generator includes capabilities such as a DBMS, graphics, built-in functions, modeling analysis, statistical analysis, and optimization and simulation models. These generators include macro programming, which is more powerful than using high-level languages such as FORTRAN and COBOL. DSS generators continue to gain popularity. Interactive Financial Planning System (IFPS) by Comshare and Express by Information Resource, Inc. are two examples of these generators. By using IFPS, many different specific DSS in the areas of finance, simulation, and statistical analysis can be developed.

In the microcomputer environment, spreadsheet programs such as Excel, Lotus 1-2-3, and Quattro Pro are becoming powerful generators. The basic requirements for construction of small-scale specific DSS are readily available in these packages.

DSS Tools

DSS tools are computer hardware or software used to develop either a specific DSS or a DSS generator. For example, either a graphics package or COBOL may serve as a DSS tool. A DSS tool deals with part of the DSS, but not all of it. In general, development of specific DSS from a DSS generator is faster, and it may be more economical than the development of these systems from DSS tools. This area of technology has improved continually. For example, computer languages have gone through several generations, developing from machine language to assembly, to high-level languages, to fourth-generation languages; finally the developers are working on natural language processing systems. Another example of such improvement is the enhancement of operating systems for the microcomputers. Very soon these operating systems should simulate the same level of sophistication first found in larger computers. Hardware technology has improved in parallel with the software technology. For example, graphic terminals, laser printers, and sophisticated modems all are examples of DSS tools. Figure 4.1 illustrates these three technologies of DSS and their relationships.

OTHER SOFTWARE PACKAGES FOR BUILDING SPECIFIC DSS

In addition to DSS tools and DSS generators, there are some other packages that can be used for building specific DSS. Generally speaking, these packages are more powerful than programming languages and less powerful than full-featured DSS generators. Let us briefly explain these software tools.

Database Manager or File Manager Systems

Database manager or file manager systems (sometimes called flat-file systems), the most basic type of DBMS, perform basic data retrieval tasks. They cannot integrate data from several files, but they are useful as personal filing systems, allowing a decision maker to recall data quickly when it is needed for

Figure 4.1
Three Technologies of DSS

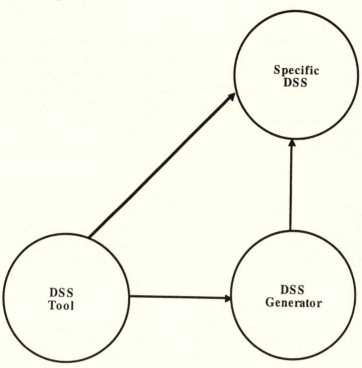

decision-making purposes. These systems can perform various sort and search operations and can be quite useful for retrieving various data items from a single file. The next step beyond a data manager system is a true DBMS, which is capable of performing sophisticated data management tasks.

Specialized Modeling Languages

Specialized modeling languages allow the construction of various modeling techniques used in constructing a SDSS. A popular example of this type of package would be SPSS or SAS, both of which include the facility for building various modeling techniques. They also include readily available modeling routines for performing modeling tasks (e.g., a MLR routine for forecasting purposes, or a linear-programming routine for optimization purposes). DSS generators, including spreadsheet programs include modeling facilities and built-in functions as well. However, specialized modeling languages offer more diversity and sophistication.

Statistical and Forecasting Packages

Specialized software packages are designed to determine the relationship among variables in the system and to generate forecasts based on the past behavior of the system. Regression analysis is the most popular type of analysis in this group. A regression model determines the correlation among variables and generates a forecast. For example, you may want to determine the correlation between the advertising budget and total sales. You may also want to estimate the total sales based on a certain advertising budget. A regression model, which is available in numerous packages, can perform this task for you. Among the popular statistical and forecasting packages are SAS, Minitab, SPSS, Statgraphics, and Systat. Also, spreadsheet programs such as Lotus 1-2-3, Excel, and Quattro Pro include various statistical and forecasting models.

Graphics Packages

Graphics software has been designed to present data in graphic format. Data can be converted into a line graph to show a trend, into a pie chart to highlight the components of the total, and into other types of graphs for various analyses. Masses of data can be converted to a graph, and, at a glance, the reader can discover the general pattern of the data. Graphs can easily highlight patterns and the correlation of data items. They also make data presentation a manageable job. Graphics can be created with spreadsheet packages such as Lotus 1-2-3, Excel, or Quattro Pro or with dedicated graphics packages. Five popular graphics packages are Aldus Persuasion, Hollywood Graphics, Harvard Graphics, Freelance, and PowerPoint. One limitation of graphics analysis is that graphs cannot convey differences among numbers smaller than about 1 percent of their full scale. Because DSS applications are more concerned with trends and correlation among data items, this limitation does not present a serious problem.

DIFFERENT PLAYERS IN THE DSS ENVIRONMENT

To design, implement, and utilize a DSS, several different groups of individuals must be involved. Throughout this book we recognize three roles for the design, implementation, and utilization of a DSS and other MSS. These roles are user, designer, and intermediary.

User

The user is the individual for whom the DSS is designed and may be an individual, a department, or an organizational unit. Specific DSS must address and incorporate the specific requirements of the user into its operation. The success and failure of the system is heavily dependent on the user(s).

Designer

The designer may include two different groups: the managerial designer and the technical designer. A managerial designer is the individual(s) who defines the management issues related to DSS design and utilization. This role is very similar to the role of an architect building a house in that the architect provides the general design of a house. Without getting into specifics, he or she highlights the important aspects of the house. In a DSS environment, this individual may be the MIS specialist in the organization, the decision maker, or anyone else who can define the requirements of the DSS. For example, in developing an online forecasting DSS, some of the managerial issues may include the following:

- What data must be collected?
- From what source must the data be gathered?
- How recent must the collected data be?
- How must the data be indexed?
- How must the data be updated?
- What should be the balance between aggregated and desegregated data?

The technical designer usually is not concerned with the issues specified under the managerial designer's domain. Instead, his or her role is very similar to the role of a construction engineer charged with the task of building a house. The technical designer is concerned with the technical issues related to the DSS design and use. Some of the questions addressed by a technical designer would be

- How must the data be stored?
- What type of file structure must be implemented (sequential, random, or indexed sequential)?
- What type of user access must be implemented?
- What type of response time is required?
- How must the security measures be installed?

This role may be occupied by the computer specialist, a consultant from outside the company, and so forth. The technical designer may incorporate these facilities into a specific DSS by using a DSS generator, DSS tools, or inventing new capabilities from scratch.

Intermediary

An intermediary is the liaison between the user and the DSS. This individual(s) may play different roles. For example, during the design phase for the forecasting DSS cited earlier, the intermediary may explain the user's needs to the managerial designer or technical designer of the system. This same individual, at a later date, may explain the provided output to the user or may explain the output of the regression analysis provided by the forecasting DSS mentioned earlier. He or she may tell the user about the assumptions underlying the model, the limitations, strengths, and so forth. He or she may also suggest new or different applications of the system. Figure 4.2 illustrates these roles in a DSS environment.

Figure 4.2
Different Roles in the DSS Environment

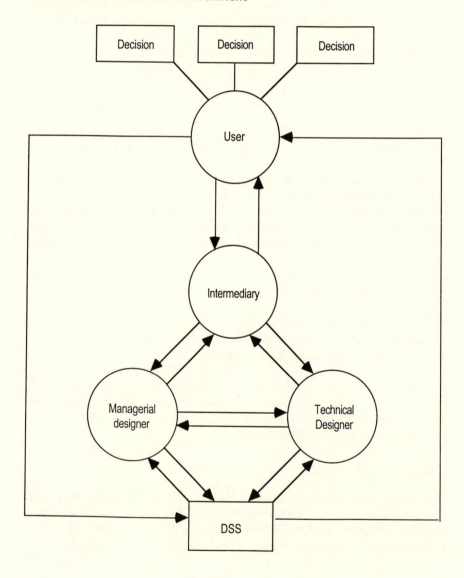

COMPONENTS OF A DSS

A DSS includes three major components: a database, a model base, and dialog management (user/system interface) [8]. The database component includes both internal and external data. Internal data are either transaction data or data collected internally from other subsystems in the organization. External data may come from various sources, such as competitors, the government, the financial community, and so forth. Associated with the database is the DBMS. This software creates, modifies, and maintains the database as required by the user. The database component enables a DSS to perform any type of data analysis operation.

The model base component includes a series of mathematical and statistical models. These models, in conjunction with the database, enable a DSS to perform any type of modeling analysis. Modeling analysis was explained in detail in Chapter 3.

Finally, the dialog management component is the user/system interface, which provides a user with different interface procedures that enable him or her to access the DSS. This component, from the user's point of view, is probably the most important part. It is imperative that this component be as flexible and as user-friendly as possible. Because the majority of DSS users are discretionary in their usage, user-friendliness is an even more important consideration in such a situation.

Figure 4.3 illustrates a graphic model for DSS within the organization. As this figure indicates, a DSS user who may occupy a position in any one of the three management levels of the organization (operational, tactical, or strategic) may be faced with the need to make a decision. The decision process may include the three stages of intelligence, design, and choice. The user, through the dialog component, may query the database, model base, or both for decision help.

ADVANTAGES OF A DSS

A comprehensive DSS that has followed and incorporated the objectives of an organization into its architecture should provide all the advantages and features offered by any computer-based information system such as the following:

- faster decision making
- more comprehensive information
- improved communication
- improved accuracy
- improved customer service
- increased comfort level

As we mentioned earlier, the major objective of a DSS is to improve the effectiveness of a decision maker. The following five factors highlight how a DSS

Figure 4.3
DSS in the Organization

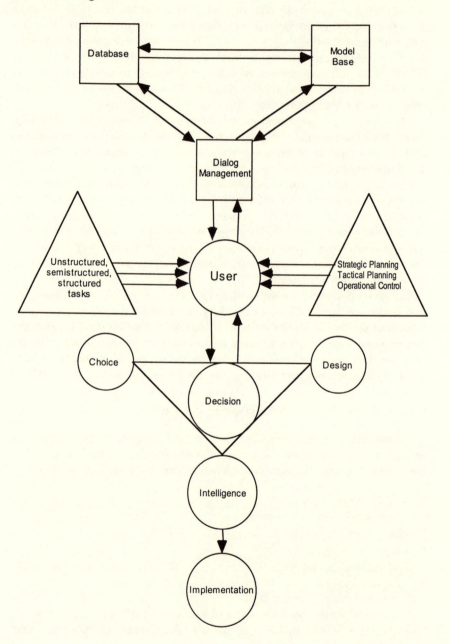

may improve the effectiveness of a decision maker [1]: improving personal efficiency; expediting problem solving; facilitating interpersonal communication; promoting learning or training; and increasing organizational control.

A decision maker who has online access to a DSS capable of providing timely, integrated, accurate, and comprehensive information can spend his or her time making effective decisions rather than wasting time searching for information that should have been available initially. A DSS can expedite problem solving by providing rapid turnaround, increased accuracy, detailed examination of different scenarios, and improved consistency. Capabilities such as what-if, goal-seeking, and sensitivity analysis discussed in Chapter 1 are all instrumental in accelerating the problem-solving process.

Interpersonal communication is facilitated and improved because everyone using the DSS has a new channel to access, a "language" common to all participants. DSS provides "tools for persuasion" [1], a vocabulary, and discipline that facilitates negotiations and coordination across the organizational boundaries. As an example, consider a situation in a high-tech company, that did not have a cost-based DSS. Because of the absence of such a system, different division managers were providing different prices for a finished product in bidding process. The establishment of an online cost-based DSS significantly improved the interpersonal communication generated among these executives. Also, the coordination among the individuals was improved because of the use of the new system.

A DSS can have an impact on learning or training by telling the user why and how a particular decision must be made in a particular way. This may not be a common practice in today's DSS. However, as mentioned earlier, through the integration of artificial intelligence products and ES into DSS architecture, the learning and training features of a DSS can be improved significantly.

Again, by providing comprehensive information regarding the entire organizational boundaries, the overall control of the organization will be improved. This may include control over costs, inventory, and personnel.

UNIQUE FEATURES OF ES

As you will learn, ES offer unique features that are not provided by DSS. In many cases, ES can complement DSS by offering added features not found in DSS. In this chapter, we will provide an overview of these features, and a detailed explanation will be given in future chapters. The following are situations that are suitable for ES applications [2, 9, 10]:

- When a great degree of expertise is available
- In situations that are not oriented toward mathematical models
- In situations that have been successfully solved by human experts
- In situations that require consistency and standardization

- When subject domain is limited
- When uncertainty is involved
- When many rules are involved
- When explanation capability is needed
- When there is a scarcity of experts
- When key experts are retiring
- In hazardous situations

Unsuitable applications of ES are summarized bellow [2, 9, 10]:

- Problems that include very few rules
- Problems that include too many rules
- Well-structured numerical problems
- Problems in areas that are too broad
- Problem areas in which there is disagreement among experts
- Problems that are solved by human experts better than ES

THREE TECHNOLOGIES OF ES

ES similar to DSS include three technology levels: ES tools, specific ES, and ES shells. ES tools include artificial intelligence languages such as LISP or PROLOG or high-level languages such as PASCAL or C. ES shells are readily available commercial products that include many of the features needed for the construction of specific ES. There are many such products available on the market. VP-Expert, First-Class, and EXSYS are three examples of ES shells. Specific ES performs a specific task in a particular field. These systems, developed from either ES tools or shells, are designed to perform a specific task in a given discipline. XCON, XSEL, and XSITE, developed by Digital Equipment Corporation and Carnegie-Mellon University, are examples of specific ES.

COMPONENTS OF AN ES

A typical ES may include the following components (Figure 4.4):

- knowledge acquisition facility
- knowledge base (rule base and database)
- knowledge-base management system (KBMS)
- inference engine
- user interface
- explanation facility

Let us briefly explain these components.

A knowledge acquisition facility is needed to assure the growth of the system. This subsystem should provide methods to acquire new rules and facts. The

Figure 4.4
ES Major Components

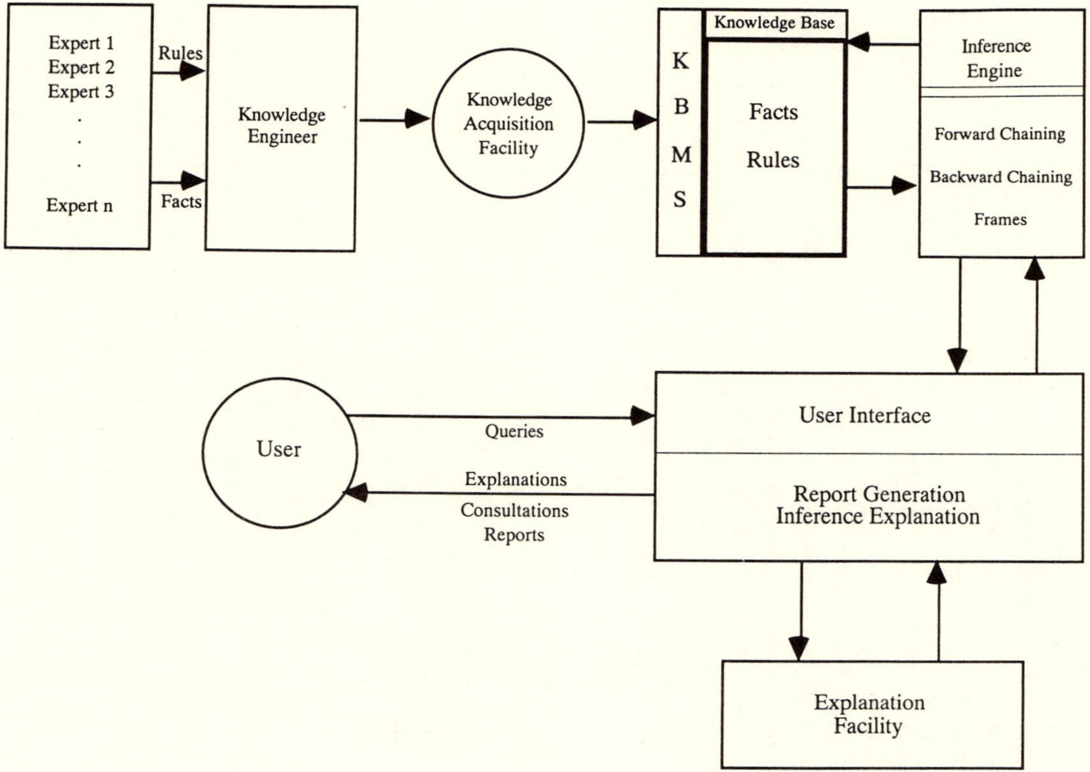

availability of new facts creates the opportunity for the KBMS to modify the existing rules and incorporate the new facts into the knowledge base. The knowledge acquisition facility and KBMS work in conjunction with each other to keep the knowledge base in its most updated form. Manual, automated, or a combination of each technique may be used to acquire knowledge for the ES's construction.

The knowledge base is very similar to the database of a DSS. However, a knowledge base not only stores facts and figures, it also keeps track of a series of rules and explanations associated with the facts. For example, the knowledge base of a financial ES may keep track of all the figures that constitute the current assets. This may include cash, deposits, accounts receivable, and so forth. It also keeps track of the fact that the current assets are that type of assets that can be converted to cash within one year.

An ES in an academic environment may include all the facts regarding a classified graduate student, such as number of deficiencies, GMAT score, and GPA. At the same time, it may include a rule that indicates a student may be classified only if he or she has no deficiencies, has a GMAT of 600 or better, and has a GPA of 3.4 or better.

The knowledge base of an ES must include three types of knowledge to be considered a true ES [4]: factual knowledge; heuristic knowledge; and meta-knowledge.

Factual knowledge consists of facts related to a specific discipline, subject, or problem (e.g., all the facts related to kidney problems, such as size, blood components, pain duration, and location). Heuristic knowledge consists of the rules related to a particular problem or discipline (e.g., all the general rules that indicate a patient has a kidney problem such as a serious pain in the lower left or lower right of the abdomen).

Incorporation of metaknowledge in an ES may be the ultimate goal of ES designers. This knowledge enables an ES to use and examine the facts, extract those facts, and direct the path used to obtain a solution. In simple terms, metaknowledge is the ability of an ES to learn from experience. This is the area that has not been fully developed and is yet to be seen in future ES. The integration of ES and neural networks is one approach for achieving this goal.

A KBMS is similar to a DBMS in a DSS environment. Its major task is to keep the knowledge base updated with all the facts, figures, and rules. If new facts become available or new rules are added to the existing system, it is the job of the KBMS to update the knowledge base of the ES.

An inference engine is similar to the model base of a DSS. Through different techniques, such as forward and backward chaining (explained later in this section), an inference engine manipulates a series of rules. In forward chaining, a series of IF-THEN pairs are performed. The condition IF is evaluated first, then the appropriate THEN is performed. For example, if the temperature is less than 80 degrees Fahrenheit and the grass is three inches long, then cut the grass. In a medical diagnostic ES, the system may ask the following:

What is the body temperature of the patient? Does the patient have a headache? The system then may conclude it is very likely (95%) the patient has the flu.

In backward chaining, the ES starts with the goal, the THEN part, and backtracks to find the right solution, (i.e., to achieve this goal, what conditions must be met?). As an example, consider a financial ES that provides advice for financial investment for different investors [7]. In forward chaining, the system may ask fifty questions to determine which of the five categories of investments is more suitable for a perspective investor as follows: oil–gas, bonds, common stocks, public utilities, or transportation.

Let us further assume a particular investor is in a given tax bracket and each investment scenario provides him or her with a different tax shelter.

In forward chaining, the system evaluates through all the IF-THEN conditions, then makes the final recommendation. In backward chaining, the system starts with the goal, the THEN part. In this example, let us say investment in public utilities is under investigation by an investor. The ES starts with this goal and then backtracks through all the IF conditions needed to achieve this goal to see if a particular investor qualifies for this type of investment. The backward chaining inference engine may be faster in a particular situation by not considering the irrelevant rules to a given situation. However, the solution recommended by the system may not be the optimum one.

Some inference engines work from a matrix of facts that may include several rows of conditions and rules, similar to a decision table. In this case, a number of rules are evaluated at a time and then the advice is provided. Also, some inference engines learn from doing.

User interface is very similar to dialog management of a DSS. It provides a method of user-friendly access to the ES for the user. The goal of artificial intelligence technology is to provide a natural language for the user interface. Natural language processing (NLP) is the ideal goal for the user/system interface for any MSS. There are many problems associated with NLP that must be overcome before a full-featured NLP can be introduced. However, with the introduction of the GUI, this component of ES has been significantly improved.

Explanation facility performs tasks similar to a human expert. It explains to the end user(s) how recommendations are derived. For example, in a loan evaluation ES, the explanation facility will tell you why an applicant was approved and another applicant was turned down. In a medical ES such as MYCIN, this component explains why the system concluded that the patient has a kidney stone. The explanation facility is important for ES success because having explanations assures the user of results and provides a feeling of confidence.

DIFFERENT PLAYERS IN THE ES ENVIRONMENT

Similar to DSS, the major players in the ES environment include user(s) and top management. In addition, a knowledge engineer performs tasks similar to the systems analysts and programmers in the DSS environment. The knowledge engineer interacts with the expert(s) to collect all the necessary facts and rules and then, using an ES tool or shell, constructs the expert system. We will talk about these major players in detail in Chapter 8.

DSS AND ES: AN INTEGRATED TECHNOLOGY

There are situations that can be successfully solved by DSS, and there are situations that can be successfully solved by ES. On the other hand, there are situations that can be successfully solved by an integrated DSS and ES. You should remember that ES and DSS are more similar than different. In many cases, the strong feature(s) of each technology can be used to provide a better and unified solution to a growing number of business problems.

SUMMARY

This chapter highlighted the unique characteristics of DSS and ES, compared DSS to EDP, MIS, DSS, and ES, and discussed the power of DSS and ES and their potential for decision making and decisions implementation in all levels of an organization. It explained three different levels of DSS, which include specific DSS, DSS generators, and DSS tools, and reviewed the three technologies of ES that include specific ES, ES shells, and ES tools. This explanation should clarify the options available to a DSS and ES user and designer for construction of DSS and ES. The chapter also briefly introduced other software packages for building specific DSS, such as database managers and specialized modeling, statistical and forecasting, and graphical packages, and discussed different players in the DSS and ES environments. This chapter also introduced some advantages of a DSS and ES.

REFERENCES

1. Alter, Steven L. *Decision Support Systems: Current Practice and Continuing Challenges*. Reading, Mass.: Addison-Wesley Publishing, 1980: 110–112.
2. Blanning, Robert W. "Expert Systems for Management: Research and Applications." *Journal of Information Science* (September 1985): 153–162.
3. Keen, Peter G. W., and Michael S. Scott-Morton. *Decision Support Systems: An Organizational Perspective*. Reading, Mass.: Addison-Wesley Publishing, 1978: 1–15.
4. Keim, Robert T., and Sheila Jacobs. "Expert Systems: The DSS of the Future?" *Journal of Systems Management* (December 1986): 6–14.
5. Klaas, Richard L. "A DSS for Airline Management." *Data Base* 8 (Winter 1977): 2–8.
6. Little, John D. C. "BRANDAID: A Marketing-Mix Model, Part I: Structure." *Operations Research* 23 (July/August 1972): 628–655.
7. Luconi, Fred L., Thomas W. Malone, and Michael S. Scott-Morton. "Expert Systems: The Next Challenge for Managers." *Sloan Management Review* 27 (1986): 3–13.

8. Sprague, Ralph H., Jr. "A Framework for the Development of Decision Support Systems." In *Decision Support Systems: Putting Theory into Practice.* edited by Ralph H. Sprague, Jr. and Hugh J. Watson. Englewood Cliffs, N.J.: Prentice-Hall, 1980: 7–32.

9. "What Is Happening with Expert Systems?" *EDP Analyzer* 23 (December 1985): 1–11.

10. Yoon, Youngohc, Tor Guimares, and Quinton O'Neal. "Exploring the Factors Associated with Expert Systems Success." *MIS Quarterly* (March 1995): 83–103.

CHAPTER 5

Executive Information Systems

This chapter introduces executive information systems (EIS) as a growing application of MSS. The chapter provides a definition of EIS and outlines their major features and characteristics. A conceptual model for an EIS and reasons for developing an EIS are explained. The chapter also introduces factors that assist designers of EIS to increase the chances of successful design and utilization of an EIS. Several real-life applications of EIS will be introduced. The chapter introduces several EIS products and concludes with a brief discussion on multimedia and hypermedia and their roles for improving the effectiveness of an EIS.

DEFINING EIS

EIS, executive support systems (ESS), or executive management systems (EMS) are a branch of MSS that are gaining in popularity. Although some authors have tried to differentiate these various applications, in this text, we use them interchangeably and refer to all of them as EIS. For the purpose of this text, we define an EIS as a computer-based information system that provides executives with easy access to internal and external information with drill-down capability related to the critical success factors for running current and future business operations.

The following are the key features of an EIS: ease of use; access to both internal and external data; critical success factors; and drill-down capability.

Ease of use plays an important role for the success of an EIS. Because the majority of EIS users are not computer-trained personnel, simplicity of the system is crucial. By using various types of user/system interfaces, the designer(s) of the EIS provide a variety of options for using the system. GUI have been well received by typical users. Pull-down menus, context-sensitive help, multimedia, virtual reality, and possibly voice input/output can further enhance the ease of use of an EIS.

Access to both internal and external data is a critical consideration for an EIS. To be able to spot trends and forecast and analyze various scenarios, an EIS should have access to both types of data. External data may come from a variety of sources such as competition, government, and financial communities, and internal data may come from within the business itself. The real challenge is the collection and proper manipulation of the external data.

Critical success factors are those issues that make or break a business. Different organizations, divisions, and individuals have different types of critical success factors. For example, in a financial institution, the interest rate may be considered the critical success factor. For a car manufacturer, the location of a dealership and style may be considered critical success factors. An EIS should be designed to be able to provide related information for the critical success factors of the organization, division, or individual.

The drill-down capability of an EIS provides access to multilayer information on request. For example, at the first level an EIS may report the performance of a company in eight sales regions. In the next layer, a marketing executive may be interested in the northwest region, and this analysis can be further broken down. By doing these types of analyses, an executive is able to zero in on a particular situation and then make an appropriate decision.

To ascertain the features discussed above, various authors have identified different characteristics for an effective EIS. The following are some of these characteristics [4, 12, 15]:

- They are tailored to meet executives' information needs.
- They have the ability to extract, compress, filter, and track critical data.
- They have the capability to provide online status access, trend analysis, and exception reporting.
- They can access and integrate a broad range of internal and external data.
- They are user-friendly and require minimal or no training to use.
- They are used directly by executives without the assistance of intermediaries.
- They provide graphical, tabular, and/or textual information.
- They discover and report relationships among data items.
- They provide statistical-analysis techniques for summarizing and structuring data.
- They perform data retrieval across a wide range of platforms and data formats.
- They analyze data in a variety of methods.
- They create ad hoc reports.
- They contain customized application-development tools to build an application that automatically performs routine tasks.
- They support electronic communications (e-mail, voice mail, and computer conferencing).
- They include organizing tools such as calendars, automated Rolodex, and tickle files.

In the remaining part of the chapter, we further examine these features and characteristics of EIS.

A CONCEPTUAL MODEL FOR AN EIS

EIS are popular today because they provide the most crucial information in a usable format. How information relates to the decision maker is very important. Corporate data comes in a number of formats: It can be internal or external data and can also be "hard" or "soft" data. Internal data are mostly provided by a corporate database but can also come from operational data, reports, and documents and directly from corporate personnel. External data might come from external databases, news services, surveys from customers, information from vendors or trade services, surveys from competitors, and information from vendors or trade associations. Internal and external data from these two sources can be "hard" data, such as database information, or "soft" data, such as rumors, opinions, ideas, or predictions. The real challenge is the collection and manipulation of external data.

To effectively collect and manipulate both internal and external data and provide critical information in an easy-to-follow format, an EIS may utilize some or all of the following technologies:

- GUI
- touch-sensitive screens
- voice input
- color screens and displays
- voice and e-mail
- LAN, MAN, and WAN
- message distribution systems
- teleconferencing
- spreadsheets
- facsimile and image-transmission systems
- laptop, notebooks, and hand-held computers

The dialog between the executive and the EIS is one of the most critical elements of a successful EIS. Whether it is through the use of touch-sensitive screens or light pens, simplicity of use and access is essential. The diagram presented in Figure 5.1 illustrates a conceptual model for an EIS.

WHY DO EXECUTIVES NEED EIS?

There are many good reasons for executives to use EIS. EIS put a full array of powerful analytical and business decision-making tools at their fingertips and provide data analysis and graphical presentation functions that enable them to make critical decisions quickly using relevant information. In addition, by using

Figure 5.1
Conceptual Model for an EIS

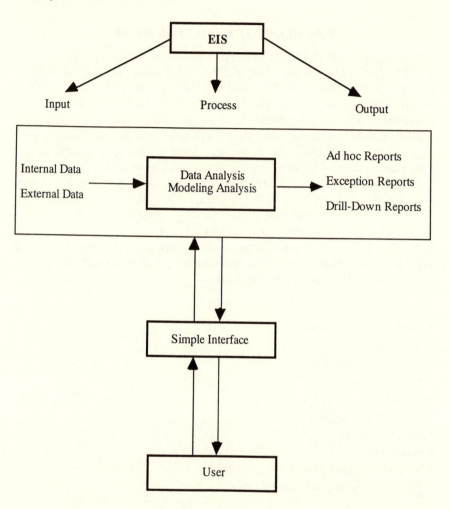

EIS, executives can share information with others more quickly and easily. All of these can dramatically increase the efficiency and effectiveness of the decision-making process in the following ways: EIS increase an executive's productivity by providing easy access to relevant information in a timely manner. They also provide all critical information at the executive's desktop. Information can be transformed to various formats in order to analyze different business scenarios. This will help an executive to see the effect of certain decisions on the organization. And EIS spot trends and report exception-type situations. For example, from his or her desktop, an executive can easily get the information on profitability and production costs at a particular manufacturing plant and determine whether closing the plant is more beneficial for the corporation than keeping it open.

A study conducted by Hugh Watson and Rex Kelly Rainer [18, p. 46] identified a number of specific factors that lead to EIS development. These factors are listed here:

- Need for timely information
- Need for improved communication
- Need for access to operational data
- Need for rapid status updates on different business units
- Need for increased effectiveness
- Need to identify historical trends
- Need for increased efficiency
- Need for access to corporate (internal) databases
- Need for more accurate information
- Increasingly competitive environment
- Rapidly changing external environment
- Need to be more proactive in dealing with the external environment
- Need to access external databases
- Increasing government regulations

AVOIDING FAILURE IN EIS DESIGN AND UTILIZATION

Similar to other management support systems, an effective EIS design and utilization require top management support, active user involvement, and an appropriate technology. Watson and Satzinger [19] identified several specific factors that lead to failure of an EIS. Among these factors are the following.

Executives may be a factor themselves. Because many of today's senior executives missed the computer revolution, they may feel uncomfortable using computers. Ongoing education and increasing "computer awareness" should resolve this issue.

The nature of executive work may inhibit successful implementation of an EIS. Executives' busy schedules and travel requirements are not amenable to long training sessions, do not permit much uninterrupted time for system use, and do not allow a system to be employed on a daily basis. The result is that senior executives are unlikely to employ systems that require considerable training and regular use to be learned and remembered. A user-friendly interface should encourage executives to use EIS more extensively.

The provided information may not be useful. Many previous EIS have contained little information of value to senior executives, which is related to a lack of understanding of executive's work. Systems designers who often possess excellent technical knowledge but little business or "big picture" knowledge have exacerbated this problem. This is why we have recommended all along using a task force design team that improves the chances of success by delivering systems that are tailored to the specific needs of the decision maker. The bottom line is that in order to develop a successful EIS, it is necessary to be aware of all functions that are to be touched by the EIS and be sensitive to the executives' decision-making requirements. An EIS can then be developed that allows information to flow cross-functionally to improve decision making. In order to solve this problem, senior management should use its leadership and influence to achieve this type of cross-functional design. They should involve all departments in the design process, not just the department that the system is being designed for.

Another common mistake usually made in acquiring information requirements is that the executives are interviewed on an individual basis instead of as a group. This method of interviewing places the executive in a limited position. Having an executive singled out impedes his or her ability to properly react to any inquiries being made. This is why Joint Application Design (JAD) has been recommended. A significant advantage of using JAD is that different functional areas of corporations have different agendas when it comes to creating a new system. Using JAD, an organization can be assured that all executives representing various departments are together in group interviews. This will help the organization avoid collecting narrow and one-dimensional information [22].

Another common mistake made while gathering information requirements is that designers usually ask the wrong questions, such as, What information do you need from the new system? System analysts should not assume that managers know exactly what they need. Instead of being an order taker, the analyst should be a problem solver, asking indirect questions that will help properly identify the information requirement. As discussed in Chapter 2, the design team should use a combination of top-down and bottom-up techniques to identify the information needs of executives. Examples of such questions are the following: What are the major problems encountered in accomplishing the goals of the organizational unit you manage? What are good solutions to those problems? How can information play a role in any of those solutions? What are the major decisions associated with your management responsibilities? Questions like these can help determine what information will be required to assure that the executives' information needs are met.

Another mistake usually made in determining information requirements is that executives are not permitted to visualize their ideas or plans. This is possible through a trial-and-error type of modeling. With prototyping, specific screens and reports can be produced for management to examine. Trial and error is important in determining information requirements. By using readily available software and hardware, a prototype of a new system can usually be constructed in a short period and presented to the executive decision makers for their reaction [22].

Glover et al. presents the results of a detailed study that clearly highlights characteristics of failed EIS [8, p. 12]. The result of this study is shown below:

- Inadequate technology
- Lack of sponsorship
- EIS too complicated
- EIS perceived as unimportant
- EIS failed to meet objectives
- Insufficient information systems resources
- Management not committed
- EIS was not cost-justified
- Corporate culture not ready for EIS
- Unknown objectives
- Executives lost interest
- Inability to define information requirements
- Data integrity in doubt
- Organizational resistance
- Insufficient depth of information
- EIS not linked to critical success factors
- Sponsor turnover
- Too much time needed to develop applications
- Information requirements too detailed
- Vendor support discontinued

GUIDELINES FOR EFFECTIVE EIS DESIGN

Similar to other management support systems, prior to the design of EIS, the goals and objectives of the system should be clearly defined. After defining the objectives of the system, methodologies similar to the ones discussed in Chapter 2 can be followed. Because the purpose and users of EIS are somewhat different than other MSS, we describe the important steps for designing an EIS as follows [1, 16, 17, 19, 20]:

1. Get the top management involved. Support and commitment must come from the top. Without a full commitment from top management do not build the system because the chances of failure are high.

2. Clearly define the objective and the benefits of EIS. Because the majority of the benefits of an EIS are intangible, this step is a challenging one. The costs are in hard dollars, and the benefits are qualitative. The design team should spend enough time to identify all the costs and benefits and present a convincing scenario to top management.

3. Identify the information needs of an executive. The decision-making process of executives should be examined to find out what kinds of decisions they are making. What are the critical success factors in meeting those goals or objectives?

4. Keep the communication lines open. Make sure the communication lines are open at all times among developers and executives and the entire design team who directly or indirectly will be users of the system.

5. Hide the complexity. Use common language when talking with executives. There is no need to explain the underlying technologies used in the EIS. Executives may lose interest if they perceive the system as too technical. Remember that typical executives are not interested in a particular platform or software. All they are interested in is getting the needed information in the simplest terms and format.

6. Keep the interface simple. The system must be simple and intuitive, otherwise it would be too difficult for executives to learn and use. Keep in mind that executives should be able to use an EIS with no training or a short training session. To a typical executive, the interface is the system. The ease of use of this component of the system is the make or break determinant of success or failure.

7. Keep a consistent look and feel concept. Developers should design standard layouts, formats, and colors through all windows. These standards offer many advantages such as a consistency of look and feel, and the gained knowledge and training can be transferred to other systems.

8. Design a flexible system. Almost all aspects of an EIS, including the user interface, change in time. It is quite possible that the system will require some changes a few months after implementation because of a dynamic business environment, as well as changes in technologies.

9. Provide a fast response time. EIS developers must continually monitor the response time of the system. Executives are intolerant of slow response time. When the system function takes more than a few seconds, a message should always provide feedback that the system is processing their request.

EIS IN ACTION

In the following sections, we briefly introduce several successful applications of EIS in the real world. For a detailed coverage, consult the provided references.

Washington, D.C., Hospital Center

Different executives at the Washington, D.C., Hospital Center are currently using an EIS. The president can review patient admissions and discharges on his monitor, plus review revenue trends to prepare for meetings. Before having the EIS, the president had to use other methods for retrieving valuable information. Information was accessible, but to obtain it he had to filter through numerous reports. If some information was missing, he had to have someone produce a report for him, which could be quite time consuming. Now the information is downloaded daily from the mainframe.

In addition to the president being able to use the system, other executives are starting to realize its capabilities. It was estimated that by the following month thirty decision makers were expected to use it. A few months later that number was supposed to reach 150 to 200. Ken Samet, president of the organization, stated, "All of our managers need data to make decisions, and they need it just as fast as I do" [2, 11].

Hertz Car Rental Company

It is very important for executives in the car rental business to be able to electronically sift through important information. This information can be about cities, climates, holidays, business cycles, tourist activity, past promotions, and market forecasts that allow a company to make immediate marketing decisions. This kind of decision making has become a requirement for competing in the car rental business.

Hertz, in order to have a competitive edge, has implemented a mainframe-based DSS and an EIS—a PC-based front end to the DSS that gives executives the tools to analyze the mountains of demographic data and make real-time marketing decisions.

With this EIS, Hertz's DSS now has a front end in the form of tools that executives use to analyze essential information from all over the nation, which includes both internal and external information. These include Hertz's own rental agreements, fleet purchases, and computer reservation system reports on the number of calls made to Hertz's toll-free number. It also includes airport reports on comparative revenues for the various car-rental companies stationed there.

One way that Hertz has measured the success of its system is by comparing its operations and level of customer service with its competitors. According to the designer of the system, this is due to the fact that their executives can maneuver and refine data to be more meaningful and strategically understandable to them. In addition, they have the ability to store needed data on their PCs and perform all sorts of what-if analysis. According to an executive of Hertz, Scott H. Meadow, using an EIS does not ensure prosperity, but "how you use it" will have an impact [14].

Harvard Coop

Harvard University is one of the world-renowned business schools, and the Harvard Cooperative Society (Harvard Coop or the Coop) is the nation's largest collegiate bookstore chain. It operates in six locations, and the inventory turns over about three times a year. With its growing business, the Coop management identified the need for an EIS.

CEO Jerry Murphy hired the CFT Consulting firm to build an EIS that analyzes sales, watches cash flow, and tells top management what is selling and what is not. CFT Consulting used an EIS software package known as Forest

& Trees, from Trinzic Corp. in Palo Alto, California, as a development tool for creating the EIS for the Coop [5].

Among the Coop's requirements are a system that will be easy to expand in the future, is easy to use, reliable, and includes central control and tracking of exceptions. After implementation, CEO Jerry Murphy said that the investment in the EIS revitalized the business, allowing him to juggle prices and inventory to make overall sales goals. The EIS receives all the information about customers, suppliers, products, competitors, and industry. In turn, the EIS is now able to report critical information with a high degree of efficiency and effectiveness.

Texas Instruments

Before Texas Instruments implemented Lightship, information was spread around in a variety of reports, and it was difficult to anticipate problems. With the EIS, managers and engineers at many levels (e.g., cost center, project and site managers, and chemical and hardware engineers) can control spending on both internal and research and development (R&D) projects.

The main office used to run a series of damage reports to find out what had gone wrong when costs for the process-automation systems were out of line. But since the reports were run after the fact, it was too late to do anything to fix the problems.

Using a hot spot on the screen (i.e., an area that has been programmed to perform other actions when you click on it), managers can "drill down" (in hypertext fashion) from the project level to actual cost elements and compare budgeted dollars to actual costs as they occur. Thus they can see not just how much money is left in a certain budget, but whether the money is going too fast.

Texas Instruments considered several packages before making its final choice to use Lightship. Reports that used to take days to compile can be generated in few seconds now. The change from damage reports to damage control that Lightship made possible is one of taking control of your information [12].

Dr. Pepper

The Dr. Pepper/7 Up Company uses PowerPlay to give upper management access to sales and demographic data at the company's corporate headquarters located in Dallas, Texas. PowerPlay's extracted database is updated monthly and then downloaded from a VAX to the regional PCs. This monthly extract allows the field sales offices to evaluate the sales performance of local bottlers. Because the extracted regional data files are less than two megabytes in size, the local office can optionally load the data onto a portable computer to graphically review and report the data at the customer site.

Although PowerPlay does not contain live data links, Cognos has a package that Dr. Pepper uses called Database Host Connector that provides some of that functionality. With PowerPlay, Dr. Pepper sales executives can complete most reporting functions in the field. The program has also eliminated a considerable amount of rekeying of information [12].

EIS TOOLS AND CAPABILITIES

EIS are generally designed with two or three components: an administrative module, where data access is managed; a builder module, where a developer sets data mapping and builds a sequence of screens; and a run-time module that the executive or knowledge worker runs. Sometimes the first two components are combined. Data access and consolidations vary depending on the package. Some EIS provide their own data storage system, and some only package the data and route it into a more accessible database, usually on a LAN. Finally, almost all of today's EIS come with a standard GUI, such as Windows.

There are generally six tasks that managers do for which an EIS will be useful: tracking, flagging exceptions, ranking, comparing, spotting trends, investigating, and exploring. The features most EIS tools provide perform these tasks. They present summarized and consolidated data in both report and chart format, or they allow sequencing of screens to produce executive slide shows. Locations that users can click on to get more information and other drill-down techniques help users navigate through varying levels of detail.

Exception reporting is another extremely useful technique managers use to flag data that is unusual or out of bounds. Variance reporting is the most common form of exception output. Both unusual and periodic events can be defined to trigger visual cues or activate an intelligent agent to perform a specific task.

SELECTION AND EVALUATION OF EIS PRODUCTS

Before selecting an EIS product, a detailed evaluation must be conducted to select the right package among the competing products [3, 7]. The evaluation of an EIS product should include the following dimensions: software, hardware, vendor, database capabilities, modeling capabilities, user/system interface, and advanced features.

Software Analysis

One of the most important components of an EIS product is the software component. Because the software is usually run on the existing hardware, in many cases the software is the entire system. From the user's viewpoint, software is always the entire system. There are several important factors that should be carefully considered before selecting an EIS product.

Ease of use, or user-friendliness, is the key factor in software analysis, because the user/system interface is one of the most important features of an

EIS. Systems that are intuitive, graphical based, menu driven, and work in an interactive fashion are more acceptable to EIS users than the other types of systems that work either in batch mode or command language mode. The emergence of the GUI has added more user-friendliness to EIS products. Generally speaking, users prefer mouse-driven and icon-based systems to those that are strictly character based and keyboard-command driven. Also, the amount of training needed to get a user started on an EIS product is important. The shorter the training time, the more acceptable the system will be.

Documentation is another important factor, and it includes all the supporting documents that accompany a product. Comprehensive documentation has been one of the poorest areas in the computer industry. Good documentation should be easy to read and understand, it should include error traps and error correction, it should help a user to enter and exit the system at any point, and it should include a help screen and a variety of internal documentation for ease of use. In recent years, particularly in the Windows environment, EIS products have been entering the market with comprehensive documentation, online help menus, and tutorial facilities. All these features add more to the level of acceptability of the product to an EIS user.

Update availability is another important feature. Software products are continually upgraded and corrected—new features are added, technical capabilities are improved, and so forth. The major concern to EIS users is whether such updates are going to be available; if they are, how much must the user pay to gain access to these updates?

Volume handling is another issue that should be considered. This may include the number of fields, records, and files handled by an EIS product. This may also include the number of users who can access the system in a network environment, processing time, and so on.

Reliability is obviously an important feature to have because an EIS product must generate reliable reports. The accuracy and consistency of the reports are of paramount importance in an EIS environment.

Maintainability of an EIS product is important, because these products are mostly used and managed by users with minimum technical knowledge. They should be easy to maintain by individuals who are not computer experts.

Technical support for the EIS product is very important. The user should have access to technical support specialists over the telephone who can assist the user in trouble spots. Technical support for an EIS product should be available twenty-four hours a day, or at least Monday through Friday during regular business hours.

Hardware Analysis

The selected EIS product either will run on the existing hardware, or hardware components of the system must be purchased when the software is selected. In either case, the following important factors should be carefully analyzed.

The compatibility of the hardware with present hardware standards of the company or with future hardware acquired by the company is important. If the hardware is compatible, it will be easier to use the system; maintenance and training new users on the system will also be easier. And it also helps the organization to stick with its standard procedure regarding the hardware acquired in the organization.

Maintainability is another important factor. The trend for hardware technology is "turnkey" systems, which are those types of systems that are ready to use as soon as they are purchased. Usually there is not any major programming or modification involved for their immediate operation. These types of systems are easier to maintain, even by individuals with minimum computer training.

Availability, another important feature, usually refers to the degree of access to the system by other users using access devices from different geographical locations in the organization. It can also refer to the number of users who can access the same program or model at the same time. This feature emphasizes the network capabilities, multiprocessing, multiprogramming, and multitasking capabilities of a system.

Reliability usually refers to the down-time of a system. How the system performs during peak times or the performance of the system under "stress" are indicators of system reliability. Organizations that have implemented EIS in mission critical applications cannot afford down-time of the system. Hardware standards in such an environment must be the highest possible, and users of such systems demand hardware with proven track records of high mean time between failure ratios. The trend is toward systems that allow hardware support technicians and specialists to perform necessary repair work on the system without taking the system down. If one hardware component (such as a hard disk) fails, the redundant hard disk(s) simply takes over while technicians repair the failed unit.

Expandability is another important feature. To keep abreast of the future growth of the company, the system must be expandable. This may include memory size, speed, throughput, input/output channels, networking capabilities, and so forth.

Vendor Analysis

There are numerous vendors offering EIS products, but not all of these vendors provide the same level of service. Careful analysis of key features that should be supported by a good vendor can increase the chances of success in EIS selection and utilization.

Training provided by the vendor on both hardware and particularly on software is very important. Some vendors provide on-site training; others provide training at vendor facilities, and some provide both. Some of these training sessions are free of charge to the user, and some are very costly. Also, some vendors provide ongoing training in parallel with the system updates. Vendors can also provide significant support and instructions on initial installation and ongoing support for both training and maintenance of the system. Several vendors offer timely upgrades and assure the user of product reliability.

Hotline availability is another important feature to consider. Many of the questions asked by EIS users can be answered through a hotline service. Access to one of these hotlines can be very helpful. In some cases there is an operator available on a twenty-four-hour basis to answer questions raised by users.

Availability of knowledgeable staff by the vendor is another important feature. Several vendors send their technical staff for on-site visits. These individuals sometimes provide consultation and introduce some of the new features that can be handled by the EIS product.

Newsletters and user groups are also very helpful. Some vendors continuously inform the users about the extended capabilities of the EIS product and support user groups by establishing a bulletin board and other online facilities.

Crisis reaction is also important. The user should investigate how a particular vendor may react to a crisis. The user can either ask other users of the system or the vendors themselves. A few vendors provide a "loaner" at the time of the crisis and quickly resolve the situation. Still other vendors provide full backup support for their clients. In this situation, if a catastrophe such as fire destroyed the client's system, the vendor would be able to fully restore the clients system to 100 percent functionality by using the mirror image backup that is updated on a daily basis. This type of vendor support can be costly, but it may be worth the cost in the event of a disaster.

The number of previous installations is very important. Naturally, if the vendor has installed systems for various organizations, this verifies the quality of a system and vendor. Talking to other users at these installations is the best safeguard for a new user regarding the purchase of a new EIS product.

Contract terms for diagnostic and preventive maintenance, maintenance contract renewal, and relocation or reassignment of an EIS product are also important factors to be considered.

Local support of the vendor is also important because it may expedite the maintenance procedure in resolving an unexpected crisis situation.

Cost is naturally a very important factor. The EIS user should consider the bundled and unbundled costs, which include the cost of the system as a whole or the cost of different components of the system.

Database Analysis

The database and DBMS components of an EIS must support some minimum capabilities. The trend for database is toward the relational, extended relational, and object-oriented data models. It seems these types of data modeling are gaining a lot of support in the user community. They are also well supported by the database vendors. The relational data model is easier to use and maintain by computer novices. The following are the basic requirements of DBMS components of an EIS:

- file creation, access, modification, and update
- data dictionary
- automatic audit trails
- simple and multicriteria search
- sort using one key field and multiple key fields
- multifile access
- file-merge and file-join facility
- access to both internal and external databases
- security and privacy protection

Modeling Analysis

The modeling and modeling analysis for EIS and other MSS were discussed in detail in Chapter 3. This component of an EIS should perform some basic analysis. Depending on the specific needs of a decision maker, one or more of these capabilities may carry a heavier weight. The following capabilities are needed for various EIS applications:

- functions (general and user-defined)
- what-if analysis
- goal-seeking analysis
- sensitivity analysis
- statistical analysis (bivariate and multivariate)
- forecasting models (time series, regression, and curve fitting)
- optimization models
- simulation models
- financial models
- scheduling models
- internal and external model access

User/System Interface Analysis

From a user viewpoint, the user/system interface component of an EIS is the entire system. EIS users are not concerned with how different analyses are performed or how a DBMS manages the EIS database. Their primary concern is how easy and effective the system is to use. The following are the key features of this component of an EIS:

- basic user/system interfaces
  menu-driven
  question and answer
  command language
- GUI
- multimedia interface
- graphic display with different scaling, labeling, and sizing
- multiple graphs per page
- query capability (procedural and nonprocedural)
- exception-type reporting
- multidimensional display
- different report generation and format
- help screens
- online tutorial

Advanced Features Analysis

The advanced technical features of an EIS product are important to some users and should be examined. They emphasize efficiency and effectiveness of the entire system. The following are the important technical features of an EIS product:

- multi-user access (multiprogramming and multitasking)
- multidimensional analysis (e.g., product line, geographical location, time, and other business variables)
- response time
- computational cost
- memory requirement
- source code for the software (some source codes are faster than others)
- CPU cycle
- type of operating system
- accuracy and speed of calculations
- linkage capabilities to other hardware/software

SELECTED PRODUCTS

There is a vast array of EIS products on the market, the cost and capabilities of which vary significantly. For a detailed analysis you should request additional documentation from the prospective vendor. The following are some of the popular EIS products on the market [21]:

- Acumate Enterprise (Kenan Technologies)
- Commander EIS (Comshare, Inc.)
- Cross Target (Dimensional Insight, Inc.)
- Data Interpretation System (DIS) (Metaphor, Inc.)
- EISToolKit (Micro Strategy, Inc.)
- Express/EIS (IRI Software)
- Focus/EIS (Information Builders, Inc.)
- Forest & Trees (Trinzic Corp.)
- Holos (Holistic Systems, Inc.)
- LightShip (Pilot Software, Inc.)
- PowerPlay (Cognos Corp.)

IMPORTANT TECHNOLOGIES FOR
EIS DESIGN AND UTILIZATION

One of the most important considerations in EIS design is the development of an easy-to-use interface because, for the executive, the interface is the EIS. As we have said all along, to a typical executive, the interface is the most important feature. Ease of use and attractiveness of this component play a major role in the success of the system. Multimedia, hypermedia, data warehouse, and other related technologies facilitate and enhance the ease of use of these systems. Let us briefly explain these important technologies.

Multimedia

Multimedia is the ability to present and transfer information through more than one medium at a time. This may include voice, data, images, full-motion video, and animation. The most compelling reason for utilizing multimedia is that when using traditional methods, chances are that the majority of your audience may not absorb the entire presentation. Multisensory presentations speed and improve understanding, and they can further attract the user's attention.

The use of multimedia is similar to comparing radio to television. Although radios distribute information through sound, television can disseminate information through a combination of sounds and visual images. Multimedia popularity is mainly due to two factors [13]: (1) enhancement and popularity of video and (2) the ever-increasing power of computers, particularly microcomputers.

Before we go any further, let me share a personal experience regarding multimedia applications. Several years ago I was trying to teach a group of school children about various birds. The first bird was a canary. First I wrote on the board a detailed description of a canary, but only a few students understood our description. Then, using a CD-ROM-based training package that includes the names and descriptions of all birds, I retrieved a textual description of the canary on the monitor. A picture of the bird appeared on the monitor and started to sing and finally flew through the monitor.

This is multimedia. By combining textual, images, sound, and video, you can convey information with minimum difficulty. The old saying "a picture is worth a thousand words" makes more sense in the multimedia environment.

Hypertext

Hypertext is an approach to data management in which data are stored in networks of nodes connected by links. The nodes are designed to be accessed through an interactive browsing system. A hypertext document includes node links and supporting indexes for a particular topic. A hypertext (usually called hypermedia) document may include data, voice, and images. In hypertext documents, the physical and logical layouts are usually different, but this is not the case in a paper document, where the author of the paper establishes the order.

A hypertext system provides users with nonsequential paths to access information, which means that information does not have to be accessed sequentially as in a book. A hypertext system allows the user to make any request that the author or designer of the hypertext provides through links. These links choices are similar to lists of indexes, and also can be links within information nodes. The user chooses which choice best suits his or her needs [15].

Some hypertext systems define their links as directed (or directed-hierarchical). In this format, the links have a direction between source and destination nodes. This type of arrangement makes it much easier for the user to navigate through the system; however, they are not as flexible as in a network of interrelated links. In a network system, links point in both directions—the system is not organized into a hierarchical format. This type of arrangement may be difficult for the user to navigate or traverse.

There is a similarity between a hypertext document and an encyclopedia-type document. In an encyclopedia you may read a topic and then look for more information on this topic in another section of the encyclopedia. Hypertext documents are designed for this type of access.

A good example of a hypertext document is the online help provided by the majority of Windows applications. When you click the help menu option, a context-sensitive help screen will be provided. You can read about a topic and then find out more about other related topics simply by clicking on any of the related-topic icons. The internal links will quickly take you to the requested topic. Also, in addition to text, you may see images as well. These images provide visual support that in turn makes information easier to retrieve.

Hypermedia

In the previous section, we explained hypertext technology as a sophisticated method for retrieving information from a variety of sources. Hypermedia is an extension of hypertext. It combines text, images, sounds, and full-motion video in the same document and allows information retrieval with a click of a button [6].

The graphics used with hypermedia can be either scanned images or object-oriented pictures. Hypermedia is encoded digitally on CD-ROM type media and played back through a highly interactive PC or workstation.

Hypermedia technology has been utilized successfully in EIS. A hypermedia-based EIS offers several advantages to executives and allows them to accomplish four basic needs [10]: (1) They can quickly track the information behind reports; (2) they have user-friendly access to information; (3) they can retrieve filtered and compressed information that focuses on critical data behind reports; and (4) they can experience hands-on navigation through detailed organizational information, which eliminates the use of their subordinates, who can then search for detailed information.

Data Warehouses and Replication Capabilities

Client/server packages with intelligent agents can automate processes such as warning a financial analyst when a key ratio has been exceeded or sending e-mail to a purchasing manager when an inventory quantity has been reached. Many organizations are meeting the challenge of providing direct access to corporate data on the mainframe by creating LAN-based data warehouses that contain read-only snapshots of host data that is periodically refreshed. This has the advantage of minimizing network traffic, expensive host CPU time, and security headaches. Vendors offer different versions of a data warehouse, such as a relational DBMS that is optimized for queries rather than data entry. Typical clients are firms that need to analyze large amounts of data, like retailers and financial institutions [9].

Replication servers are also becoming more widespread. Replication is related to the notion of data warehousing; but data warehouses usually contain only a subset of the data, while replicas are usually copies of an entire database. Vendors sell replication servers that can keep multiple copies of the database up to date, making it easier for users who may be geographically dispersed to get fast, local access to data. Lotus Notes was the first to popularize the concept of replication. Since then, replication has become a common feature in the majority of EIS products [21].

SUMMARY

This chapter provided a detailed discussion of EIS as one of the growing applications of MSS. It presented key features of an EIS, a conceptual model for an EIS, guidelines for avoiding failure, instructions for a successful EIS design, several real-life applications of EIS, and popular EIS products. The chapter concluded with a discussion on multimedia and hypermedia as these technologies become more important for EIS design and utilization.

REFERENCES

1. Barrow, Craig. "Implementing an Executive Information System: Seven Steps for Success." *Information Systems Management* (Spring 1990): 41–46.
2. Bergman, Rhonda. "From the Top Down: EIS Works for Everybody." *Hospital & Health* (September 20, 1994): 68.
3. Bidgoli, Hossein. "DSS Product Evaluation: An Integrated Framework." *Journal of Systems Management* (November 1989): 27–34.
4. Cronk, Randall. "EIS's Mind Your Data." *Byte* (June 1993): 121–128.
5. DeJong, Jennifer. "View from the Top." *Inc. Technology* (Summer 1995): 49–52.
6. Frolick, Mark N., and Narender K. Ramaraupu. "Hypermedia: The Future of EIS." *Journal of Systems Management* (July 1993): 32–36.
7. Frolick, Mark N., and Jennings Seavy. "EIS Software Selection at Georgia Power: A Structured Approach." *Information Strategy: The Executive's Journal* (Spring 1993): 47–52.
8. Glover, Harry, Hugh J. Watson, and Rex Kelly Rainer, Jr. "20 Ways to Waste an EIS Investment." *Information Strategy: The Executive's Journal* (Winter 1992): 11–17.
9. Hoven, John Van Den. "Data Warehousing: New Name for the Accessibility Challenge." *Information Systems Management* (Winter 1997): 70–72.
10. Inmon, William. "Building the Best Database." *Computerworld* (July 9, 1986): 73–75.
11. Keegan, Arthur J., and Barbara Baldwin. "EIS: A Better Way to View Hospital Trends." *Healthcare Financial Management* (November 1992): 38–66.
12. Kinland, Jim. "EIS Moves to the Desktop." *Byte* (June 1992): 206–212.
13. O'Hara, Frank. "Interactive Multimedia." *Journal of Systems Management* (November 1994): 16–19.
14. O'Leary, Meghan. "Putting Hertz Executives in the Driver's Seat." *CIO* (February 1990): 62–69.
15. Swift, Michael K. "Hypertext: A Tool for Knowledge Transfer." *Journal of Systems Management* (June 1991): 35–37.
16. Tang, Victor. "The Organizational Implications of an EIS Implementation." *Journal of Systems Management* (November 1991): 10–12.
17. Watson, Hugh J., and Mark N. Frolick. "Determining Information Requirements for an EIS." *MIS Quarterly* (September 1993): 255–269.
18. Watson, Hugh J., and Rex Kelly Rainer, Jr. "A Manager's Guide to Executive Support Systems." *Business Horizons* (March/April 1991): 44–50.
19. Watson, Hugh J., and John Satzinger. "Guidelines for Designing EIS Interfaces." *Information Systems Management* (Fall 1994): 46–52.
20. Watson, Hugh W., Hugh J. Watson, Rex Kelly Rainer, Jr., and Chang E. Koh. "Executive Information Systems: A Framework for Development and a Survey of Current Practices." *MIS Quarterly* (March 1991): 13–29.
21. Watterson, Karen. "The Changing World of EIS." *Byte* (June 1994): 183–193.
22. Wetherbe, James C. "Executive Information Requirements: Getting It Right." *MIS Quarterly* (March 1991): 53–65.

CHAPTER 6

Group Support Systems

This chapter provides a comprehensive discussion of group support systems (GSS) including group decision support systems (GDSS), electronic meeting systems (EMS), and GroupWare. It presents definitions, applications, and software support for each category. The chapter also provides a definition of three popular types of teleconferencing and offers several real-life case studies of the applications of GSS.

GSS: AN OVERVIEW

In today's business environment, decision makers increasingly work in group settings. Group or collective computing is a new buzzword for the 1990s and beyond. All major software vendors are competing to either enter or increase their share in this fast-growing market. Within this collaborative environment, there has been an increase in the use of computer-aided group support technologies. GDSS, a subfield of DSS, have evolved over the past decade. More recently, technologies such as EMS and GroupWare have found their way into the workplace. We call these various technologies "group support systems." Figure 6.1 illustrates this classification. GSS are intended to assist a group of decision makers who are working with a certain task to make a decision or to make a better decision. These systems utilize computer and communications technologies in order to process, formulate, and implement a decision-making task.

Computer-aided decision support such as GDSS can be considered a kind of intervention technology that helps to overcome the limitations of group interaction. A GDSS supports a group's natural decision-making processes. Intervention features of a GDSS reduce communication barriers and introduce order and efficiency into situations that are inherently disorderly and

Figure 6.1
GSS Taxonomy

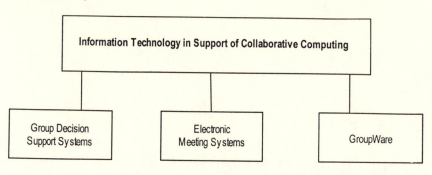

inefficient. Thus, a GDSS facilitates the decision-making process by providing a clear focus for group discussion, minimizing politicking, and organizing attention around the critical issues. The outcome of this intervention depends on (1) successfully matching the level and sophistication of the GDSS and its collaborative tools with the appropriate size group, scope of task, and proximity of the decision-making environment and (2) providing supportive management (especially at the CEO level) who are willing to champion the application of GDSS within the organization.

Other computer-aided technologies that have emerged in the 1990s for group support are EMS and GroupWare. Even though these systems are not considered to be "full-functionality GDSS" because of their decision-tool limitations, they are less expensive and provide communication and problem-solving mechanisms necessary for effective team management in a collaborative environment [6].

As discussed in Chapter 1, DSS are usually designed to be used by a particular decision maker. A decision is made from the inputs given by this particular person. GDSS are designed to be used by more than one decision maker. These systems are useful for committees, review panels, board meetings, task forces, and decision-making sessions that require input from several decision makers (required to make such decisions as whether to locate a new plant, introduce a new product, or participate in an international bid) [2].

COMPONENTS OF A GDSS

Desanctis and Gallupe define GDSS as an interactive computer-based system that facilitates the solution of unstructured and semistructured problems by a group of decision makers working together as a team [5].

This definition is very similar to the definition of DSS given in Chapter 1. The only difference is the focus on the group versus the individual decision maker. By this definition, the components of a GDSS are basically the same as those of DSS, meaning hardware, software, people, and procedures. In addition, communication technology is added for group participation from various sites. Let us provide a breakdown of each component.

Software and Hardware

The software components of a GDSS may include the following:

* database and database management capabilities
* modeling capabilities
* user/system interface with multiple-user access
* specialized application programs to facilitate group access

The hardware components of GDSS may include the following:
* general purpose I/O devices (dumb terminals, PCs, workstations, and voice I/O)
* a CPU
* a common viewing screen (for the group) or individual monitor (for each participant)
* a network system that links different sites and participants to each other

People

In addition to the hardware and software components, a GDSS is composed of people: the facilitator and the decision-making participants. Let us briefly identify these individuals: The facilitator is the individual who must direct the group through the planning process. This individual must have sound computer skills and a thorough understanding of the dynamics of group interaction. The level of control the facilitator exercises varies by meeting style. There are three meeting styles: the chauffeured meeting, the supported meeting, and the interactive meeting [3].

In the chauffeured meeting, the facilitator is the primary user and controller of the GDSS. The computer and a projector act as an electronic blackboard on which the facilitator records and updates key information as the group orally discusses the issues (the participants do not have input devices). The system also can access databases and modeling tools to analyze various alternatives.

The supported meeting is similar to the chauffeured meeting except that the participants use input devices, such as a keypad or workstation, that are attached to the facilitator's computer. Because each participant has an input device, parallel communication capabilities enable him or her to talk and vote simultaneously, which saves time.

The interactive meeting is the most common meeting format in which a meeting room provides a computer for each participant. In these meetings, the discussion among participants is done simultaneously through typing rather than verbal exchange. The facilitator's role is to keep the group focused on the issues and to direct the momentum derived from the group's synergy. Even though the cost for a facility that can accommodate an interactive meeting requires a major capital investment, the efficiency and effectiveness gained from this style of meeting quickly return the cost.

Regardless of the meeting style, the facilitator's most important duties are to identify the meeting's objectives, to select the appropriate GDSS tools and models, and to make sure the essential databases, both internal and external, will be available during the meeting. The objective of extensive premeeting planning is to minimize the time the participants will need to spend in the formal meeting and to make sure the agenda can be completely covered in the allotted time [3].

The decision-making participants are the major players in the group decision-making process. The most important factor in a computer-aided group support system is the group of people. The technology must support the group, not dominate it [3]. The impact of the technology's support often depends on the size of the group. In an unassisted environment (non-GDSS), as the number of participants increases, the potential for information exchanges rises significantly, the frequency, duration, and intimacy of information exchange decline, and consensus becomes harder to achieve [4]. Since large groups have more communication difficulties, the impact of a GDSS on such a group is more obvious. However, with small groups, the minimization of "group think" is a major benefit. Research data show that the parallel communication and voting features were of more benefit to large groups than to small groups, whereas the anonymity feature of a GDSS was of greater benefit for small groups [3, 6]. A conceptual model of a GDSS is provided in Figure 6.2 [5].

LEVELS OF SUPPORT PROVIDED BY GSS

The features that GSS provide to facilitate the decision-making process can be divided into three distinct levels of support, each suited for different needs [4].

Level 1 Support

The purpose of GSS at this level is to improve the decision processes by removing common communication barriers and providing communication support (i.e., a large screen to gather and display ideas, features to solicit and compile votes and results anonymously, and electronic messaging capabilities). Most GDSS and EMS provide this level of support, whereas some GroupWare products provide limited capabilities at this level of support.

Figure 6.2
Conceptual Model of a GDSS

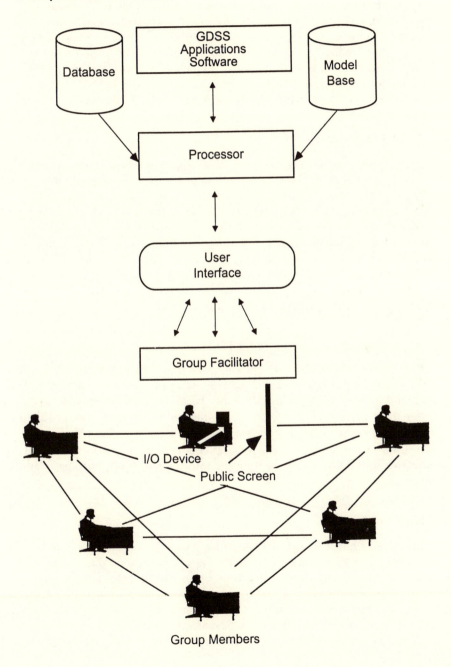

Level 2 Support

GSS at this level are enhanced versions of those at level 1 because they provide quantitative modeling and planning tools (i.e., Delphi Technique, or PERT and CPM). The purpose of level 2 support is to reduce uncertainty and permit groups to work on problem identification and solutions while viewing their analyses. Full-functionality GDSS such as the University of Minnesota's SAMM, the University of Arizona's (Ventana) GroupSystems, IBM's TeamFocus, Collaborative Technology's VisionQuest, and RONIN Development Corporation's RONIN War Room provide level 2 support.

Level 3 Support

GSS at this level use ES and artificial intelligence technologies. A level 3 GSS can actually control the pattern, timing, and content of group interaction using rule-based features and heuristics to adapt to the meeting environment, changing the interaction patterns as needed. A GSS at this level eventually will provide advice to help the group select the most suitable rules for enhancing group discussion. The systems available at this level are experimental, such as Argnoter, an "intelligent" enhancement for Xerox's COLAB designed to assist decision makers in evaluating proposals [15].

Tables 6.1, 6.2, and 6.3 provide a concise overview of the three GSS levels and the group problems or needs that GSS support.

GSS TOOLS

Full-functionality GDSS are differentiated from other GSS like EMS and GroupWare by the sophistication and availability of planning tools and decision models [6]. The following GSS tools, basic and advanced, have been developed for problem identification, deliberation, planning, and problem solving by a group. The basic tools can be found in some GroupWare products. EMS usually have the basic tools and many of the advanced tools. Full-functionality GDSS usually include the full range of tools, both basic and advanced.

Basic Tools

Electronic brainstorming and voting are considered generic tools and can be applied to a wide range of problem identification, idea generation, and problem-solving situations. Electronic brainstorming (EBS) helps group members generate ideas by allowing them simultaneously to share comments in response to a specific question. The anonymity of EBS encourages objectivity and creativity. EBS is based on the manual method. With the individual brainwriting pool technique, each member of a group writes a comment on a

Table 6.1
GSS Level 1

Group Problem or Need	GSS Feature
Ability to send and receive information efficiently among all parties or specific group members	Electronic messaging, broadcast or point-to-point communication
Access to personal data files or corporate data during the course of a meeting	Computer terminal for each group member; gateway to a LAN or central computer and e-mail systems
Display of ideas, votes, data, graphs, or tables to all members simultaneously	Large common viewing screen or "public" screen at each group member's terminal
Reluctance of some members to speak due to their shyness, low status, or controversial ideas	Anonymous input of ideas and votes from particular sites
Failure of some members to participate due to laziness or tuning out	Active solicitation of ideas or votes from each group member
Failure to organize and analyze ideas and votes efficiently	Summary and display of ideas; statistical summary and display of votes
Failure to quantify preferences	Rating scales and/or ranking schemes that can be solicited and displayed
Failure to develop a meeting, strategy or plan	A mock agenda that the group can complete and/or modify
Failure to stick with the meeting plan	Continuous display of the agenda; a time clock; agenda items automatically displayed at the appropriate time

Table 6.2
GSS Level 2

Group Problem or Need	GSS Feature
Need for problem structuring, planning, and scheduling	Planning models, such as PERT, CPM, Gantt chart, and responsibility matrix
Decision-analytic aids for uncertain future events	Utility and probability assessment models, such as decision trees, risk-assessment models, and probability models
Decision-analytic aids for resource allocation problems	Resource allocation models, such as linear programming
Decision-analytic aids for data-oriented tasks	Statistical models, multicriteria decision models
Insufficient knowledge or time to use the structured technique	Automated Delphi, brainstorming, other idea-gathering and compilation techniques; on-line tutorial for the group or a human facilitator

Table 6.3
GSS Level 3

Group Problem or Need	GSS Feature
Desire to enforce formalized decision procedures	Automated parliamentary procedure
Desire to select and/or arrange an array of rules for discussion	Rule based; facility for rule selection and application
Uncertainty about options for meeting procedures	Automated counselor, giving advice on available rules and appropriate use
Need to develop meeting rules	Rule-writing facility

piece of paper and then places it in the center of the table for another member to read before adding a comment. This process continues until the group runs out of comments on the topic that is under consideration [16].

Voting can offer a variety of prioritizing methods, such as true/false, rank ordering, and multiple-choice questions. All the participants cast private ballots, and then the accumulated results are displayed in graphic and tabular formats that are appropriate for the method used. Using voting techniques will result in a listing of prioritized alternatives for further elaboration by the group [3].

Advanced Tools

The next groups of tools offer advanced problem-solving decision models that are often customized to a particular class of problems. Group-decision situations concerning strategic planning, contingency planning, problem formulation, and resource allocation can benefit from these tools, which are summarized and explained here [6]. The following is a brief explanation of these advanced tools.

Stakeholder identification and assumption analysis are used to systematically evaluate the implications of a proposed policy or plan. Stakeholders and their assumptions are identified and rated in terms of importance, and then are presented graphically to the group for discussion and analysis. Stakeholders are the entities, individuals, or groups of individuals upon whose actions the organization depends or who will be affected by the organization's proposed plan or course of action [16].

An alternative evaluator provides multicriteria decision-making support. Alternatives are examined by applying flexible weighted criteria to evaluate decision scenarios and tradeoffs. Results are displayed in tabular or graphic format.

Policy formation supports the group's development of a policy or mission statement. Sample text is contributed and then edited through group discussion. The process is iterative until a consensus is reached.

Topic commentor helps the group solicit ideas and provides for additional details in connection with the list of topics, which may also include subtopics. Group participants enter, exchange, and review information on self-selected topics.

Idea organizer helps the group identify and consolidate text of the key items and also supports the integration of external information to support the identified items.

Issue analyzer helps the group condense the combined topic list to a manageable size by identifying the topics that merit further consideration.

Questionnaire supports researchers and facilitators in designing online questionnaires. The questionnaires are "dynamic," meaning that the additional questions are triggered based on the responses received.

Enterprise analyzer is an organization-modeling tool used to support any user-definable approach by capturing characteristics of a business subsystem such as IBM's Business System Planning [10].

Semantic graphics browser is used to examine information from the enterprise analyzer by allowing the users to zoom in on specific areas of interest for more detail [10].

File reader is an efficiency tool that allows the group members to browse (read-only) previously stored material at any point in a group discussion and then return to the discussion at their own discretion.

Group dictionary permits a group to formally define a word or phrase or create references for future group work. The process is iterative to encourage group participation in arriving at a consensus.

CLASSES OF GSS

GSS can be classified in two ways: input devices and geographic devices [4, 7]. Figure 6.3 illustrates these classifications.

Input Devices Classification

Three major GSS fall under the input devices classification: software-only, keypad response, and full-keyboard workstation systems. Let us briefly explain each type [7].

Software-Only Systems. The simplest form of GSS is a single-computer, software-only system. Although these systems often are marketed as GroupWare, they are single-user decision-support tools that use a video display monitor to allow the meeting participants to view the decision-making outcome. They do not have the anonymous input capabilities of the more sophisticated keypad response and full-keyboard systems, but they are portable and relatively inexpensive.

Decision Pad (Apian Software) and AutoMan (Sterling Software, Inc.) are examples of software-only systems that provide support for evaluating alternatives. For example, a group could evaluate a capital-budgeting decision using

Figure 6.3
GSS Classes

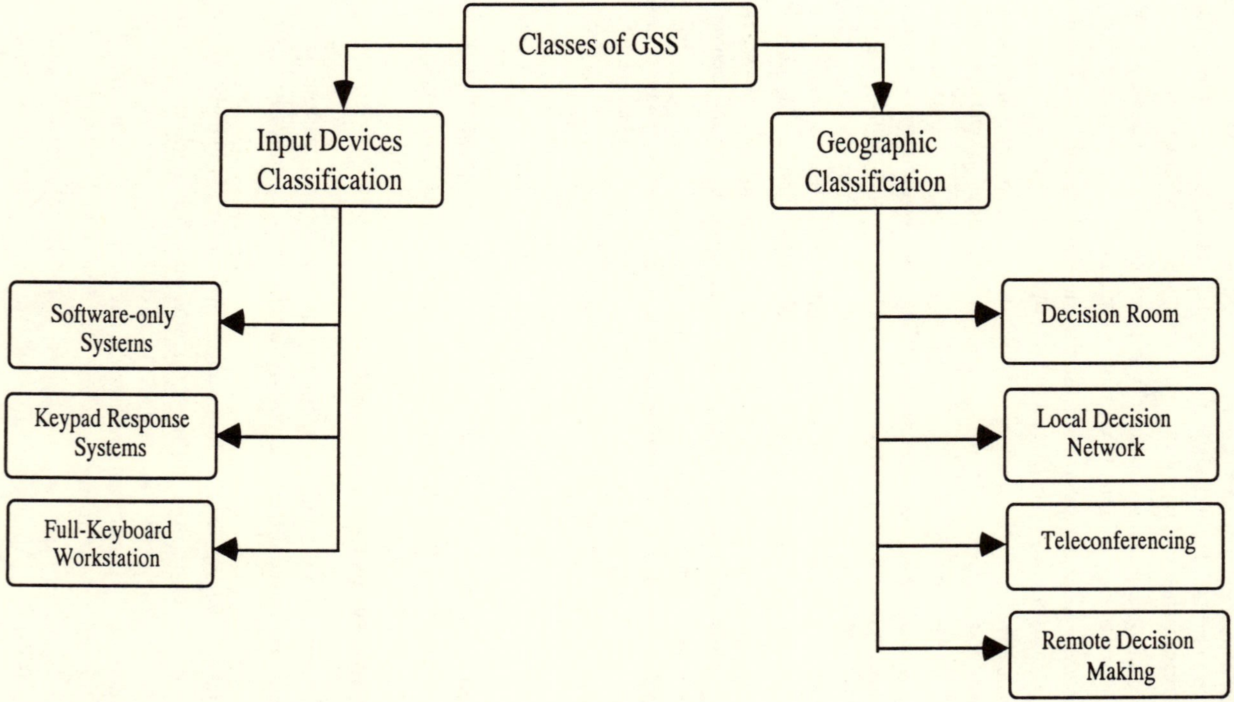

multiple criteria such as payback, return on investment, and investment risk. The group may assign weights to each criterion, then rate each alternative based on the three criteria. The system manipulates the ratings, considers the criteria's weights, and ranks the alternatives accordingly.

If meeting participants should disagree with the outcome (e.g., some might argue that the group did not put enough weight on investment risk), what-if analysis can quickly find how alternative weights might affect the outcome. For instance, the outcome might not change even if the group weighted investment risk four times as heavily as the other two criteria. In this case, the group chooses the desired alternative and saves time by avoiding further discussion.

Keypad Response Systems. The second level of GSS is the keypad response system, which consists of a host PC and wired or wireless hand-held keypads. Group members respond to questions or evaluate alternatives using the electronic keypads. The host PC processes the participants' input and displays the analysis on a display screen.

Keypad response systems have an advantage over software-only systems in that they allow a meeting facilitator to gather participants' input instantly and anonymously. They also have two important advantages over the more sophisticated keyboard-based systems: They are portable, and they are relatively inexpensive.

OptionFinder (Option Technologies, Inc.) and Data-Back System (Macro 4, Inc.) are two commercial keypad response systems. Both systems allow re-defined rating scales, such as yes/no, multiple-choice, and five-point Likert-scales questions. They also allow users to design their own rating scales, and they support graphical display of the data, such as bar charts and line graphs. A keypad response system also can be used to make capital budgeting decisions. As an example, consider a group that is considering six investment alternatives. The keypad response system provides several methods for prioritizing the six alternatives. They could be ranked from one to six by each participant, or each alternative could be evaluated separately using a five-point Likert scale. It is also possible to evaluate each alternative using multiple criteria, such as return on investment, payback, investment risk, and so forth. Criterion weighting is also possible. The group's input would be tabulated to provide immediate feedback and identify where the group agreed and disagreed. Thus, the group can save time by bypassing areas of consensus and by concentrating on disagreement.

Full-Keyboard Workstation Systems. The third type of GSS under this group is the full-keyboard workstation system. Typically, these systems are configured in a meeting room with workstations connected using a LAN. Workstations are arranged around a U-shaped table, with a facilitator station and projector screen at the front of the room. Some companies place file servers, workstations, CPUs, and printers in a separate room to reduce the noise level and improve room aesthetics.

The full-keyboard workstation systems support the following: alternative evaluation, rating, and voting; brainstorming; idea organization; issue analysis;

and strategic planning, such as developing mission statements, identifying critical success factors, and developing master plans.

Alternative evaluations, ratings, and voting tools are similar to those in key-pad response systems, but full-keyboard systems allow the participants to talk through their computers. Anonymous talking provides an ideal method for involving a heterogeneous, broad-based group in brainstorming and strategic planning activities.

During a brainstorming session, each participant submits an idea to the system, then receives other participants' ideas, comments on them, and sends the comment back to the system—all via the workstation. This technology improves traditional brainstorming in several ways. First, anonymity helps provide a supportive atmosphere because ideas are more likely to be evaluated based on their merit, independent of the source; thus, criticism is less likely to be seen as a personal attack. Second, ideas are processed in parallel. No one has to wait until everyone else has stopped talking in order to be heard. Third, having the participants write their comments forces them to be more concise and focused. Fourth, all comments are captured in memory, so no ideas are lost. Last, cross talk, side talk, and chitchat are reduced.

After using the brainstorming tool to generate a diverse list of ideas or suggestions, the idea organizer tool can be used to combine similar ideas. Several service organizations use this technique to generate suggestions on how to improve customer satisfaction.

Geographic Classification

Four major GSS fall under the geographic classification: decision room, local decision network, teleconferencing, and remote decision making. Let us briefly explain each type [5].

Decision Room Systems. In this type of GSS, decision makers sit around a horseshoe-shaped desk facing a large screen. Each participant has access to a terminal, which is used for individual input, and at the same time everybody can see the large screen, which is used to summarize the input from different participants. This configuration is equivalent to the full-keyboard workstation system.

Local Decision Network (LDN) Systems. In this type of GSS, the participants are dispersed in a limited geographic area, but they can participate from their own offices and express their views. This configuration includes a central processor with dedicated software for storing the results.

Teleconferencing Systems. This architecture enables different decision makers in scattered geographic regions to participate in a group decision-making process. Teleconferencing can include one of the following: real-time computer conferencing, video teleconferencing, and desktop conferencing.

Real-time computer conferencing allows a group of users, who are either gathered in an electronic meeting room or physically dispersed, to interact synchronously through their workstations or terminals. When a group is physically dispersed, an audio link, such as a conference call, is often established.

Two basic approaches are used to implement a real-time computer conferencing system [17]. The first approach is to embed an unmodified single-user application in a conferencing environment that transmits the application's output to each participant's display terminal. Input comes from one user at a time, and floor-passing protocol exchanges input control among users. For example, terminal linking allows several terminals to communicate at the same time. The second approach is to design the application specifically to account for the presence of multiple users (e.g., meeting scheduling systems and real-time group note-taking systems).

Video teleconferencing, the most familiar example of teleconferencing, requires special rooms and sometimes trained operators. Video teleconferencing approximates face-to-face meetings, and television sets and cameras are used to transmit live pictures and sounds. This is markedly more effective than the telephone and limited image conferencing; however, it is more costly. Newer systems provide workstation-based interfaces to a conference and make the process more accessible. Xerox, for example, established an audio/video link to be used by a project team split between Portland, Oregon, and Palo Alto, California. Most video interactions occurred between large common areas at each side, but project members could also access video channels through their office workstations. However, video teleconferencing is not only relatively inaccessible, but it also has the disadvantage of not letting participants share text and graphics. Real-time computer conferencing does not offer video capabilities.

Desktop conferencing, a third type of computer-supported conferencing, combines the advantages of video teleconferencing and real-time computer conferencing while mitigating their drawbacks. Desktop conferencing still uses the workstation as the conference interface, but it also runs applications shared by the participants. Modern desktop conferencing systems support multiple video windows per workstation. This allows for the display of dynamic video images of participants. An example of desktop conferencing is the MMConf system. MMConf provides a shared display of a multimedia document, as well as communication channels for voice and shared pointers. Another example is the Rapport multimedia conferencing system, which is designed for workstations connected by a multimedia network. The system supports various forms of interaction, from simple telephone-like conversations to multiparty shared-display interactions.

Remote Decision-Making Systems. These configurations advocate uninterrupted communication in geographically dispersed organizations that include a fixed number of decision makers on a regular basis [5]. In this type of architecture, there is no need to schedule meetings in advance as with video teleconferencing. A participant may send his or her input to the central database (electronic mailbox), then the other participants will respond to this input. Eventually a decision is made by consensus.

Figure 6.4 illustrates the four configurations just discussed [5].

GROUPWARE: AN OVERVIEW

The goal of GroupWare is to assist groups in communicating, collaborating, and coordinating their activities. For the purposes of this book, we define GroupWare as a MSS that support groups of decision makers engaged in a common decision-making task by providing access to the same shared environment and information. The shared environment may be in the form of a memo, a single file, or an entire database.

A very different type of GroupWare focuses on managing (accessing, collecting, parsing, sorting, storing, and distributing) information. Lotus Notes

Figure 6.4
GSS Based on Geographic Classification

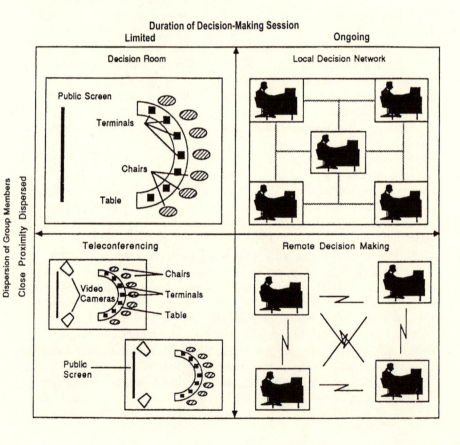

(Lotus Development Corporation) is an example of this type of GroupWare. Lotus Notes provides distributed database support with built-in wide-area connectivity, automated documents routing, and e-mail. With these tools, users can easily build databases, track data, and open discussion applications that can be connected via phone lines. Classic example (used in routing help requests) archives previously handled problems and solutions, archives support-staff discussions, and distributes messages.

LANs, WANs, and MANs are the backbone of GroupWare. Recently, the Internet has also become a key participant in GroupWare utilization. In turn, the software foundation of GroupWare is e-mail—in simple terms, the transport of text messages across the network. Although e-mail is not GroupWare per se, it is vital for some communications facilities that do have workgroup implications.

Today, GroupWare is in the early stages of development. Viable products are here, but businesses are only beginning to adopt them. The available commercial products vary significantly in their functions, complexity, and cost. At one end of the scale, a product like Futurus Team (Futurus Corporation) offers communications with a workgroup twist at an affordable price with minimal setup or administrative demands. At the other end, industrial-strength products, such as CM/1 (Corporate Memory Systems) and Keyfile (Keyfile Corporation), can cost tens of thousands of dollars to implement, often requiring setup procedures and extensive training to run.

GROUPWARE CLASSIFICATION

GroupWare software can be classified based on two features: type of group meeting and type of software [14, 18]. Figure 6.5 shows this classification. Let us briefly explain each type.

Type of Group Meeting

This class of GroupWare includes software support for four types of groups: the small group, the planetary group, the decision-making group, and the worn-sneakers group.

The small group (or task group) is made up of four or five coworkers who tend to interact extensively on projects. The small groups are not necessarily everlasting—they may dissolve and be recreated on a per-project basis. Keyfile (Keyfile Corporation) and Office IQ (Portfolio Technologies, Inc.) are suitable software products for this type of group. One member of the group may create, copy, or scan an initial set of files or documents, while the other team members enhance, adjust, suggest changes, and generally refocus the work. All collaborative notes can appear on one document; the document can have a tracking provision to log whose changes came first, second, third, and so forth. These comments and changes can then be incorporated into the final project.

Figure 6.5
GroupWare Classification

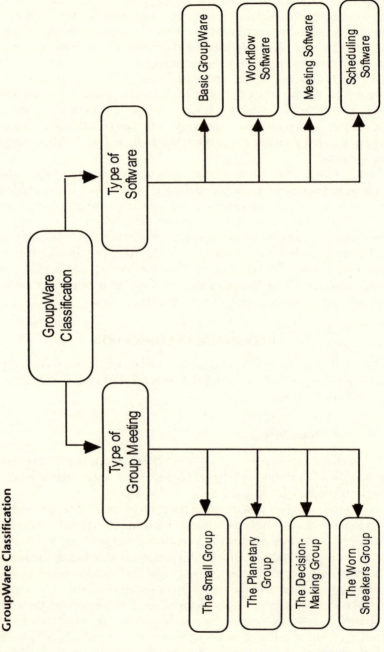

The planetary group is made up of participants who work in different places. They have to contact each other in order to transfer the information and gain the updated information. Lotus Notes is a good example of software support for this type of group. Beyond being a highly successful product, Lotus Notes is rapidly becoming the nucleus of a whole new GroupWare development community, as vendors develop Lotus Notes add-ons and products that work in conjunction with Lotus Notes.

With offices all over the world, a company can have a hard time managing all its wide-reaching information. For example, salespeople in every location need to know whether the account for the XYZ Company, with offices in the United States and Germany, shows that it has agreed to buy peripherals for all its locations. A shared database with some application development tools could be the perfect answer. With this facility, up-to-date customer and account information would be available at all locations. With sales-order tracking tools built into the application development environment, all invoices are automatically filled and copied to the product distribution center.

The decision-making group is the management team that has to make a decision in a specific location. CM/1 (Corporate Memory Systems) is an example of software for this type of group. This tool helps the management team members discuss the issues involved from their individual locations (over a proprietary leased-line network), remember past discussions, arguments, and conclusions, and save time.

For example, the Organization for Petroleum Exporting Countries (OPEC) oil ministers regularly meet to decide whether they should slow production to hike up oil prices. The problem is, they have to meet face to face and discuss the same issues over and over again every time in different places. This software can assist them significantly by bringing up all the past discussions, arguments, and comments made by each member. By doing this, the members can concentrate on the new issues and expedite the decision-making process by attacking fewer issues.

The worn-sneakers group is made up of participants who work in a small business environment. They are constantly hand delivering goods, products, invoices, messages, and even appointment notices from one desk to another for approval and changes. BeyondMail (Beyond, Inc.) is a good software candidate for this type of group. Some small-business owners cannot afford secretaries, so when they are out of the office, work may pile up on their desks. They need to automate the workflow from one desk to another in order to keep things moving in their absence or when they are busy with other tasks. GroupWare with BeyondMail capabilities can significantly improve the productivity of such worn-sneakers groups by providing e-mail capability, automated routing slips, form integration, and form delivery.

Type of Software

This class of GroupWare includes four types of software support: basic GroupWare, workflow software, meeting software, and scheduling software.

Basic GroupWare, for which Lotus Notes has almost the entire market share, combines a sophisticated messaging system with an extensive database containing work records and memos. It changes the way information flows in an organization and creates a kind of corporate online service similar to the Internet of the office. Unlike plain e-mail, Lotus Notes does not require you to figure out who needs to know a fact or hear an idea. Instead, you simply forward your memo to the appropriate bulletin board. Several hundred large and medium-sized organizations, such as Price Waterhouse, Andersen Consulting, Compaq Computer, Chase Manhattan, General Motors, and Texaco, have been successfully using this very powerful software. Since its inception in 1989, Lotus Development Corporation has sold more than 15 million copies of Lotus Notes to more than 3,000 companies at around $300 for each PC that uses it.

Workflow software is designed to remake and streamline business processes, especially in paper-clogged bureaucracies. It helps workers understand the steps that make up particular processes and allows them to redesign those steps. It also routes work automatically from one employee to another. The most popular software product in this group is Action Works (Action Technologies, Inc.). This software allows a user to draw charts, create documents, and print a map of business processes. It identifies process inefficiencies based on prespecified business rules.

Meeting software allows participants in face-to-face or videoconference gatherings to "talk" simultaneously by typing on PC or workstation keyboards. Because people read faster than they speak, and because with this system users do not have to wait for others to finish talking, the software can significantly speed progress toward consensus. It also ensures that everyone gets a chance to participate. The most prominent software product in this group is GroupSystems (Ventana Corporation).

Scheduling software uses a network to coordinate colleagues' electronic datebooks and figure out when they can all get together. This can be a powerful tool, especially when there are several executives involved and they have diverse schedules. Of the several software products in this group, Network Scheduler (Powercore International, Inc.) is one example.

ADVANTAGES AND DISADVANTAGES OF
TELECONFERENCING AND OTHER GSS

A teleconferencing system may include some of the following unique advantages [1, 13]:

1. *Cost savings.* Because participants do no need to travel from place to place, the organization avoids paying high costs for planes, hotels, and meals.

2. *More contacts.* Because the decision makers are not traveling long distances, they may have more time to talk with each other and resolve organizational problems.

3. *Problems caused by shyness reduced.* Issues of shyness may not be as severe in a teleconferencing environment as they are in face-to-face meetings. This is particularly helpful to those decision makers who are hesitant about speaking up in face-to-face settings.

4. *Less stress.* Because fewer hours are spent traveling, the decision makers may be able to spend more time with family and friends, which may improve their morale.

However, with all the advantages, teleconferencing systems may also include some disadvantages:

1. *Lack of human touch.* In a teleconferencing system, gestures, face-to-face impressions, handshakes, and eye contact are lost. This in turn may hinder the effectiveness of the regular meetings. At this point, only two of the five senses (sound and vision) are present in a teleconferencing system. Taste, smell, and touch cannot be expressed through teleconferencing. With the new development in virtual reality (VR) technologies, some of these shortcomings may be resolved in the near future.

2. *Unnecessary meetings.* Because it is relatively easy to arrange a teleconference meeting, some of these meetings may not be necessary, and time and energy may be wasted.

3. *Security problems.* Teleconferencing has the same security problem as any other telecommunication system. Some valuable and private organizational information may get into the hands of unauthorized individuals. This issue dictates the implementation of tight security measures that allow only authorized individuals to have access to the data and information being transferred among the participants.

Other GSS include all the advantages and disadvantages of teleconferencing systems described. In addition, they include the following specific advantages:

- Help improve meeting satisfaction, which may improve group morale
- Provide both electronic and hard-copy documentation of the meeting activities
- Save decision-making time by providing online support to the group
- Save money by requiring fewer people to perform the same task
- Improve group effectiveness by advancing collaboration

Other GSS include the following disadvantages:

- It is difficult to reward someone for quality input; and an electronic shouting match is no better than a verbal one.
- A strong member who could dominate meetings may lose that power when an anonymous GSS is used.
- They are more difficult to introduce to an organization than more traditional, less threatening software.
- The costs of GSS implementation are high because the system includes many features; a company must identify its needs before getting into this expensive venture.

GSS IN ACTION

Numerous GSS-related studies have been performed by academia in conjunction with private businesses. The results are not always successful, as illustrated by the Department of Indian Health Services (IHS) case presented later in this chapter. Overall, however, most cases reveal more successes than outright failures.

The studies are conducted either at the university's campus meeting room facilities, as was the case with Burr-Brown Corporation, or in a "decision room" installed on-site at the place of business, as was the case with the multiple Texaco sites. The Burr-Brown and Texaco cases are representative of the overall positive outcome that many companies that have used GSS have experienced. The IHS and IBM cases are discussed to contrast one GSS failure (IHS) and one overwhelming success (IBM). The last case illustrates the successful application of a GroupWare in a large corporation.

Burr-Brown Corporation

Burr-Brown Corporation is a Tucson-based international electronics company that used the meeting room at the University of Arizona to develop several divisional five-year strategic plans and a one-year action plan. Among the benefits Burr-Brown derived from using a GSS was the ability to expand its planning group from an average of eight to ten managers to thirty-one senior managers. Even with a significantly larger group, Burr-Brown achieved its objective in three days (although it usually took months with fewer people). The managers gained more input and spent less time. The company's CEO expressed that the most notable benefit, which is not quantifiable, was his managers' improved understanding of the planning process and direction of the company [12].

Texaco Incorporated

The University of Minnesota constructed SAMM (software-aided meeting management) decision rooms on the premises of Texaco, Inc., in Houston, Tulsa, and Midland. The two-year program was deemed a success, despite SAMM's initial user-unfriendliness (as compared to commercially available software). The success was measured by the extensive use of SAMM by all levels of management for issues that ranged from the broad to the highly technical. The voting and brainstorming features were the most popular. The reduction of time spent in meetings, the quality and quantity of ideas generated during the meetings, and the completion of meeting agendas were considered major accomplishments. The most important benefit for Texaco was the ability to use SAMM for dispersed meetings (Texaco uses cross-functional teams extensively within the organization). With SAMM, team members in the Tulsa and Midland office, for example, did not need to travel to Houston for meetings. The future use of SAMM within the Texaco organization, as well as other GDSS and EMS, is being evaluated [6].

Department of Indian Health Services, Tucson

The significance of this case study is that it exemplifies a GSS that failed because of management resistance and political pressures within a company's environment. In 1988, an IHS doctor saw that the limited productivity of IHS meetings could be assisted with EMS technology. The University of Arizona supplied GroupSystems on-site at IHS, at no charge. From its inception, myriad difficulties had to be overcome to simply install the system. IHS managers did not perceive a need for this technology and were unwilling to commit proper resources. Among the problems, fewer chairs arrived than were requested, improper lighting washed out the Barco (public screen), and getting a dedicated room was a major hurdle because space was a scarce commodity. There were political disagreements concerning equipment liability and a fundamental disagreement between the administrative core (IHS management) and the technical core (the doctor who suggested the GroupSystem's idea). Once the system was finally installed, the initial results were positive. The most noticeable benefit was the increased level of participation. One observation was that Native American participants were quiet during verbal sessions but contributed actively during the nonverbal sessions. However, due to lack of use over a year's time (it was employed fewer than a dozen times), the system was dismantled and returned to the university [9].

There are two reasons for the failure of this system. First, the management did not perceive a need for such a system. Second, there was no one to champion the system by illustrating how IHS could benefit from its use in the long term. This case illustrates a very important point. Success of any computer-aided group decision system requires that (1) there be a perceived need for the technology; (2) the technology be well matched with the users' needs; and (3) there be a strong commitment from top management to support the use of the system within the organization.

International Business Machine

IBM is a well-documented example of a GSS success story. The benefits that IBM derived using its system are cited in numerous studies related to computer-aided group decision support. Initially, IBM used the meeting room site at the University of Arizona to test the technology by doing some strategic planning. The measurable success of the sessions prompted IBM to work with the university from 1983 through 1989 to develop its own in-house system

[10]. The result was a sophisticated EMS named TeamFocus equipped with extensive planning and modeling tools and remote meeting capabilities. Currently the company has more than fifty facilities at IBM sites around the world. Each facility costs approximately $20,000 to $300,000 to develop, and each facility is equipped and designed with the user-group in mind (i.e., the differences between metropolitan administrative needs and remote manufacturing site needs are considered). The sites are used by IBM but are frequently leased to outside companies for $2,000 to $7,000 a session [8].

IBM uses its facilities for strategic planning and problem solving, that is, for factors contributing to cost overruns, workload elimination, and functional area data-processing needs. The tasks are usually complex, require creativity, have no known right answer, and require input from a group [10].

The cost–benefit results are astounding and attest to why IBM is committed to making this technology an integral part of its organization. Without the aid of GSS, it is estimated that managers spend anywhere from 35 percent to 70 percent of their time in meetings. IBM wanted to make better use of its managers' time. IBM's use of its facilities, ranging from the administrative to manufacturing orientation, averaged 55.6 percent savings in labor hours [10]. In addition, "administrative costs fell, calendar time was reduced, and the number of meetings necessary to complete a project diminished" [10]. The average time an IBM group spent completing a project was reduced by 90 percent [8]. IBM's data and experience also show that the larger and more difficult the task, the greater the savings realized. During the first year of using TeamFocus, when the costs of development were compared with the savings in time and increases in productivity, IBM indicated that it realized a full return on its investment within the first year. Some of the success factors cited by IBM are as follows [8]: organizational commitment; executive sponsorship ("the champion"); dedicated facilities; communication and liaison improvements; training improvements; cost and benefit evaluation improvements; software flexibility; and realization of managerial expectations.

The IBM case illustrates that, ultimately, the success of a GSS is measured by how appropriately the technology meets the needs of the business. In IBM's case, the technology was appropriately matched with the business needs and the tasks of the decision-making group, and management championed the use of this technology throughout the organization.

Price Waterhouse

Price Waterhouse, one of the largest accounting and consulting firms in the world, used Lotus Notes to win a multi-million-dollar consulting contract [14]. This is how it was done. One Thursday, Price Waterhouse was invited to submit a bid. However, there was a catch: The bid was supposed to be submitted on the following Monday. Meanwhile, a Price Waterhouse competitor had been working on its own bid for several weeks. The four executives who were supposed to write the bid were in three different states, but they were able to work together using Lotus Notes. Lotus Notes allowed them to conduct a four-way dialogue on-screen. First of all, they were able to extract major components of the proposal from various databases on Lotus Notes. From one end they were able to pull resumes of the Price Waterhouse experts from all over the world who were supposed to work on this assignment; from the other end they were able to borrow passages from similar successful proposals from various Lotus Notes databases. Several drafts were generated, all four executives reviewed them carefully, and Lotus Notes kept track of all the changes. Other executives were able to review the proposal over the weekend. Price Waterhouse submitted the proposal and won the bid on Monday. Its competitor did not even meet the deadline.

SUMMARY

This chapter covered the definition, capabilities, and uses of computer-aided support technology, including GDSS, EMS, and GroupWare, which provide a wide range of collaborative decision-making support. However, the successful use of this technology requires that the capabilities of the GSS be appropriately matched with the decision-making group's needs and that management be supportive and champion its use within the organization.

The virtual organization of tomorrow is flat, team driven, downsized, global, and very competitive. In such a dynamic business environment the winners are those who make complex decisions in a timely manner with input from the key decision makers. With decreasing costs and increasing sophistication in communications and computer technologies, a GSS can play a significant role in keeping the organization ahead of the competition. The outlook for the continual development and application of computer-aided group decision support technologies like GDSS, EMS and GroupWare is very promising [2, 11].

REFERENCES

1. Baldazo, Rex, and Stanford Diehl. "Workgroup Conferencing." *Byte* (March 1995): 125–128.
2. Bidgoli, Hossein. "Group Support Systems: A New Productivity Tool for the 90's." *Journal of Systems Management* (July/August 1996): 56–62.
3. Dennis, Alan R., J. F. Nunamaker, Jr., David Paranka, and Douglas R. Vogel. "A New Role for Computers in Strategic Management." *Journal of Business Strategy* 11 (1990): 38–43.
4. Desanctis, Geraldine, and Brent Gallupe. "A Foundation for Study of Group Decision Support Systems." *Management Science* 33 (May 1987): 589–609.
5. Desanctis, Geraldine, and Brent Gallupe. "Group Decision Support Systems: A New Frontier." *Data Base* (Winter 1985): 39.

6. Desanctis, Geraldine, Gary Dickson, and Marshall Scott Poole. "Texaco University of Minnesota Research Project: Status Report and Project Summary." *Brainstorm* 1 (1992): 12–16.

7. Donelan, Joseph G. "Using Electronic Tools to Improve Meetings." *Management Accounting* (March 1993): 42–45.

8. Eisenhart, Tom. "Systems That Support Group Decision Making." *Business Marketing* 75 (1990): 50–51.

9. George, Joel F., J. F. Nunamaker, Jr., and J. Valacich. "Electronic Meeting Systems as Innovation: A Study of the Innovation Process." *Information & Management* 22 (1992): 181–195.

10. Grohowski, Ron, and Chris Mcgoff. "Implementing Electronic Meeting Systems at IBM: Lessons Learned and Success Factors." *MIS Quarterly* (December 1990): 369–383.

11. Jacob, R. "The Search for the Organization of Tomorrow." *Fortune* (May 18, 1992): 90–98.

12. Jessup, Leonard M., and S. Kukalis. "Better Planning Using Group Support Systems." *Long Range Planning* 23 (1990): 100–105.

13. King, William R. "Strategic Issues in GroupWare." *Information Systems Management* (Spring 1996): 73–78.

14. Kirkpatrick, David. "GroupWare Goes Boom." *Fortune* (December 27, 1993): 99–106.

15. Mockler, Robert J., and D. G. Dologite. "Using Computer Software to Improve Group Decision Making." *Long Range Planning* 24 (1991): 44–57.

16. Nunamaker, J. F., Jr., Lynda M. Applegate, and Benn R. Konsynski. "Computer-Aided Deliberation: Model Management and Group Decision Support." *Operations Research* 36 (November/December 1988): 826–848.

17. Sarin, S., and I. Greif. "Computer-Based Real Time Conferencing Systems." *IEEE Compute* (October 1985): 33–45.

18. Stevenson, Ted. "GroupWare: Are We Ready." *PC Magazine* (June 15, 1993): 261–272.

CHAPTER 7

Geographic Information Systems

This chapter offers an overview of geographic information systems (GIS) as a growing decision-support tool both in the public and private sectors by discussing the components of a typical GIS and guidelines for developing a successful GIS, which include performing needs assessment and a cost and benefit analysis and choosing the right platform and implementation. The chapter then concentrates on the popular applications of GIS. It concludes with an outlook for GIS as a rapidly growing information system.

WHAT IS A GEOGRAPHIC INFORMATION SYSTEM?

Executives in a growing number of organizations are faced with questions such as

Where should we locate a new store?

Where should we locate a fire station?

Where should we locate a fast-food restaurant?

Where should we locate a new school?

Where should we locate a new airport with a minimum environmental impact?

What route should our delivery truck follow for a minimum of driving time?

A properly designed GIS can answer these questions and more. A GIS utilizes spatial and nonspatial data and specialized techniques for storing the coordinates of complex geographic objects, including networks of lines (roads, rivers, streets) and reporting zones (zip codes, cities, counties, or states).

There are numerous definitions for GIS. In its promotional literature, the Environment Systems Research Institute, in Redlands, California, one of the major vendors of GIS, defines GIS as follows: "A GIS is an organized collection of computer hardware, software, geographic data and personnel, designed to effectively capture, store, update, manipulate, analyze and display all forms of geographically referenced information."

GIS use three typical geographic objects:

point—the intersection of lines in a map (e.g., a customer location, a dealership location, the location of a fast-food restaurant, or the location of an airport).

line—usually a series of points on the map (e.g., a street, a road, or a river).

area—usually a section of the map (e.g., a particular zip code such as the zip code for the southwest region of Portland, Oregon, or the San Diego Zoo).

Digitized maps and spatially oriented databases are two major components of GIS. Imagine a company wants to open a new store in the southwest part of Portland, and you would like to find out how many people live in walking distance of this new store. With a GIS you can start with the map of the United States, zoom in on the state of Oregon, then zoom in on Portland and finally end up with a street map on your screen. Your tentative store location becomes a marked point on the map. You can draw a circle around your desired location to highlight the area that you feel is within walking distance. Now you can ask for a summary of the U.S. Census data on all the people living inside the circle who meet certain conditions such as income level, age, marital status, and so forth. A GIS can provide information that enables you to zero in on individual customers and individual marketing objectives [4, 6].

A GIS integrates and analyzes spatial data from a variety of sources. The ever-increasing power of the microcomputer and the significant cost reduction in computing equipment makes GIS an attractive alternative for a wide variety of organizations.

GIS have been around for almost thirty years. Their major applications have been in government and utility companies, mostly for analyzing census data. As will be explained later in this chapter, GIS are increasingly utilized by various business organizations, particularly in marketing, manufacturing, insurance, and real estate.

Typical GIS can perform the following tasks: They enable the user to digitize maps, associate spatial attributes with points, lines, and polygons on the maps, and integrate the maps and database data with queries.

The query language available in GIS supports the following sophisticated query operations:

single criteria search (e.g., all the customers with income over $50,000)

multiple criteria search (e.g., all the female customers with income over $54,000 who live in the southwest part of the city)

searches with logical operators, AND, OR, and NOT (e.g., all the customers who are either female or have an income below $27,000; all the male customers except those who make more than $100,000)

GIS are differentiated from DBMS and computer-aided design/computer-aided manufacturing (CAD/CAM) in addressing fundamental, theoretical, and technical problems that geographic information presents. The spatial interdependence among geographic entities, termed spacing autocorrelation, requires filtering to compensate for the spatial proximity between two entities, which creates interdependency. A sophisticated GIS can resolve these issues by using different filtering techniques. GIS spatial displays account for the spatial autocorrelation, as required for the statistical analysis of the data in an attempt to identify relationships between "independent" entities [26]. CAD technology is also designed to deal with spatial objects and is similar to GIS in this respect. However, GIS differ at this level because they link spatial objects with their distinguishing attributes, allowing access to records through their geographical locations.

A GIS with analytical capabilities evaluates the impact of decisions by providing interpretation of spatial data. Modeling tools and statistical functions are used for forecasting purposes, including trend analysis and simulations. Multiple windows provide simultaneous viewing of the mapped area and the relative nonspatial data. The display of points, lines, and polygons can be color-coded to the nonspatial attributes. The zoom feature can provide the viewing of geographic areas in varying detail levels. Several maps of varying features can be consolidated with map overlays. A map overlay might be used to view all the gas lines, public schools, or fast-food restaurants in any specified region. A buffering feature creates pin maps by highlighting locations based on queried criteria. The new store location just described is a good example of this type of analysis.

COMPONENTS OF A GIS

A typical GIS consists of the following components:

1. GIS software: This component includes one of the commercial GIS software packages available on the market. As you will see later in this chapter, there are several types of software packages on the market for virtually all platforms, including Macintosh, DOS, Windows, and UNIX operating systems. Some of the popular GIS software includes ARC/INFO, Atlas GIS, Tactician, MapInfo, and GeoQuery. Using GIS software, an executive can view the names of customers and competitors overlaid on streets, together with demographic information showing population density, gender, income, age, and ethnicity. Geographic objects such as customers or locations can then be analyzed, evaluated, and presented in maps, tabular reports, and graphs [19]. GIS software usually does not include data sets such as demographic and census information, city, county, and zip code boundaries, and major road systems. These kind of data are purchased from public agencies or private vendors.

2. graphics workstation or a high-powered PC: This component is used for display of data and maps. It should be in color, with a very high resolution in order to be able to view the details of maps and graphs with clarity. The workstation or PC

should utilize a CPU sufficiently powerful to handle massive data files in a graphic display format. Ideally, the screen should be oversized (e.g., 20 or 21 inches), in order to accommodate large viewing areas easily.

3. plotter: This output device is used to generate hard-copy maps and drawings in large sheets and letter-sized formats.

4. digitizing tablet: This component is equipped with conductors that receive electrical signals emitted by a cursor and convert a hard-copy map mounted on the surface of the tablet into a digitized map.

5. a scanner: This is used to optically read and convert images such as a hard-copy map or photograph into digital format. Scanners vary in price and sophistication.

6. vast storage device: A huge storage device is required to accommodate the immense storage requirements of both spatial and nonspatial data created and used by a GIS. Ten gigabytes or more of storage space is recommended.

7. CD-ROM: This accommodates the distribution of a large GIS database. For example, one CD-ROM may include all the maps of Seattle, and another may include all the maps of Los Angeles.

8. cursor/puck: This is a palm-sized input device for digitizing that consists of a glass or plastic lens with a cross-hair target and multiple buttons. It is used with the digitizing tablet to create lines or boundaries around specific areas and to trace the outline of map objects by tracing over the hard copy map while it is laying on the digitizing tablet.

9. a mouse: This device controls a cursor or pointer on the screen and they come in a variety of shapes with different capabilities. By moving the mouse on the surface of the desk or a mouse pad, the user moves the pointer on the screen. To select an item, after positioning the mouse pointer on the desired location, the users clicks on the left or right mouse button.

10. a database: This component includes spatial and nonspatial data with related attributes about the objects. It stores and manipulates the data within the GIS. It also includes a query language for various query operations. The spatial database consists of a digitized representation of maps in cartographic layers. When stored with specific coordinates, the maps can be overlaid to create new maps. For example, let us say that you have started with a map of Chicago. Next, you zoomed in on a particular region of the city, then overlaid the map with the coordinates (locations) of all stoplights within that region. Then you overlaid the map with the coordinates of all emergency roadside call boxes in that same region. This custom map can then be saved in a separate file for later editing or analysis.

Three important elements of data are required for each feature on a map: the location of each feature in geographic space; each feature's spatial relationship (i.e., the distance and orientation to their features); and what each feature is (e.g., consider the top of Mt. Rainier: its latitude and longitude, how far from what used to be Mt. St. Helens, and that it has all the attributes of a mountain peak [whatever they are]).

In the GIS environment, there are two spatial database approaches: raster and vector models. The raster structure divides the coverage area into grid cell series in either a detailed or thematic basis. The detailed raster model is generated by remote sensing systems in data acquisition. The thematic model is useful in application-specific analysis projects. A thematic map displays different quantitative ranges of data by varying colors, textures, symbols, or embedded charts. The vector model stores maps as spatial attribute tables for each type of map element, containing the point and line coordinates [14]. The vector model is either unstructured (spaghetti) or topologically structured (intelligent) [22]. The vector model is typically used in data acquisition, and the raster model is useful in the integration of data across multiple sources.

The nonspatial database uses a relational database structure for storing records with reference connections to the spatial database. It is used for queries and provides the basis for examining the relationship among the data elements.

Figure 7.1 provides a conceptual model for a geographic information system.

DEVELOPING A SUCCESSFUL GIS

Design and implementation of a successful GIS similar to other MSS is a multidimensional venture. A methodology similar to the life-cycle approach discussed in Chapter 2 can be utilized. The diagram presented in Figure 7.2 shows the important steps for developing a successful GIS.

Needs Assessment

The first step before establishing a GIS is to define the mission for the system. The tasks and types of analysis performed by the GIS must be clearly understood. A clear needs analysis should help the design team to design an appropriate system for a particular organization. GIS vary in sophistication. A GIS can be a simple computerized mapping system or a sophisticated decision-support tool for diverse analysis. An organization must decide the following issues:

- storage volume
- format of the provided output
- types of data to be included
- level of sophistication of the end-user(s)
- types of statistical analysis needed
- types of modeling capabilities needed
- types of simulation analysis needed

An organization should establish a GIS planning and implementation team. The participants of this team should include individuals with a comprehensive understanding of how geographic data are created, manipulated, interpreted, and distributed throughout the organization. The key users of the

Figure 7.1
Conceptual Model for a GIS

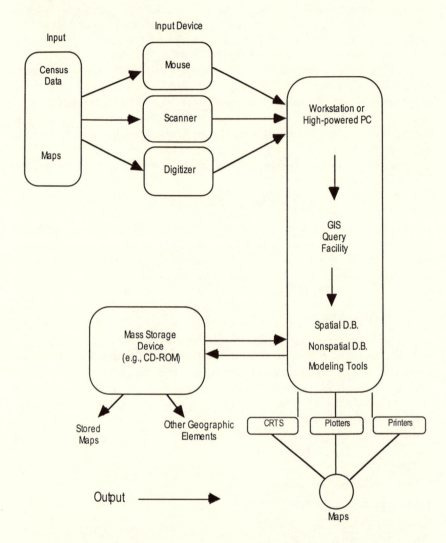

proposed GIS should be included in this team. This team is similar to the MSS task force discussed in Chapter 2.

Selection of a GIS administrator is imperative. Qualifications should include familiarity with mapping and map terminology, superior computer proficiency, and information management experience. Familiarity with the organization operations is preferred. Since GIS is a relatively new technology, staffing is critical,

Figure 7.2
Important Steps for Developing a GIS

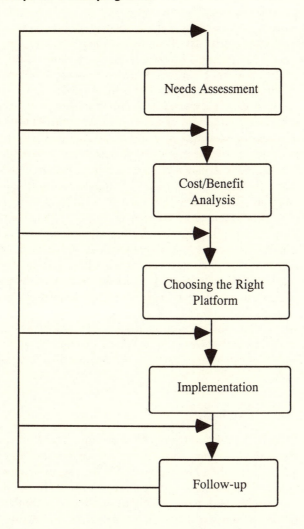

and the development of an effective GIS administrator often entails a year or more of training and experience. The GIS authority must be established within or outside of the control of the information systems department. The relationship of the GIS administrator to the information systems department must be defined.

The initial phase of the project also must be clearly defined. One of the most important decisions is the selection of the base map to construct. It is of primary importance to the organization, as it establishes the foundation for further map developments. Pertinent decisions include which geographic areas to choose, scale, resolution, and level of accuracy.

The data sources must be identified. These may include in-house development of data, purchasing the data from government agencies, or purchasing them from private companies. Database redundancy control must be established to avoid duplication of central information services. Whether integration of the organizational data is used, a central repository is accessed, or individual vendors are used, conversion requirements must be established.

Data acquisition and conversion require the integration of multisource data and are complicated by varying scales and coordinates, as well as imprecise measurements. The census data offered by private vendors are superior to the government offerings due to data refinements and an improved user interface. The U.S. Census Bureau maintains a list of Topologically Integrated Geographic Encoding and Referencing (TIGER) file-related products and services. Digital mapping is faster and more accurate than topographic conversion and reduces costs significantly. Topographic features define elevation information, sometimes called third dimension. To achieve particular levels of accuracy, specific densities of vertical control points must be available. Digital ortho mapping is based on aerial photographs that have been digitally scanned after airplane tilt and ground relief is rectified. Scaling is possible, unlike U.S. Geological Survey maps [28].

Data acquisition and conversion costs may be reduced in the future by more extensive commercial and government database availability, automated digitalization of maps, and sharing of data among organizations with similar geographic interests.

Cost and Benefit Analysis

The cost of a GIS, similar to other MSS, includes hardware and software costs and personnel. Data acquisition is probably one of the most important costs for developing a GIS. As explained in the next section, a GIS may run on the existing hardware, or specialized hardware might be purchased. The amount of time, energy, and money required to effectively implement a GIS can be significant, in addition to the long-term costs of updating and maintaining the software and data. A leading GIS consulting firm, Plan Graphics, Inc., estimates that data conversion comprises 50 percent to 60 percent of implementation costs [28]. The basic GIS package and optional data files cost, such as street data and geographic detail files, should be evaluated, as each vendor requires proprietary file format for geographic data. Although most of these data are publicly available from the U.S. Census Bureau, the format will differ, requiring conversion; the third-party vender often provides enhancements. The U.S. Census Bureau offers a forty-four-disk set of street maps and a seventeen-disk set of population and economic data. Shortly this data will be available on CD-ROM, making it cheaper and more compact.

The elements of specialized hardware and software require extensive training and a steep learning curve for users. Sufficient time must be allocated to train users in the full capabilities of the GIS. The hardware requirements should not be compromised. Substantial processing power, immense storage, and an oversized high-resolution monitor are essential.

A properly designed GIS can easily outweigh its cost by improving the efficiency and effectiveness of decision making. A GIS produces informative maps for data analysis prior to making decisions that put resources in jeopardy. A GIS, by performing statistical and modeling analyses, provides new insight for the data prior to its utilization. The manager of marketing analysis at Ostram/Sylvania commented on the use of GIS (they are using Tactician by Tactician Corporation) in presentations to their customers (wholesale distributors): "Of course, we could have given them the same data on reams of spreadsheet printouts, but illustrating the information with a map is a much more powerful tool." He referred to the use of a GIS as a "sensory approach to bring customers" [24].

The use of GIS overcomes the drawbacks of using maps for decision analysis, including the following:

images contain limited amounts of information

requirement of extensive knowledge of map interpretation due to limited detail

difficulty in the assessment of multiple maps due to inconsistencies in map sizing and presentation

complications of overlaying maps for information consolidation

difficulty in updating and manipulation [14, 15]

In addition, electronic storage is more compact than maps and the associated manual records. The capability of obtaining data from a variety of sources is improved by the ability to digitize maps.

All database and DBMS include the following benefits: automated data entry and retrieval; data consistency enforcement; both logical and physical data views; and presentations of data in a format appropriate to specific problems. The unique features of a GIS query identify its power by offering the following capabilities [22]: The merger of voluminous data sources from dissimilar data models is required; both spatial and nonspatial data must be interpreted and abstracted; and a rapid response time is required.

Choosing the Right Platform

The discriminating factor in assessing GIS software is the task performed by the software. Each has a particular focus and a variety of strengths and weaknesses; thus the needs assessment will narrow the criteria and number of products to evaluate. The annual *International GIS Sourcebook*, published by GIS World, Inc., includes comprehensive descriptions of hardware, software, and suppliers. In addition, the periodical *GIS World* provides current technical articles.

The market is divided into software for two hardware platforms: workstations and microcomputers. The size of the application determines the necessary hardware. However, due to the ever-increasing power of microcomputers, the gap between these two platforms is narrowing.

Workstation-Based GIS. There are more than 150 companies competing in the GIS market. Two software vendors dominate the market with a combined share of approximately 50 percent—Environmental Systems Research Institute, Inc. (ESRI) and Intergraph [16]. The three major vendors of workstation GIS include ARC/INFO ESRI, Intergraph, and Earth Resources Data Analysis Systems (ERDAS). ARC/INFO ESRI is the leading workstation product. A wide variety of data formats are supported, including TIGER, digital line graph (DLG), ETAK (this format was developed by ETAK Corporation to represent street information), and dual independent map encoding (DIME) (this format is the predecessor to the U.S. Census Bureau's TIGER format). Hardware platforms include Apollo, Hewlett-Packard, SUN, and DEC-VAX. The ARC product processes vector-based cartographic data; the INFO product is a relational DBMS.

Intergraph of Huntsville, Alabama, provides vector-based turnkey systems for a variety of applications. ERDAS, a raster-based system, is typically used for natural resources management and military intelligence applications and requires remotely sensed data.

Microcomputer-Based GIS. ARC/INFO is a PC-based GIS of complexity and depth consisting of a cohesive unit of individual modules. Its strengths lie in providing a mapping front end to database queries. An application programming language and compiler is included (simple macro language), which enables command line and shell procedures to be sequenced for application development. The complexity of the product requires a high learning curve; the vendor suggests a six-month familiarity period.

Atlas GIS (Strategic Mapping, Inc.) focuses on map generation, has a propriety geographic file format, and is vector based. A map-layering capability is included, and data from different sources can be combined. Several thematic presentation maps are available: ranged maps, ranking data by color, symbol, and fill pattern; proportional maps, representing data with varying fill patterns in proportion to the data value; and dot-density maps, proportioned to the data values. The ease of digitizing new maps and adding detail to existing maps is a prominent feature. Atlas GIS is not designed as an interface for querying databases; no programming language is provided. However, simple queries by map features, map feature relations, and attribute relations can be performed. A data file format common to dBASE and FoxBASE is used, and other database files can be imported with translation utilities.

Site selection is a typical use of Atlas GIS. A model is developed from defined parameters that identify "where stores do best." Electronic scouting for the areas that meet the criteria is performed, producing selected sites for physical review.

Tactician (Tactician Corporation) is a vector-based GIS designed for sales and marketing applications. It includes superior data retrieval and recompilation speed due to the fact that it was migrated from the DEC VAX/VMS platform. It can integrate with varying hosts and database systems with an Ethernet connection. Foreign cartographic files can be imported. Thematic maps using color and dot density are accompanied by a corresponding chart display of the data. All layer data must be of the same type, but when map layering is used, select, reveal, and hide features of the display serve to provide only pertinent geographic data. Tactician is a complex program of considerable difficulty for users lacking technical knowledge [9]. It is available for both Windows and the Macintosh environment.

In 1989, Sears Roebuck and Company implemented Tactician for various analytical applications. Their marketing database contained seventy million households from their retail, credit, insurance, brokerage, and real estate entity marketing files. They performed site location analysis for new and relocated stores, redistricting for reorganization, and physician location for their managed health care program [21].

MapInfo (MapInfo Corporation) focuses on map data analysis, combining map drawing and map query features. It is targeted for sales management and offers two query methods: the user interface (Windows) and the MapBasic programming language. Turnkey applications can therefore be generated. Alternative map sources include those provided with the software, digitized maps, and imported maps in alternative formats. Alternative data source formats that can be imported include ASCII, dBASE, Lotus 1-2-3, and Excel. During data import, the geocoding process assigns relative map locations. If no match exists, a manual assignment is asked for a later assignment or can be made in aggregate by an alternative database. Analytical functions are relational with assessment of multilayer relationships. MapInfo is available in both MS-DOS and Windows versions.

GeoQuery (GeoQuery Corporation) is a Macintosh GIS with data analysis emphasis designed to search preexisting imported databases and maps for details by query. It provides full relational analysis and is supported by the 4th Dimension (Acius) Relational Database Management System (RDBMS). A unique feature is the ability to load and manipulate data from within a custom application by using Apple Events. Map zooming is available by map scale definition. Table 7.1 provides a summary of popular commercial GIS software [23].

Implementation

GIS development requires a multiyear commitment due to an extensive database development process [15]. Massive amounts of data must be compiled,

Table 7.1
Popular GIS Software on the Market

GIS Name	Vendor	Features
ARC/Info	ESRI, Inc.	Command-line interface Application programming language Screen, digitizer, printer, support and plotter support Relational database
Atlas GIS	Strategic Mapping, Inc.	Menu-driven Extensive tools for developing thematic maps Digitizer, printer, support and plotter support dBASE oriented
GeoQuery	GeoQuery Corporation	Macro interface Relational database Strong market analysis and reporting
MapInfo	MapInfo Corporation	Windows interface Screen, printer, plotter, support and Windows device support SQL database query Full-featured map drawing and query application programming
Tactician	Tactician Corporation	Menu-driven Spreadsheet oriented Strong market analysis and reporting Flexible fitting for external data query and importing

standardized, and input into the system. A major cost can be the development of a customized database if products or services are not available to meet the organization's specific requirements.

GIS software varies in integration capabilities with other database software. This feature greatly extends the usefulness of the software in applications for which retrievable data exists. The lack of data standards and state or nationwide GIS data inventories limits data availability, and the resulting cost of collecting data must be factored. A common misconception about GIS is that the required data "already exist" in a GIS-accessible format. This is not true in the majority of cases. Efforts to overcome the fact that the majority of geographically referenced information does not adhere to common data format standards are being undertaken by the U.S. government's TIGER and DLG data formats. The former was developed by the U.S. Census Bureau for compiling the 1990 census of population, the latter by the U.S. Geological Survey. A data quality issue of the federally provided GIS data has been identified; the accuracy of the first national digital map is only to 200 feet. Vendors offer improved versions that correct and enhance the TIGER and DLG data formats.

The effects of the positioning of a GIS within an organization must be considered. Often, a GIS is considered to be important by small units within an organization, yet not necessarily by information systems departments, who must be relied upon for evaluation and implementation. Conversely, the organizational impact of GIS implementation must be evaluated, as individuals may be threatened by the perceived loss of control over information within their arena when organization-wide projects are undertaken. Sufficient resources should be allocated to alter the potential resulting resistive attitude.

The users and designers of GIS should also be aware of some of the possible downsides of this powerful technology. GIS may create ethical and legal issues. Can the organization be sued if it based decisions on data that was incorrect in a GIS? Who is responsible for such a lawsuit? Does anybody have the right to photograph my property from a satellite and use that information for various purposes without my permission? If an aerial photograph showed someone building bombs on their property, would that be probable cause for an arrest? What if the photograph was false or mistaken? Does the Census Bureau have the right to sell or give away information I provide to them? How does it ensure that information is not combined with other information in such a way that my privacy is invaded? Are there industries (e.g., title search) that may disappear as a result of GIS? How could GIS be used for positive environmental purposes? These are all important issues and will become more important with the widespread applications of GIS. Careful planning and considerations are needed to minimize the negative impacts of this very powerful technology.

GIS APPLICATIONS: AN OVERVIEW

Although GIS applications started with government agencies and utility companies, it now covers a diverse spectrum. GIS applications can be broadly classified within the following category [1, 2, 3, 4, 12, 13, 17]:

business applications

transportation and logistics

urban and regional planning

education planning

election administration

map and database publishing

oil, gas, and mineral exploration

real estate

surveying and mapping

research and education

The range of public sector applications of GIS is extensive. Operation Desert Storm during the Gulf War used a GIS from Intergraph corporation to support supply logistics and determine cruise missile targets.

City and county administrators rely on GIS for dispatching personnel and equipment to crime and fire locations, as well as maintaining crime statistics and locating fire hydrants. GIS education applications include making changes on school district boundaries to alter the total school population and racial diversity. GIS land use applications include area zoning, boundaries, classification, and taxation. A GIS can track the shifting ridership on local transit systems for analysis purposes. Based on this analysis, new political districts can be developed. Disaster management and recovery can benefit from GIS use: Public services can provide quicker emergency response, and insurance companies can provide faster customer response for dispatching services and adjusters to the most devastated neighborhoods.

Marketing

Marketing and sales applications are extensive. For target marketing purposes, GIS pinpoint the area of the greatest concentration of a retailer's ideal customers with the display of sales statistics in geographic terms. Evaluating demographic and lifestyle data can identify new markets. New products and services can be targeted at specific population groups. Analysis of customer distribution, including market share and population growth relative to store locations, can be performed. A company's current position in the marketplace based on industry, company size, and geographic location can be evaluated [25].

The need for new stores can be determined based on mapping the success of existing stores, the location of competitors, and the areas not penetrated. Site selection is a critical application of GIS because stores succeed or fail mainly based on location. By combining data on demographics and traffic patterns, PepsiCo, Inc. uses a GIS to help pinpoint the best locations for new Pizza Hut and Taco Bell restaurants.

With a GIS, sales territory management for retail and wholesale products can be improved. Historically, sales territories have remained static due to the complexity of redefinition. Modifications are crucial in response to competitive pressures and productivity improvements. Sales territories are not always contiguous geographic zones and do not always have balanced sales potential. Sales figures can be evaluated in order to balance territory assignments. As sales territories are redefined, the cumulative sales potential and size and shape of the territory are examined to minimize travel time.

An interesting marketing application of GIS is in political campaigns. Marketing in political party organizations and campaigns can be effectively supported with a GIS in developing target campaigns for promoting contributions and candidates. Census data and voter registration files provide the same data. The Clinton presidential campaign used Atlas GIS, from Strategic Mapping, to improve volunteer efforts and enhance media efforts [18]. Specific uses of GIS in political campaigns include securing union endorsement by mapping AFL-CIO members; enlisting volunteers from organized labor; improving responses to negative advertising by mapping their origination; and identifying voters who could determine election results.

Similar applications include political action committees, labor unions, and grassroots movements.

Transportation

The transportation industry and industries that use transportation services and involve logistics can benefit from GIS use. GIS is used for dispatching and vehicle fleet management as route and scheduling optimization reduces fleet operating costs. Delivery addresses are geocoded, a routing algorithm is applied, and a street network is produced that enables the estimation of actual driving time. Geocode is the key by which one can quickly retrieve a geographic object such as a point, line, or area. A simple example would be a street address. However, you can generate your own keys from the longitude, latitude, and map layer, or any method that you want. All geocodes within a map must be unique. This is similar to the key in a relational database [23].

Home delivery and taxi company delivery zones can be defined and factored for efficient dispatching. Emergency vehicle, repair, and parcel pickup services can benefit from dynamic dispatching and updating recent knowledge of required service calls. Commercial delivery services, such as Federal Express and UPS, have benefited from GIS use. For example, Federal Express uses a GIS to place its drop boxes and estimate the number of trucks and planes it needs during peak periods [5].

The distribution problem of delivery trucks returning to the warehouse empty results in a waste of time and resources. Development of a scheduling system to pick up supplier merchandise on returns from customer deliveries can improve the effectiveness of the system. A GIS can identify the stores and suppliers, develop a map showing those closely related, and schedule the routing accordingly.

Insurance

Insurance agencies are using GIS for various demographic information. Their most common application is for guarding against classification errors. Insurers and their agents are frequently pressed by market demands to act quickly on a potential new customer's request for coverage. Researching for information such as risk and premium rates mean hours of searching various books and a variety of maps. With GIS, the insurance company can identify an appropriate premium in a few seconds without ever having to pick up a telephone or look at a map. A GIS combines community boundaries, street addresses, postal carrier routes, and zip codes, plus four codes with search capabilities to locate a risk; it also provides key hazard information in four areas as follows [11]: windstorm, including wind pool eligibility, proximity to nearest large body of water, historic wind events at the site, extended coverage as well as group II zones and territory codes for personal and commercial lines; auto rating variables, including territory codes and distance between an insured's home and work address, measured as the probable minimum driving distance; indexes that measure crime rates, including auto theft, robbery, aggravated assault, burglary, crimes against persons and properties, and overall crime hazard index; and public fire protection information that gives data about the public protection of the community in which specific property is located.

In addition, the system is capable of providing information on earthquakes and brush fires, as well as environment risk data collected from federal and state agencies.

The benefit of an insurance GIS is that it can help insurers uncover fraudulent application information. In the last three months of 1993, GIS discovered ten to fifteen cases in which information regarding an insured's property address was false and resulted in premium rates that were 80 percent lower than the predefined rate. The risk factors built into the GIS system are based on information and most often misrepresented in the insured's property's proximity to fire hydrants or a fire station [7].

Real Estate

The real estate industry has benefited from GIS use in numerous applications. Real estate agents can use GIS as a tool to identify a lot for a potential buyer's preferences and price range. Using a combination of census data, multiple-listing files, and mortgage information, buyer profile can do this. Realtors can establish selling prices of homes, replacing the time-consuming task of finding comparable homes and identifying the sale prices.

GIS can survey the entire city to identify comparable neighborhoods and average sales prices. Real estate market analysis can be performed for appraisal purposes to determine the causal relationships between national, regional, and local economic trends and the demand for local real estate [26]. In addition, factors that effect the return on real estate investments can be analyzed.

Government

We already mentioned some of the GIS applications in government. Cities and counties have been some of the major users of GIS. The following is another look at this growing GIS application. With more and more constraints being placed on all forms of governments, cities and local agencies are being forced to become more efficient. The story is always the same—do more with less. In real-life practice, the only way this can be done is with increasing use of technology—GIS is an example of such technology. In recent years, only the larger cities and agencies could justify the use of such technologically advanced equipment. Now not only has cost of GIS lowered to an affordable level, but their applications are absolutely essential to operating government efficiently. There are three categories of GIS applications in government [27]: the conversion of data to information; the integration of data with maps and CAD; and the ability to provide error-free analysis.

Every city and government agency keeps track of volumes of data that are mostly found in hard-copy format scattered throughout the organization and are valuable and irreplaceable. However, access to the data is hampered by the logistics of the data storage systems. Even when data can be located, they must be manipulated and merged with all other data from other departments in order to provide the services requested. GIS eliminate this painstaking search. The database can be sorted and resorted depending on the information requested. When one department needs information from another department, with GIS the inquiring department can simply call it up on the screen. There would be no more interdepartmental memos and lost days waiting for information to be routed back. With GIS, countless hours of sorting, filing, and digging through basement files are eliminated. One benefit to using GIS is the image projected to the public. Before, if a citizen requested information, he or she was supposed to wait while the clerk sorted through numerous hard-copy reports. Now the answer is at the fingertips of the person taking the request. All cities and agencies strive for increasing efficiency and GIS project efficiency.

GIS also allow this newfound database power to be merged with existing CAD systems. Field crews equipped with a laptop, notebook, or sub-notebook can access almost unlimited information anywhere in the field. At the present time, most of the field crews carry large, bulky hard copies to the field. Due to its size, the hard copy is limited to the needs of only their department. With GIS a street crew could ask for sewer or water grid overlay on their laptop and in seconds see the location of all utilities before digging the street. Back in the engineering department, drafters could overlay all of the utilities to see the total effect of the design process. When field crews change systems or find differences, the problem could be noted and uploaded onto the database. One major improvement, as pointed out, is the ability to merge written files with CAD systems. With GIS all aspects of information transfer would be greatly improved.

Two of the main problems with any large amount of data are human error and the time required to generate and manipulate models. In the absence of GIS data, the creations of models for different situations require painstaking hand drawing and tabulation. In this manual process, error could cause days of work to be wasted. With GIS this is reduced to a simple query task, and what used to take days or weeks now only takes a few minutes. In addition to the obvious speed advantage, all work is done error free. With new GIS techniques, numerous models can be designed and simulated. Due to budget constraints, before GIS this would not have been possible. Models could have been constructed on only a few selected variables.

GIS do help government agencies to be more effective and efficient by allowing fewer people to perform more and more difficult tasks. It frees much needed technical personnel for more specific tasks, by permitting fewer technical employees to carry out these tasks. In the field, every crew has complete and total access to whatever information they need to perform the job at hand. This eliminates down time and backtracking. The system allows for an unlimited flow of information between all interested parties [27].

Emerging Applications

The integration of GIS and ES is referred to as an intelligent GIS. Two such systems have been developed for resource management. A prototype that links a GIS, an ES, and remote sensing equipment has been designed for irrigation scheduling. Plant canopy temperature is considered to be an indicator for the timing of crop irrigation, and the sensory equipment provides remote measurement for interpretation by the ES component. The results are transferred to the GIS, which prioritizes fields in the region by water need and allocates the available water accordingly [20].

A second application, integrated resource management automation (IRMA), links a GIS, an ES, and a conventional database for forest pest management. Graphic records of previous defoliation enable the visual analysis of forest stands for the determination of pesticide treatment. The area descriptions, stand conditions, and spatial relationships are transferred to the ES for treatment recommendation [20].

The integration of GIS and global positioning satellites (GPS) has the potential of transforming the aviation and shipping industries. It enables vehicles or aircraft equipped with a GPS receiver to pinpoint its location as it moves [24]. Jepson Corporation of Minneapolis currently utilizes GPS in roving vans with ten video cameras. Their goal is to record an image of every U.S. city street in digital and video output formats with digital map linking with annual updates [5].

Alliance Retail Information Systems (Englewood, Colorado) is developing GeoStore, a multidepartment GIS for retailers, to meet the customized demand. Planned uses include advertising, market research, distribution, transportation, site location, and real estate [2].

Japanese car manufacturers have started offering cars that utilize this technology by using a small device on the dash of your car. This device can give you directions and help you find needed places in a city or state with which you are not familiar.

OUTLOOK FOR GIS

Vehicle navigation systems have potential use in emergency services, utility repair vehicles, and passenger vehicles. Etak, Inc. (Menlo Park, California) has developed the Navigator, a vehicle tracking and navigation system that works with digital street maps. It includes a database of U.S. street centerlines, as well as streets of portions of the developed world [2].

Widespread acceptance of GIS and its increasing popularity in profit and nonprofit organizations indicates a very promising future for this exiting MSS. Two factors position GIS for potentially explosive growth. Accessibility to the sources of data is in place, as street maps and economic and population data are offered by the U.S. Census Bureau. The technology links spatial databases with traditional alphabetic and numeric databases.

Business applications thus far have comprised only 6 percent of the GIS market, yet they are the fastest growing segment [24]. Geographic technology can be sold by providing a competitive edge, providing the basis for accelerated expansion of the corporate market. Production, marketing, and distribution efficiencies determine business success, and a GIS can support the identification of opportunities and inefficiencies [10].

The task of site location has become more critical, considering higher costs, fewer prime locations to choose from, and the resulting increased risk in opening new stores. GIS can provide location analysis considering all the important factors.

GIS is already emerging as an embedded technology. The first database software to offer GIS is offered by OneSource Information Services, a Lotus Development Corporation spinoff. Microsoft and Lotus Development Corporation have both incorporated a mapping engine (Strategic Mapping, Inc.) to Excel and Lotus 1-2-3 spreadsheet upgrades.

In the near future, GIS technology will provide business with a better representation of its customers and competition, similar to the way that spreadsheet provided an improved view of financial information in the 1980s [8]. Technology can influence a firm's competitive ability, and GIS technology can provide access to enhanced information that will support the effort to create and sustain a competitive advantage.

The future of GIS will undoubtedly contain links to virtual reality and artificial intelligence software. In the near future we should be able to review a home from across the world, while choosing the neighborhood that we want to live in. Included here would be the ability to view the schools our children will attend, the stores we will shop, parks, and other social and economic necessities. The ever-increasing power and reduction in cost of microcomputers will expedite the adoption of this exciting technology.

SUMMARY

This chapter provided an overview of GIS as one of the growing applications of DSS in both public and private sectors; provided an overview of the components of typical GIS; explained important steps for developing successful GIS; and introduced an overview of some of the popular applications of GIS in marketing, transportation, insurance, real estate, and government. The chapter concluded with an outlook for GIS. All indications show that GIS applications will continue to grow and will become more affordable by many organizations, regardless of their size and financial status.

REFERENCES

1. Aalberts, Robert J., and Douglas S. Bible. "Geographic Information System: Application for the Study of Real Estate." *Appraisal Journal* (October 1992): 483–492.
2. Antenucci, John C. *Geographic Information Systems: A Guide to the Technology.* New York: Van Nostrand Reinhold, 1990.
3. Barnett, Albert P., and A. Ason Okoruwa. "Application of Geographic Information Systems in Site Selection and Location Analysis." *Appraisal Journal* (April 1993): 245–254.
4. Bidgoli, Hossein. "Geographic Information Systems: A New Strategic Tool for the 90s and Beyond." *Journal of Systems Management* (May/June 1995): 24–27, 66–67.
5. *Business Week* (July 26, 1993): 75–76.
6. Celko, Joe. "What You Need to Known About Geobases." *Systems Integration* (November 1991): 39.
7. Covaleski, John M. "Software Help Carriers Avoid Perilous Areas." *Best's Review* (February 1994): 82–83.
8. Dunn, William. "How to Talk to a Map." *American Demographics* (May 1992): 8–23.
9. Eglowstein, Howard, and Ben Smith. "Putting Your Data on the Map." *Byte* (January 1993): 188–190.
10. Ester, Thomas G. "The Next Step is Called GIS." *American Demographics Desk Reference* (May 1992): 2–4.
11. Gilbert, Evelyn. "GUS Guards Against Costly Classification Errors." *National Underwriter* (October 4, 1993): 5.
12. Goodchild, Michael F. "Geographic Information Systems." *Journal of Retailing* 67 (Spring 1991): 3–15.
13. Griffin, Mark, and John Hester. "New Opportunities for Capital Improvement Programming Using GIS." *Government Finance Review* (December 1990): 7–10.
14. Grupe, Fritz H. "Can a Geographic Information System Give Your Business its Competitive Edge?" *Information Strategy* (Summer 1992): 41–48.
15. Grupe, Fritz H. "Geographic Information Systems: An Emerging Component of Decision Support." *Technology Outlook* (Summer 1990): 74–78.
16. Kindel, Sharen. "Geographic Information Systems." *Financial World* (January 19, 1993): 44.
17. Lewis, Richard. "Putting Sales on the Map." *Sales & Marketing* (August 1992): 76–80.

18. Montague, Claudia. "Clinton Follows Computer Maps to White House." *American Demographics* (February 1993): 13–15.
19. Moore, Mark. "GIS Software Proliferates." *PC Week* (June 13, 1994): 34.
20. Plant, Richard E. "Expert Systems in Agriculture and Resource Management." *Technological Forecasting and Social Change* (May/June 1993): 241–247.
21. Robins, Gary. "Retail GIS Use Growing." *Stores* (January 1993): 44–50.
22. Sinton, David F. "Reflections on 25 Years of GIS." *GIS World* (February 1994): 1–8.
23. Smith, Ben, and Howard Eglowstein. "Putting Your Data on the Map." *Byte* (January 1993): 188–200.
24. Tetzeli, Rick. "Mapping for Dollars." *Fortune* (October 18, 1993): 91–96.
25. Thom, Jenny, and Linda Walters. "A Map for Marketing." *Sales & Marketing* (July 1992): 102–104.
26. Weber, Bruce R. "Application of Geographic Information Systems to Real Estate Market Analysis and Appraisal." *Appraisal Journal* (January 1990): 127–131.
27. Wilson, John P. "Reinventing Government with GIS." *Public Works* (May 1995): 38ff.
28. Wright, Andrew G., Mary B. Powers, Steven W. Stetzer, and Steve Daniels. "Going Digital: GIS Maps Out Bright Future." *EIR* (October 25, 1993): 27–28.

CHAPTER 8

Expert Systems Construction: Putting Theory to Work

This chapter provides a detailed discussion regarding the construction of expert systems (ES). It first reviews knowledge acquisition and knowledge representation processes as two key components for ES construction and puts these two important phases into practice. ES construction follows a methodology similar to the life-cycle approach discussed in Chapter 2; however, there are some differences. Important phases for the construction of an ES include problem definition, organizational readiness, expert selection, tool selection, design team selection, prototype design, final construction, validation, and post-implementation audit. Naturally, the basic mission of an ES is different from that of a traditional MSS. Also, the domain expert plays a very important role in the construction of an ES. These differences mandate a slightly different life-cycle approach to be followed for ES construction. The chapter will also provide a listing of some of the popular ES shells on the market and conclude with important considerations for ES construction that must be carefully examined before releasing the system for general use.

THE KNOWLEDGE ACQUISITION PROCESS

Knowledge acquisition involves extracting, structuring, and organizing the knowledge from a human expert or experts and representing it in machine-readable forms. In some cases, the knowledge may be in documented form. This may be in books, films, newspapers, and so forth. In such cases, the knowledge engineer does not need to involve the expert. The knowledge engineer plays a role similar to a programmer/analyst in a DSS environment. The knowledge engineer must have an extensive computer background, communication skills, and general knowledge about the field.

The knowledge engineer will use a series of techniques and tools in order to extract the expert knowledge. After extracting the knowledge and performing the validation process, it will become the basis for the knowledge-based component of the ES.

Experts in the field believe that knowledge acquisition is the "bottleneck" in the development of ES. Although an expert or experts may know precisely how a particular problem is solved, it is often difficult to transfer this expertise to others. Many issues that are obvious to the expert may not be as obvious to others.

Knowledge includes all the facts that have been accumulated regarding a particular problem or task. There are two types of knowledge: undocumented and documented. Undocumented knowledge resides in the experts' minds, and documented knowledge comes from books, notes, brochures, databases, films, movies, stories, songs, research projects, and so forth.

The knowledge acquisition process involves the following three activities [8]: (1) The knowledge engineer uses various communication techniques to elicit data and information from the expert; (2) the knowledge engineer interprets these data and information to draw conclusions on what might be the expert's underlying knowledge and reasoning processes; and (3) the knowledge engineer uses his or her conclusions to direct the construction of a model, which describes the expert's knowledge and processes for solving a particular problem. The knowledge engineer and the expert carry out an iterative process as the ES model evolves into a functional system.

STEPS IN THE KNOWLEDGE ACQUISITION PROCESS

Practitioners in the ES field generally agree on five distinct steps for acquiring knowledge [1]:

1. identification
2. conceptualization
3. formalization
4. implementation
5. testing and validation

Let us briefly explain each step.

During the identification phase, the problem and its major characteristics are identified, and subproblems, participants, and resources are clearly defined. The knowledge engineer learns about the problem, and the goal of the ES is agreed upon. The scope of the problem and its relationship to the organization as a whole are defined.

Hayes-Roth et al. [6] provide a comprehensive list of questions designed to help define the problem:

What class of problems will the ES be intended to solve?

How can these problems be characterized or defined?

What are important subproblems and partitioning of tasks?

What are the data?

What are the important objects and their interrelations?

What aspects of the human expertise are essential in solving these problems?

What is the nature and extent of "relevant knowledge" that underlies the human solution?

What situations are likely to impede solutions?

How will these impediments affect the ES?

What is the problem that the ES is intended to solve? The active participants (expert, knowledge engineer, user, and sponsoring manager) are also identified, and their roles are defined.

Conceptualization takes into account the fact that the knowledge important to the decision process can vary. Care must be taken to determine the concepts and the relationships to be used. What is the necessary information? What is the best way to extract it? Which tool should be used?

Formalization determines the format in which knowledge is to be represented and organized. In rule-based systems, knowledge must be organized in terms of rules. During this stage, knowledge acquisition is actually integrated with knowledge representation. It is also a difficult stage because here is where most of the extraction of the expert's knowledge occurs.

Questions that must be answered during this phase include the following [6]:

Are the data sparse and insufficient or plentiful and redundant?

Is there uncertainty attached to the data?

Does the logical interpretation of data depend on their order of occurrence over time?

What is the cost of data acquisition?

How are the data acquired or elicited? What types of questions need to be asked to obtain the data?

Are the data reliable, accurate, and precise, or are they unreliable, inaccurate, and imprecise?

Implementation involves the actual programming of knowledge into the ES. Refinements may occur in the acquired knowledge. A prototype ES is developed during this stage.

During testing and validation, the final stage, the knowledge engineer tests the system by subjecting it to examples, and the rules are revised if necessary. Knowledge validity is examined at this stage. Usually there are three activities in this phase: evaluation, validation, and verification. Although the terms are often used interchangeably elsewhere, each has a distinct meaning in the context of the knowledge acquisition process. Evaluation refers to the assessment of the ES's overall value. The emphasis is on its usability, efficiency, and cost effectiveness. Validation concerns the system's performance. Usually, tests are given to verify the accuracy of the ES's response relative to that of human experts. Rolston [16] developed three principles to be used for this purpose. The first principle is that for many of the domains addressed by ES, it is impossible to identify an answer that is "absolutely correct" for any given problem. Second, in ES evaluation, the correct response is taken to be that given by a human expert given the same question. Finally, an ES's response should be evaluated relative to the domain expert's and then relative to the responses given by a group of experts. Verification is focused on the system implementation activities; that is, how the system was built and how closely the implementation was carried out based on the specifications. Validation and verification are dynamic and repetitive. Any changes in each of the ES components will result in another round of validation and verification.

Selected Knowlege Acquisition Techniques

There are several techniques used for knowledge acquisition for ES construction. The following is a brief definition of some of the popular knowledge acquisition techniques.

The *observation* technique involves simply observing the expert when he or she is performing a specific task in his or her comfortable environment without interruption by the knowledge engineer. *Protocol analysis* requires that the expert "think aloud" while solving a problem. Protocol analysis, originated in clinical psychology, is a form of data analysis using problem scenarios to stimulate the experts' thinking process. *Discourse analysis* is similar to protocol analysis. Interview sessions are tape recorded, and the tapes are transcribed and analyzed later. *Interviews* are an effective technique for knowledge acquisition. There are two types of interviews used as knowledge acquisition tools: unstructured and structured. Open, unstructured, or free-form interviewing is one of the most commonly used methods for knowledge acquisition. The knowledge engineer may start by asking a question such as, "How do you solve this problem?" The advantage of the free-form interview is that the knowledge engineer can elicit unanticipated information. The disadvantage is that experts become less aware of the cognitive processes they use in performing a task. They cannot explicitly describe the reasoning used. There are also biases and fallibility in human reasoning. They tend to leave out certain components since they may be so obvious to them. The structured interview is goal oriented. It forces the expert to be organized, and interpretation problems are reduced. The *voting* technique is used to generate consensus among the experts. After identification of various alternatives, experts are asked to vote on a desired alternative. *Brainstorming* is an effective technique for generating ideas. Special attention areas can be uncovered in this process. Inhibiting behavior and confrontation can be reduced with multiple experts working together as a team. The experts must be sufficiently stimulated by a question, a scenario, or a demonstration of a system similar to the one under investigation. Each expert must submit one idea as a resolution to the problem, which is given to another expert to see if he or she can follow the same train of thought. This process continues until the experts have no more ideas. These interactions among multiple experts provide an enriched domain of expertise. The *Delphi* technique uses a series of questionnaires to aggregate knowledge, judgments, or opinions from multiple experts. This is usually done anonymously. This technique reduces the influence of dominant experts, thus preventing undue influence of strong personalities; and it allows strangers to communicate effectively.

KNOWLEDGE REPRESENTATION: AN OVERVIEW

Knowledge representation is a key component of ES construction. It is part of the knowledge engineering discipline that assists a knowledge engineer in programming and storing the knowledge gathered from the expert(s) into some types of computer codes. Knowledge representation involves recording in some language or communication medium descriptions, facts, objects, or pictures that correspond to a real world situation. It is the process of structuring knowledge about a problem in a way that makes the problem easier to solve [5].

We see knowledge as the ultimate input into ES software packages. How that knowledge is developed into a workable program and what methods are used for the representation is the focus of the knowledge representation process. If knowledge can continue to be defined for use in ES, then the future of this technology is wide open.

Representing knowledge is one of the major differences that lie between ES and other MSS. The knowledge of an expert, including facts and rules of thumb, must be implemented into software to comprise a knowledge-based system. This knowledge can be symbolically represented in various forms of logic and object relationships [17].

Representing knowledge in a computer using a computer programming language, or an ES shell, does not seem to be a difficult task. The definition of knowledge representation used earlier suggests that you simply write down the knowledge in some language acceptable to a computer. This, however, is the easy part. The difficult part, as Ringland suggests, is to represent knowledge, so that a computer can come to new conclusions about its environment by manipulating the representation [15]. He breaks down the problem of knowledge representation into three components [15, p. 3]: finding a knowledge representation language in which the domain of knowledge can be described; knowledge representation that can perform automatic inferences for the user; and how to capture the detailed knowledge base that represents the system's understanding of its domain.

These problems may not seem so difficult to surmount, but when you evaluate how much is being spent on knowledge representation in the United States you begin to get a better picture of the scope of these projects. Goel [3] cites a study that estimates that U.S. companies spent $5 billion to $10 billion exploring artificial language and used as much as 4 percent of their information technology budget on ES alone. By 1999, U.S. companies plan to spend 15 percent to 20 percent of their information technology budgets on ES. If companies are spending that much on artificial intelligence and ES and plan to spend more, knowledge representation cannot be taken as a simple or unimportant aspect of artificial intelligence and ES. Goel goes on to explain why costs are so high: Only a small fraction of the ES applications developed have been implemented in a production environment. The literature is rich with stories of magnificent failures, brilliant ideas as yet untested, systems that might have worked, and systems that will be available soon.

Knowledge representation applications failures are the result of many problems, such as a lack of standards and technology limitations. Goel suggests that lack of software standards and development methodology have caused companies to incur higher systems-development costs and risk. Knowledge representation suffers from technological limitations as well. All knowledge representation forms (e.g., production rules, frames, etc.) are based on predicate calculus. This approach has proven to be inadequate for expressing various assertions, disjunctions, inequalities, existentially qualified statements, and metalevel propositions, which include such things as a company's beliefs, attitudes, goals, value systems, cultural situations, and purpose [3].

Selected Knowledge Representation Techniques

Knowledge representation can be broadly classified into declarative and procedural methods. Declarative methods represent facts about the domain in a modular fashion. The rules are stated explicitly and independent of one another. The knowledge regarding how to use the facts resides separately in an inference engine. In our day-to-day life we use declarative methods most of the time. For example, this book has ten chapters, or John is a carpenter. Declarative methods include semantic networks, scripts, frames, and object-oriented representation methods. The advantages of declarative techniques stem from the modularity aspect. Each fact needs to be stored only once, regardless of the ways it can be used. Facts are easily added or modifyed without changing other facts or procedures.

A procedural representation is essentially a plan for the use of the information. Procedural knowledge may be such that a routine waits for conditions to trigger the procedure. If the conditions are met, then an action takes place. Another example of procedural representation is the ordering of rules. If rules are independent, then the order in which the rules are applied should be of no consequence. However, if the order of application is specified and that specification leads to additional knowledge, then the knowledge is embedded in the procedure and is not separately available to the system. Simple examples of procedural methods are changing gears in a car or building a house.

Procedural representation is used to represent knowledge about how to do things or knowledge that does not fit well into declarative schemes. Knowledge such as heuristic or probabilistic reasoning can also be represented using procedural representation. Production rules are perhaps the most popular way to represent knowledge. Let us briefly explain this popular technique for knowledge representation.

Sometimes it is referred to as the classic way to represent knowledge. A system of IF-THEN rules is used to move from condition(s) to action(s). The IF is a list of premises, and the THEN is the conclusion. To use a rule-based system it is usually assumed that the data, facts, or information consist of small, modular chunks of knowledge that can be expressed in a rule format. A production system can be in one of the following formats:

IF	(condition)	THEN	(action)	
IF	(antecedents)	THEN	(consequences)	
IF	(condition)	AND	(condition)	AND . . .THEN (action)

Rule-based systems are often referred to as production systems. Three main components must be present to have a minimum working system [15]: (1) Working memory is where the observed data enters the system. (2) In rule memory, data are compared with the stored rules to form a match. (3) The interpreter or inference engine selects the rules that were matched in the rule memory and performs the appropriate action(s). This is the action part of the system.

In addition to these three components, a fourth component is often used in more sophisticated systems. A meta-rules component can be added to store new rules that result from the processing of existing rules. Rules are distinguished from conventional conditional statements by two factors: (1) The conditional part is expressed as a pattern, not as a Boolean expression; and (2) each rule is determined separately by the interpreter and is not passed from one rule to the next in lexical sequence.

Forward and backward chaining (as explained in Chapter 4) describe the flow of data from input to output. An example of a car mechanic dealing with an automobile problem will be used to demonstrate how these components interact. The following is a simple model of forward chaining in a rule-based system [15].

The observed data is sent to working memory:

(Complaint: The car won't start.)

(low battery)

The observed data are sent to rule memory to be matched with the rules stored in the rule memory.

Rule:	low battery = dead battery
IF	(Complaint: The car won't start.)
AND	(low battery)

The inference engine then selects the matched rule from rule memory that matches the contents of working memory. This is called firing (or taking an action).

THEN   (assert [Replace the battery])
IF   (remedy [car starts])
AND   (Customer is happy.)
THEN   (Thanks for your business.)

If the customer is happy, the output would be, "Thanks for your business." If the remedy does not work, then the inference engine goes back to working memory for more data or a modification of data, and the process starts over until the customer is happy. In this example, the car won't start because the starter is not working or there may be other problems.

In backward chaining, a goal is defined and the search is directed to accomplish the goal. In this example, the goal was to make the customer happy. The interpreter would select rules to match the data that would make the customer happy. This is where the meta-rules component would come into play, because the solution to replace the battery might not correct the problem.

ES CONSTRUCTION: AN OVERVIEW

The construction of ES, similar to other MSS, is a multifaceted and complex task. A series of well-defined steps must be followed to deliver a final product that is an operational ES.

Each step of ES construction is not a step or activity all to itself, nor must the steps be completed in sequence. Problem definition should be completed first, but could be done more than once if the prototype fails to solve the problem. The problem at hand may have to be redefined, modified, or even abandoned. Organizational readiness may have to take place right after the problem definition phase, but may be just as effective if done during the entire project.

Expert selection and tool selection are separate issues, but can be done at the same time. The knowledge engineer may need to select the tools or shells to fit the expert or the type of domain knowledge under consideration. Design team selection must take place, but not all members need to be chosen at the start of the project.

Prototype design and revision are very important and must be performed carefully. Final construction will be the last step before the post-implementation audit. Many factors will affect the actual sequence in which the ES is to be constructed, and should be given some consideration before starting the project.

ES CONSTRUCTION: FROM THE BEGINNING TO THE END

The construction of ES is more than the mechanics of implementing a system. It is not enough to buy the hardware and software, hire the necessary personal, and build the system. According to Meador and Mahler, choosing a strategy that fits your company's culture and structure has a lot to do with your chances for ultimate success [10]. To have an effective and efficient system, you must consider many factors. These factors will be discussed in detail in this chapter. Construction can be carried out using the various methods that a typical system analyst would use while implementing any project. A top-down, bottom-up, or combination approach may be used. The important point is that each of the nine following steps must be given consideration while implementing the project. Some steps can be done during the project and even after the project is finished. ES construction, similar to the DSS construction, is never finished because there is always room for improvement. The following are the nine phases involved in the construction of ES:

problem definition

organizational readiness

expert selection

tool selection

design team selection

prototype design

final construction

validation

post-implementation audit

Problem Definition

The first step in the construction of ES is to define the scope and nature of the problem. This means that the organization must decide if an ES will solve the problem under investigation. ES may be the most effective way to solve the problem, but not the most efficient. It can be a very expensive way to solve a problem that can be solved in some other, less expensive manner. A basic feasibility study should be conducted to determine the costs and benefits of the project.

The feasibility study in the ES environment is similar to the feasibility study described in Chapter 2 for a MSS with some minor variations. As you may recall, the feasibility study first investigates the costs and benefits of the system. In other words, first its economic desirability, then its social, technical, and time dimension are carefully analyzed. The various dimensions of feasibility study for ES development are summarized: economic, social, technical, and time. Let us briefly explain these various dimensions of a feasibility study for ES development.

The economic dimension usually is concerned with all the costs and benefits of the system. Both costs and benefits include tangible and intangible items. The assessment of tangible costs and benefits is relatively straightforward. The most noticeable benefit of an ES is the preservation and distribution of rare expertise throughout the organization. As an example, consider the ES developed in Campbell's Soup Company. This system has preserved forty-four years of the expertise of a rare expert in the organization. The benefit of such a system is tremendous. In addition to tangible benefits, an ES may include numerous intangible benefits such as improving communication, developing a better problem-solving process, improving customer service, and so forth. The tangible cost of an ES involves the cost of hardware, software, and personnel. The cost of personnel in an ES environment is somewhat different than the cost of personnel in the DSS environment. In an ES environment, the personnel costs include not only the cost of programmers, knowledge engineers, and support staff, but also the cost of the expert whose expertise will become the core of the system development process. The expert's time is very expensive, and in some cases, the expert may request additional compensation.

In an ES environment, the social feasibility is also somewhat different than in the DSS environment. The design team not only should consider the user acceptance of the system, but they should carefully investigate the reaction of the expert(s) and the user(s) toward the system. ES are associated with the notion that they may replace the expert(s). Widespread education and participation are needed to alleviate these problems. The user(s) and the expert(s) must be actively involved in the entire ES development process. The user(s) and expert(s) must be responsible for both the success and failure of the system. Careful planning should minimize some of the social issues of ES development.

The technical dimension investigates the required expertise, organizational readiness, and availability and willingness of the key expert(s) to be used for the ES development. The time dimension investigates the availability of the system within the required time frame. If the system will not be ready within the desired time frame, we conclude that the system is not feasible from the time dimension standpoint. Other types of feasibility do not matter.

The problem definition phase should include a survey of the rules to be used in the ES. It is more cost effective to choose another method of solving the problem if the rules are few—say, less than ten. On the other hand, if there are too many rules (more than 10,000), it may cost too much and take too long to develop an ES. If the problem can be solved numerically, there may be no need for the ES. A complete understanding of the quantity and quality of the rules to be used will help in deciding if an ES is the right application.

The suitability of the problem at hand for ES implementation is very important. It is important that a specific problem domain be narrowly defined. Too broad a domain will make the coding of the rules to apply to the knowledge base a time-consuming task. In other words, the efficiency might be at risk. ES perform well when they are applied to a narrow and deep area. This means a limited problem area that we know a lot about. The design team must make sure that the problem at hand falls into one of the following categories:

- A high degree of human expertise is needed
- Available experts are retiring or scarce
- The problem area does not call for extensive mathematical modeling, such as with those found in the DSS environment
- There is always some degree of uncertainty
- The existing experts are willing to share their expertise for the ES construction
- Recognized experts exist
- Experts agree on solutions
- The task under investigation requires reasoning and informed judgments, as opposed to just common sense
- The task is well understood
- Typical example cases or situations are readily available
- The task requires symbolic manipulation

Richardson and Defries [14] use the following two considerations to determine the suitability of a problem for ES implementation:

1. Does the task have a quantitative or procedural content or structure that would best be solved by using a more conventional computer tool, such as a spreadsheet or a database management application?
2. When a situation involves a decision or task encountered only a few times a year, then it is probably best handled by a human expert.

Just as in the number of rules, the type of rules to be used is very important. Time and money can be associated with each type, and this must be taken into consideration [11]. *Completely innumerable rules* are usually limited in number and are completely known. They are simple and do not have many arguments. *Partially innumerable rules* is a situation where many rules are known, but many others are not. This may require additional rule development with a human expert involved. *Unknown rules* are the most complex of the three because there is no way to know the magnitude of the number of rules. This type of system must be developed in a way that allows easy modifications as new information comes to light.

Organizational Readiness

Management support and user readiness must be taken into consideration before attempting to construct ES. Management and users may have no understanding of how ES work. They will need a minimum level of general computer understanding and some understanding and appreciation of what an ES will do for them. Management must be committed to the project and must be able to justify the expenditures in terms of the benefits. The users must be able to see the importance of the system and how it will affect them. The same involvement that is needed when developing any MSS should be provided. Management and the users must be involved in every step of the project from beginning to end. This gives them a sense of commitment to the project. Both management and users can cause the project to be a failure, even if the system functions according to the specifications.

The best method of providing organizational readiness is through education and ongoing education. All impacted personnel should be told about the functions of the new ES, its costs and benefits, and its overall impact on the organization. When the system is put to work, the management should provide ongoing education to expose the user group to the new features and the overall effectiveness of the system. By doing this, the management is significantly improving the chances of success.

Expert Selection

During this stage of ES development, the expert(s) must be selected. The expert(s) could be a collection of knowledge available in documented form such as books, notes, manuals, or videos, or an actual human expert. The expert has the knowledge that is being transferred to the ES. If the knowledge of the experts has been written down and collected in some manner to make it compatible with the ES, then very little, if any, involvement of the human expert will be needed. This usually is not the case. Not only will the human expert need to be involved, there may be more than one expert needed to complete the acquisition of knowledge.

Knowledge acquisition occurs at this stage as discussed earlier. Knowledge acquisition involves eliciting, analyzing, organizing, and interpreting the knowledge that the expert possesses. The knowledge engineer uses techniques such as structured interviews and protocol analyses to extract the expert's knowledge. The expert will not always be able to articulate his or her knowledge accurately, and will work with the knowledge engineer to develop the knowledge needed for the ES. It is important to note that the proper knowledge acquisition method is very important to the development of a successful ES and cannot be taken lightly. The knowledge engineer must be chosen as carefully as the expert.

Various tools and techniques must be examined to select the right tool for a given situation. The knowledge engineer may have to utilize a combination of tools for optimum results.

Expert identification can be a complex task in some situations, while in others it may be a simple task because many fields have a small number of people who are clearly world-class experts. This is very true in fields such as medicine, and it certainly was true in the case of Campbell's Soup Company.

But in many cases the selection of the expert may be difficult, because the task under investigation may require expertise in more than one area, or no outstanding expert may be available. Also, choosing one expert over another may present a problem because of status or standing in that field of expertise. The expert may not be willing to share and communicate his or her expertise. There are two types of experts: the expert with the theoretical knowledge and the expert with practical hands-on knowledge [13]. The expert with theoretical knowledge usually has extensive education and practical, high-level experience. The hands-on expert has apprentice-style training and little formal education, but many years of experience. The expert should stand out from the norm and bring some personal motivation to the project. If several experts must be used because the project scope overlaps several areas of expertise, a different set of criteria should be applied to select the experts. Experts should be able to communicate what they know and be able to work with abstract concepts. They should be able to use their knowledge to solve problems. The level of detail at which the expert works should correspond to that of the user. A familiarity with computers or a willingness to learn is very helpful.

The involvement of the expert can range from total control to limited participation with the system development process. A complex situation may require total control. In a situation where large amounts of past experience are available, the involvement of the expert could be minimal, using the expert only to review and modify the rules, if needed.

Tool Selection

The selection of a specific type of ES tool or ES shell must be carefully considered. An ES tool is a programming language, and an ES shell is the product of a programming language that allows for a comparatively easy-to-use format in which to construct the ES. Shells provide a ready-made interpreter that allows a fast design, edit, prototype design, revision, and run for the debug cycle. Most tools will fit into one of the following four types [11]:

1. Algorithmic programming languages. These can be any standard procedural computer languages such as C, FORTRAN, BASIC, or PASCAL. The code is written to record IF-THEN rules. These languages allow for portability between applications and sites and require an experienced programmer. For example, PUFF, a pulmonary function ES, was developed using BASIC.

2. Symbolic programming languages. These languages include LISP, PROLOG, or some dialect of these languages. These languages process symbols, and they can reach conclusions on a logical level unlike the algorithmic languages. Symbolic languages can categorize, analyze, and reach conclusions with symbols. Generally speaking, these languages are more suitable for ES development than algorithmic languages. Developing ES using algorithmic programming and symbolic languages may be more expensive than using shells. It usually takes a longer time to develop ES using the first two groups of tools; however, the final product will be more customized, and it usually fits closely to the specific user's requirements.

3. Shell-based expert system. Shells are relatively easy to use because the system provides all the tools necessary for developing an ES. These are like empty ES. For example, EMYCIN, a popular ES shell, was used to develop MYCIN. Two methods of development are usually found in these systems: deductive and inductive. The deductive method uses a decision-tree rule structure, and by examination of a series of IF-THEN rules reaches the conclusion. In the inductive approach, a number of actual examples whose results or conclusions are known are examined using some standard algorithm to drive efficient branching rules. An ES shell usually includes word processing, graphic, spreadsheet, and tracing components. Exsys EL by Exsys Corporation is a good example of a PC-based ES shell.

4. Knowledge-engineering environment. This approach usually is done through an elaborate multiwindow, icon and graphic, blackboard-like environment. They are expensive and require high-powered PCs or workstations. KEE and ART are two examples of this environment. KEE, the Knowledge Engineering Environment (by IntelliCorp, Mountain View, California), is a large hybrid ES development environment that requires at least the power of a workstation. KEE has rule-based and object-oriented representations, and has image processing and windowing capabilities. It also has a number of functions that allow the developer to control the inference process. ART, adaptive resonance theory, has been successfully utilized for neural network construction. It was developed by Stephen Grossberg in 1976 and later was used in ART 1, ART 2, and ART 3 neural networks (developed by Stephen Grossberg and Gail Carpenter in 1987 and 1989, respectively).

When a programming method is chosen, the hardware must be taken into consideration also. The computer must be able to work with the software and grow as the system grows. Careful consideration must be given to the hardware. Depending upon what is already available in an organization, the selected language or shell may or may not run on the existing hardware. If the selected language or shell does not run on the existing hardware, then a line of budget must be devoted for the acquisition of the hardware. The availability of one type of hardware may dictate (in some cases) which software (shell or language) must be chosen.

Design Team Selection

The design team includes programmers, systems analysts, knowledge engineers, experts, users, and top management. This is similar to the MSS task force discussed in Chapter 2. In some cases, it may not be a bad idea to involve a representative of the vendor community, at least for the first couple of meetings. These representatives may be able to provide some insight regarding the suitability of the project at hand and the commercial platform that will be used to design and implement the system. Each member must have a commitment to the project. Programmers and systems analysts may not be needed, depending on the type of ES. Most ES projects will need them in some capacity. The top management role is his or her commitment to the project. This is very important to the success of the project. Without top management support, the project may not even get off the drawing board. Top management participation can improve the chances of success for the ES development by providing both financial support and a sense of commitment. This, in turn, encourages others in the organization to be committed to the project as well. The user is another very important participant of the design team. The ES must be designed with the user in mind. Users may not be able to contribute much in the technical areas, but they can contribute to the overall success of the project. They will be using the system and can make or break a project if they feel the project is not of much value to them. Having the user on the team will help to insure that the project will be accepted by the company and will be a useful tool. Knowledge engineers and experts are unique to ES. Knowledge engineers, experts, and users must all be involved and actively participate in the design team. The knowledge engineer works with the expert and the user to transfer the knowledge, rules, and data to the knowledge base of the ES. The expert should know about the rules and facts of the problem domain.

Prototype Design

As discussed in Chapter 2, a prototype is a small-scale version of the larger system. The prototype should be constructed before the final system is implemented. Although the prototype is not the entire system, it is significant enough to provide the user with a good representation of the actual system. This allows all members of the design team to view the system, and also allows for a demonstration to the user and management. This is a good way to discover any flaws in the system or misconceptions about its purpose and operation. The prototype should be revised until all possible corrections have been made. This should be an ongoing effort throughout the system's implementation process.

As discussed in Chapter 2, there are several kinds of prototypes. In the ES environment either a throwaway or an evolving prototype should be used. Initial problem definition should take place, and knowledge acquisition and knowledge representation should be performed. The cycle should continue until a workable system is developed. Prototyping should be used as a rapid system development process. This means the prototyping process phase could be done with little or no programming. Using a shell will allow for a much faster prototype design. When a shell is used, it allows a wider range of individuals to test the system. Each time the prototype is revised it becomes more complete and complex. This problem is further complicated if a dedicated programming language is used. Not all the rules need to be defined at this time, only enough to test the design. However, at a later point the programming of all the identified rules will be needed to control and test the inference engine, run-time efficiency, customized graphic interface, interface with other external software and hardware applications, and any other issues that may arise from testing the prototype [13].

One of the major similarities of ES with transaction processing systems is that both systems try to model the real world, consider users' cognitive limitations in handling complexity, leave room for future growth, and accommodate the heterogeneity of the computing environment [7]. This implies that rapid prototyping and incremental growth are essential elements of both systems. Logical and physical designs are needed in both systems.

Final Construction

This phase is the transformation of the final prototype into the final product. Some experts also call this system integration. The final product is either the final result of the evolving prototype or a brand new system constructed-based on the throwaway prototype.

Although ES construction is never really finished and it will always go through changes, this is the point where the system is delivered to the user as a finished product.

As mentioned earlier, the majority of ES evolve over time. This is mainly because of all the new exposure that the system receives after the initial construction. A good example is XCON developed by Digital Equipment Corporation and Carnegie-Mellon University. The system started with a few hundred rules and has gone through several revisions. At the present time, the system includes more than 10,000 rules.

To progress with the construction of the ES, we should examine its architecture once again (Figure 4.4). Depending on which tool is selected, either some of these components are readily available, or they must be coded from scratch. The knowledge acquisition facility is designed for acquiring rules and facts. It is essential for the growth of the system. The knowledge engineer uses this facility to capture the expertise of the domain expert.

The knowledge base is where all the knowledge, facts, and rules are stored. It usually includes three types of knowledge: factual knowledge, heuristic knowledge, and metaknowledge. Using the selected tool, this component must be coded.

The knowledge base management system (KBMS) is usually available within the majority of ES shells. If an algorithmic programming or symbolic programming language is used, then this component must be developed. Its purpose is similar to DBMS in the DSS and MIS environments. It allows the creation, manipulation, and maintenance of the knowledge base.

The inference engine applies rules to the knowledge and facts available in the knowledge base. Again, ES shells provide a readily available inference engine. In the case of the first two classes of tools, this component must also be developed.

The last component, the user interface, is probably the most important component from the user's standpoint. The ES designer's goal is that this component be very user-friendly. That is why some types of natural language with GUI will be ideal. Again, this component is readily available in ES shells and must be constructed in the case of algorithmic or symbolic programming languages.

Validation

Validation is the process of analyzing the knowledge and decision-making capabilities of the ES. There are several approaches to validation that deal with different aspects of the ES. As a holistic approach, you can treat the system as a black box and test it on cases to determine if it makes the right decisions for the right reasons, or you can evaluate each of the components of the system. You can analyze the knowledge base for accuracy and completeness, test the inference engine, analyze condition–decision matches for decision quality, and condition–decision matches to determine whether the right answers were found for the right reasons. When test cases fail, the explanation or trace facility will point to the problem component (e.g., knowledge base or inference engine). Then the design team should fix the particular component and continue the test [12].

The testing process should provide enough test cases to demonstrate the variety of knowledge needed by the expert. This can be a difficult task. Usually, cases where the decisions are evenly spaced between the two extremes provide the coverage of knowledge. In situations where a discrete number of decisions is possible, you must ensure that each decision is represented. It is also advisable to include multiple cases for each decision where the starting conditions are different.

The most important component of an ES that must pass all the tests is the knowledge base. Direct examination is the best way to analyze the accuracy of the knowledge base for relatively small systems. For large systems, analyzing the most important rules or frames can adequately test the accuracy of the knowledge base.

The validation and delivery of an ES is much like any other system. The system must be approved or validated by the expert, the end-user, and the management team. The system will be put into use for final acceptance in much the same way as any other computer system. Training the user, installing the user interface, setting up the hardware platform, and dealing with any software issues are all part of the final construction. Validation of the system should include the following:

1. Testing. This should be done to make sure that the system is usable outside the prototype environment. The more complete the testing, the fewer problems will be discovered after the system is in the hands of the user. After all the testing, real-world problems will still arise. Testing can take several forms and shapes. You may test the system based on an existing case and see how close the system generates responses. Although experts believe that no system is fully debugged, testing will minimize a lot of future problems that may occur after the final release of the system.

2. Expert validation. The system answers should be compared with the answers given by the expert. All incorrect answers or advice by the system should be recorded in detail. If the system logic breaks down under certain conditions and cannot be corrected immediately, the system should inform the user that the advice may not be correct. It may also be useful to request other experts who have not been involved in the construction of the system to validate the system.

3. End-user validation. This is testing of the system's overall usability. It should be done by a few selected users and after the expert has validated the system. The goal is to detect any deficiencies in the user interface and determine training requirements. This stage of the testing is mostly concerned with the usability of the system and its soundness as it appears to the user with a minimum computer background.

Post-Implementation Audit

This is the stage in which the system has been up and running for some time. The validation and testing is finished, and the users are working with the system. This is the real test that determines the true value of an ES. No system is ever perfect. There is always room for improvement. At this stage, an audit of the system is performed to find any possible areas for improvement. These improvements can be to any component of the system. Some areas to look for when performing the post-implementation audit are listed below [3].

1. Operational performance. This can include any area in which the user is involved: Is the system easy to use? Does it respond quickly enough to be effective? These are the same types of operational performance issues found in any computer system.

2. Face validity. This is much like the expert validation found during the construction phase. It differs in that the system has been running for a while and should have developed a level of experience. This means the system should be able to remember and use previous case experience in solving a problem or providing an answer, then be able to use this past experience to solve a similar case at the present time. This should be done without any bias that may have been built in by the expert(s). The expertise of the system should be tested to confirm the results after some running time has elapsed.

3. Objectivity. The objectivity of the system should be examined by using a library of test cases and scenarios to test for average cases, boundary conditions, and error conditions. This is to insure that expert bias and difference in judgment have not become part of the system.

4. Reliability. Reliability is not a question of system performance. System performance and reliability are performed when measuring operational performance of an ES. Reliability refers to the solution that the ES generates. The stability of the system and its ability to generate identical solutions should be tested when given identical input. Changing input variables and parameters to see the effect on system performance should complete a systematic sensitivity analysis.

5. Economics. Economics should be evaluated to see if the system would indeed pay for itself. Is the system cost effective? Are the solutions given by the ES cost effective

and will they put the company at risk? More emphasis should be placed on the cost of the solutions and answers from the ES than on the cost of implementation. System implementation cost should have already been evaluated in the feasibility study before final construction.

SELECTED EXAMPLES OF ES SHELLS

The following are examples of ES shells on the market. For detailed descriptions and capabilities of these systems, the specific vendor should be contacted [1].

ACQUIRE (Acquire Intelligence, Inc.) offers a set of knowledge-based products designed for nonprogrammers. The knowledge-acquisition system creates knowledge bases, and the ES shell tests them on actual cases. Finished applications can be delivered as stand-alone systems using Acquire-RTS (run-time system) or fully embedded using Acquire-SDK (software development kit).

DPL (Applied Decision Analysis) offers a decision-analysis software program that combines decision trees and influence diagrams to create a complete modeling environment. DPL uses the logical framework of decision analysis to make decisions based on what the user knows, can do, and prefers. Features include spreadsheet links, automated sensitivity analysis, policy summaries, and more.

FORECAST PRO (Business Forecast Systems) offers a business forecasting application using artificial intelligence. The program does not require any background in statistical forecasting. Instead, an ES examines the data, and the program guides users to exponential smoothing, Box-Jenkins, or regression—whatever method suits the data best. A standardized set of diagnostic screens helps users compare and evaluate models.

BUSINESS INSIGHT (Business Resource Software, Inc.) offers an ES for strategic analysis and gathers information about your prospect, the product or service, and competition. Then, using the knowledge of more than thirty business experts, it identifies strengths, weaknesses, inconsistencies, and gives a thorough explanation. Service Industry Knowledge Base, software to be used with Business Insight, contains the rules and data relationships from business planning and marketing experts in the services industry.

DCLASS (CAM Software) offers an ES development tool used to capture and process logic for manufacturing applications. It uses decision trees, including features for controlling decision points, manipulating variables, calculating, and calling other subsystems.

PENSION PLANNER (Foundation Technologies, Inc.) offers an ES facilitating the establishment of employee-benefit management programs. The system validates and speeds the input process, ensures completeness of data, and outputs administrative documents for defined contribution and defined benefit programs. Pension Manager, additional software, integrates Pension Planner to manage employee health and welfare benefits as well.

IMPORTANT CONSIDERATIONS FOR ES CONSTRUCTION

ES have proved to be cost effective for the majority of organizations who have properly introduced them in their organizations. The number of ES in use has been steadily increasing in recent years [4]. The increasing power and sophistication of PCs and their very affordable cost will expedite this transition and the adoption of this powerful technology. However, organizations must be aware of several issues before they commit large budgets to this technology.

First and foremost, an organization must choose a strategy that best fits its culture and specific environment. A well-known example is the case of DuPont and Digital Equipment Corporation [9]. Both of these companies share the fundamental goal of implementing ES to improve decision making and decision implementation throughout the organization by putting relevant and scarce information into the hands of key decision makers. But each company chooses a route specific to its organizational culture.

DuPont uses a "dispersed" approach for developing ES. This means end-users develop their own systems using standard, low-cost tools. Digital Equipment Corporation from the other end uses centralized development centers with trained knowledge engineers and programmers. These systems are more complex, involve more rules, and solve more high-level problems than the ones solved by DuPont using the dispersed approach. Each approach has advantages and disadvantages. For example, the dispersed approach usually is fast, has a low cost, and enjoys broader support throughout the organization. However, the final product may not have the highest possible quality. On the other hand, the centralized approach is more costly and takes more time; however, the final product has a higher quality.

Second, the integration of ES technology into the existing information systems technology may also be a challenging task. ES more or less will utilize some of the existing data resources available in the organization. This may create a compatibility problem. ES applications have many of the same requirements as conventional applications, including the need to access databases, to interface with external systems, and to operate efficiently in a network-intensive computing environment [2]. The issue of compatibility forces organizations to take a more comprehensive look at the entire information systems resources before committing large budgets to ES technology.

Third, regardless of the type of product that is introduced to the market, there is always a need to consider its legal ramifications. The same holds for ES. In the case of ES, this issue is even more important, because ES are used as decision-making tools; and when people use them to make a decision there is always the chance that their actions, based on what was given by the ES, can have detrimental effects on the company. Of course, this in turn means that someone must become liable for any damages done. But the challenging question is who is liable? Is the knowledge engineer? Domain expert? Sponsoring manager or the user? Who exactly is at fault? This is one of the major issues that has to be examined very carefully. At this point, this issue has not been resolved [8].

Fourth, cost must be considered. ES do not come cheap. Not only is it time consuming to build one, but many of the components of an ES cannot be built with the existing hardware and software. Although some applications can be written in low-level languages such as BASIC, COBOL, PASCAL, or C, most are written in symbolic languages such as LISP and PROLOG. The need to acquire hardware and software that can run these languages will be a necessity.

From what we have seen, we can conclude that ES have a bright future. According to Ashish Goel [3], the worldwide growth of ES will continue in both the public and private sectors. American businesses have seen the payoff of using them, and many are now looking toward this technology to be able to stay competitive in today's highly competitive environment.

SUMMARY

This chapter provided a detailed discussion of the construction of an ES. After knowledge acquisition and knowledge representation, ES construction is the third phase in the sequence. The chapter introduced a methodology similar to the life-cycle approach introduced in Chapter 2. Since uncertainty and human knowledge play an important role in construction of ES, the life-cycle approach should be modified accordingly. The phases introduced for the construction of ES include problem definition, organizational readiness, expert selection, tool selection, design team selection, prototype design, final construction, validation and post-implementation audit. The chapter introduced several popular ES shells, and concluded with several important considerations for constructing an ES and releasing it to the public as a "product."

REFERENCES

1. Byrd, Terry A., Kathy L. Cossick, and Robert W. Zmud. "A Synthesis of Research on Requirements Analysis and Knowledge Acquisition Techniques." *MIS Quarterly* 16(1) (March 1992): 118–138.
2. "Expert Systems Resource Guides, Products and Services Directory." *AI Expert* (April 1995): 26.
3. Goel, Ashish. "The Reality and Future of Expert Systems: A Manager's View of AI Research Issues." *Information Systems Management* (Winter 1994): 53–61.
4. Griesser, John W. "Experts Among Us." *Business Horizons* (May/June 1992): 77–80.
5. Gum, Russell, and Steven C. Blank. "Designing Expert Systems for Effective Delivery of Extension Programming." *American Journal of Agricultural Economics* 72 (August 1990): 540.
6. Hayes-Roth, Frederick, D. A. Waterman, and D. B. Lenat. *Building Expert Systems*. Reading, Mass.: Addison-Wesley, 1983.

7. Jih, W. J. Kenny. "Comparing Knowledge-Based and Transaction Processing Systems Development." *Journal of Systems Management* (May 1990): 23–28.
8. Kidd, A. L. *Knowledge Acquisition for Expert Systems.* New York: Plenum Press, 1987.
9. Lynn, Marc P., and William N. Bockanic. "Legal Liability of the Domain Expert." *Journal of Systems Management* (November 1993): 6–10.
10. Meador, Lawrence, and Ed Mahler. "Choosing an Expert Systems Game Plan." *Datamation* (August 1990): 64.
11. Nelson, Carol, and R. Balanchandra. "Choosing the Right Expert System Building Approach." *Decision Sciences* 22(2) (Spring 1991): 354–368.
12. O'Leary, Daniel E. "Methods of Validating Expert Systems." *Interface* (November/December 1988): 72–79.
13. Payne, Edmund C., and Robert C. McArthur. "Developing Expert Systems." In *A Knowledge Engineer's Handbook for Rules & Objects*, edited by Edmund C. Payne and Robert C. McArthur. New York: John Wiley & Sons, 1990.
14. Richardson, Jeffrey J., and Marjorie J. Defries. *Intelligent Systems in Business: Integrating the Technology*, edited by Jeffrey J. Richardson and Marjorie J. Defries. Norwood, N.J.: Ablex Publishing, 1990.
15. Ringland, Gordon A. *Approaches to Knowledge Representation: An Introduction.* New York: John Wiley & Sons, 1983.
16. Rolston, David W. *Principles of Artificial Intelligence and Expert Systems Development.* New York: McGraw Hill Book Company, 1988: 9–10.
17. Slater, John R., Susan J. Hazen, and Sachi Sakthivel. "On Selecting Appropriate Technology for Knowledge Systems." *Journal of Systems Management* (October 1993): 10–15.

CHAPTER 9

Fuzzy Logic and Its Business Applications

This chapter discusses fuzzy logic as one of the growing concepts within the MSS field, introduces commonly used fuzzy logic terminology, and explains the working process of a fuzzy logic system. The chapter then reviews the hybrid systems that can significantly benefit from fuzzy logic, introduces several popular applications of fuzzy logic, and concludes with an outlook for further development of fuzzy logic systems.

BACKGROUND FOR FUZZY LOGIC

In our day-to-day life we hear and use terminology that is not yes and no, but within the context we understand the statement (e.g., phrases such as "it depends," "most likely," "he is tall," "she is short," and "the movie was crowded"). What do we really mean by these phrases. How tall is tall? How short is short? Is 6'2" tall? What about a 6'8" person?

Have you ever been given a questionnaire that asks ambiguous questions and then expects you to give a straightforward, yes or no response? Did you wish that you could use words such as "usually," "often," "sometimes," "it depends," "probably," "only if," or "most likely?" You probably have had this feeling, but you still answered the questions with yes or no, because you know that the survey could not be analyzed if only descriptive answers were given. Even the survey did not give such an option. You must answer yes or no or at best leave it blank. The computers that the surveyor uses to analyze the questionnaire simply cannot deal with anything but clear-cut, crisp, black-and-white yes and no answers. Today, this is no longer true; computers can analyze information to whatever degree of accuracy you wish with the help of fuzzy logic.

The computer industry has been dominated by digital computers. These binary machines only understand either-or answers. Fuzzy logic allows a slow and smooth transition between our vocabulary and the ones used by computers. Fuzzy logic can deal with linguistic terms by using a degree of membership. For example, you might consider a 6' tall individual a tall person, a 6'3" tall individual taller, and what about a 6'8" tall person? Fuzzy logic is designed to help computers simulate the various types of vagueness and uncertainty in our everyday lives.

When fuzzy logic is applied to computers, it recognizes the complex approximation of the human reasoning process and provides a crisp conclusion. Professor Lotfi A. Zadeh, an Iranian citizen, invented fuzzy logic. Professor Zadeh has been with the University of California at Berkeley as a professor and chairman of the Electrical Engineering Department. He developed fuzzy logic theory by using a form of mathematics called fuzzy sets. This theory allows precise computations using approximations that deal with vagueness. Professor Zadeh explained how in conventional computers everything is crisp (e.g., 0 or 1), but fuzzy logic can deal with items that are between 0 and 1.

According to Zadeh, the trouble with classical approaches is that the classes or categories that one is allowed to deal with have boundaries that are clear-cut, but most real-world classes do not have clear boundaries [13]. Aristotelian logic can deal with only true and false boundaries; however, highly complex systems such as those concerned with power distribution, transportation, air traffic controllers, and economic modeling do not lend themselves to precise analysis. They involve many variables and uncertainties.

Zadeh found out that he could use a branch of mathematical set theories and membership functions to recognize handwriting, since every person has a distinct writing pattern. According to Zadeh, membership in a set is a matter of degree. For example a 6' tall individual may have a .8 membership in a set of tall people and a .15 membership in a set of short people. Based on this principle, the programmers would not need to make thousands of rules to make computers "think"; computers could "judge" by themselves using fuzzy logic. According to this theory, computers can deal with vagueness rather than just manipulations of clear-cut items.

At the beginning, fuzzy logic was not accepted by many American scientists. In the 1970s, Ebrahim Mamdani at Queen Mary College in London introduced the first industrial application of fuzzy logic. Mamdani and coresearchers started studying ways to use fuzzy rules of thumb directly in automating process controls. They applied their algorithm to control the speed and pressure in industrial process control, automating engine control, and other fields.

At that time, fuzzy logic was also utilized in an industrial application with ES. By applying fuzzy rules of thumb with IF-THEN rules, the ES can solve complex problems somewhat like human experts do (e.g., when the temperature exceeds 82°F, turn the temperature down a little bit). In 1980, F. L. Smidth & Company of Copenhagen began marketing the first commercial fuzzy ES: a fuzzy logic controller that controlled the fuel-intake rate and gas flow of a rotating kiln used to make cement.

During the 1980s, the United States and Europe seemed less enthusiastic about fuzzy logic, because some scientists thought that uncertainty and imprecision could be solved by use of the probability theory. Only NASA used fuzzy logic as part of its space program. In Japan, fuzzy logic received widespread attention, and in the mid-1980s the first industrial applications were developed.

FUZZY LOGIC TERMINOLOGY

When dealing with fuzzy logic, a number of terms are commonly used. To be able to understand a discussion of fuzzy logic, you should be familiar with the following terminology [3, 28, 29]:

crisp logic: another name for traditional logic to differentiate it from fuzzy logic. In crisp logic, the three logical operations AND, OR, and NOT return either a 1 or a 0 (e.g., pass or fail, accepted or rejected, hot or cold, dry or wet, dark or light).

crisp set: traditional, classical, or crisp sets have strict membership criteria in which an object is either completely included or excluded from the set. They are mathematical sets with definitive boundary points (e.g., the score of 70 is passed; less than 70 is failed).

defuzzification: a process in which fuzzy output is converted into crisp, numerical results (e.g., most likely means 70 percent of the time).

fuzzification: the process of fuzzifying an element by combining actual values (e.g., the temperature of a liquid) with stored membership functions to produce fuzzy input values.

fuzziness: a term that expresses the ambiguity that can be found in the definition of a concept or the meaning of a word or phrase (e.g., usually, most often, or rarely).

fuzzy logic: a kind of logic using graded or qualified statements rather than ones that are strictly true or false. The results of fuzzy reasoning are not as definite as those derived by strict logic, but they cover a larger field of discourse.

fuzzy modifiers: operations that change the membership function of a fuzzy set by spreading out the transition between full membership and nonmembership, by sharpening that transition, or by moving the position of the transition region.

fuzzy sets: sets that do not have a clearly defined membership but rather allow objects to have grades of membership from 0 to 1.

fuzzy inference: the process of using the degree of truth in production rule premises to select an appropriate rule to execute. Production rules are a series of IF-THEN statements. They are commonly used in ES.

membership: the degree of inclusion in a set. Fuzzy sets have values between 0 and 1 that indicate the degree to which an element has membership in the set. At 0 the element has no membership; at 1 it has full membership.

set: a collection of objects (e.g., heights of 4, 5, 6, and 7 feet may constitute the set of heights for a population).

To better understand the membership functions, consider Figure 9.1. This is an example of a conventional or crisp set. Based on this diagram, 79.9°F is warm, and 80.1°F is hot. A small change in the temperature could cause a large response in the system.

Figure 9.2 shows the same set using fuzzy logic conventions. For example, in this figure, 80°F has a membership degree of .30 in the fuzzy set warm and .40 in the fuzzy set hot. All the temperatures from 40° to 100°F are the universe of discourse.

WHAT IS FUZZY LOGIC?

Fuzzy logic allows the computer to reason in a fashion similar to humans. Traditionally, a computer would analyze problems using straightforward AND, OR, and NOT functions, providing true or false or 0 or 1 answers from clearly defined inputs. With fuzzy logic, one can use approximations and vague data and yet produce clear, definable answers. Fuzzy systems use three steps for solving a problem: fuzzification, rule evaluation, and defuzzification.

In the first step, fuzzification takes actual values (e.g., room temperature) and combines them with stored membership functions to create fuzzy input values. In step two, rule evaluation, also known as fuzzy inferencing, decides which rules are appropriate to a given situation. In step three, defuzzification analyzes all of the possible outputs, finally providing a crisp output (an actual number). According to Ruggiero, there are three parts to a fuzzy operator [16]:

membership functions: relates the data to the concept of each rule

fuzzy rule logic: performs the reasoning and thought processes

defuzzifier(s): map the fuzzy answers back into identifiable "real-world" answers.

You should bear in mind that fuzzy logic could produce exact results. Fuzzy logic can deal with any degree of precision from input data and can react just as precisely in returning the results or processed information. As you will study later in this chapter, numerous commercial applications of fuzzy logic verify this claim.

FUZZINESS VERSUS PROBABILITY

Mathematicians and scientists who still have not been convinced of the notion of fuzzy logic have argued that fuzzy logic is merely an extension of traditional probability functions. Bart Kosko, one of the pioneers in fuzzy logic development, proves that uncertainty is not the same as randomness and that being unsure about something is not the same as being left to chance [10]. He proceeds to discuss the differences between ambiguity and randomness and whether versus how much. The premise of his argument is based on "whether an event occurs is random," but "to what degree it occurs is fuzzy." For example, if the possibility of John's passing his computer course is .75, this is random. However, how well he will pass the course (with which grade) is fuzzy.

Figure 9.1
Example of a Conventional Set

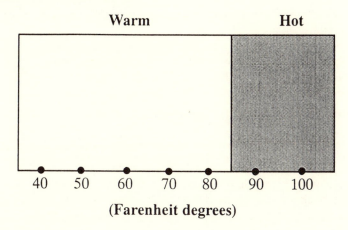

Figure 9.2
Degree of Membership in a Fuzzy System

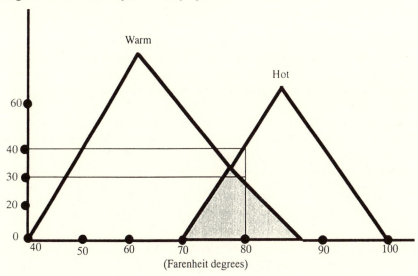

Probability is concerned with undecidability in the outcome of clearly defined and randomly occurring events such as customers' arrival in a service station. Fuzzy logic is concerned with the ambiguity or undecidability inherent in the description of the event itself, such as a tall person, a warm temperature, or a sweet drink [24].

IMPLEMENTING A FUZZY SYSTEM

To implement a fuzzy system, the following six steps are usually recommended [3]:

1. analyze and understand the problem
2. identify degrees of membership
3. define a rule or a series of rules
4. identify a procedure to fuzzify and process the problem
5. interpret and evaluate results
6. fine-tune results

Implementing a fuzzy logic system is essentially a learning process. Relatively simple applications will not need much refining, and this does not create a problem. The time saved in reduced programming far outweighs the time taken to fine-tune the rules and membership sets. Also, the ability to keep ambiguous and contradictory rules in a system allows much more flexibility in analysis. Moreover, it allows every avenue of thought to remain open instead of closing off possibilities using traditional straightforward logic. Designing the rules and membership functions can, however, become quite complicated if a system requires a high level of complexity. In these circumstances the front-end learning processes will become the most significant part of implementation.

To better understand this process, consider the following example of a fuzzy logic application, which tries to balance an inverted pendulum [2]. This problem can be likened to trying to balance a broomstick in the palm of one's hand.

The first step in implementing the system is to make sensible, logical rules that will manage the control of the pendulum movement. If regular programming were to be used, this program could add up to hundreds of lines of coding, all with specific, "clear" parameters being identified. In this example, only seven simple rules are needed. Each rule outlines a simple rule of thumb or expected behavioral characteristic for the system. These production rules are IF-THEN statements, which are broken down into the IF (antecedent) block, and the THEN (consequent) block. They are as follows:

Rule 1	If the stick is inclined moderately to the left and is almost still	Then move the hand to the left quickly
Rule 2	If the stick is inclined a little to the left and is falling slowly	Then move the hand moderately to the left a little quickly
Rule 3	If the stick is inclined a little to the left and is rising slowly	Then do not move the hand much
Rule 4	If the stick is inclined moderately to the right and is almost still	Then move the hand moderately to the right quickly

Rule 5	If the stick is inclined a little to the right and is falling slowly	Then move the hand moderately to the right a little quickly
Rule 6	If the stick is inclined a little to the right and is falling slowing	Then do not move the hand much
Rule 7	If the stick is almost not inclined and is almost still	Then do not move the hand much

From the set of rules, one can see that there are only two variables that need to be controlled. The first is the angle from the vertical (that is, the voltage input from a potentiometer), and the second is the rate of change of the angle due to the speed of the corrective movement. Both can be positive or negative, and both are governed by ambiguous words stated in the production rules.

Once the production rules have been identified, membership functions must be constructed. The membership functions partially quantify the ambiguity in the production rules. Words such as "moderately," "slowly," "quickly," and "a little" are all modifiers in controlling the two variables. The system developer must decide how each word is represented in special codes or labels. "A little" to the left could be translated as –1 to –3 volts; or "vertical" (zero position) could be allowed between a range of –1 to +1, depending on the degree of accuracy set by the developer. Everything is set by the discretion of the developer. If more accuracy is required, more rules with tighter constraints could be added.

After establishing the rules and membership functions, the system can be put to the test. The developer will be able to see how each rule affects the system by adding or deleting one rule at a time. If a rule appears to have no effect whatsoever, it can be permanently deleted from the system. Perhaps the system will not be accurate enough, so the developer will make smaller ranges for each label. Finally, the developer will be happy with the system after much trial and error, and the system will be ready for implementation. Trial and error and the reliance on the developer's judgment is the only way to get to the finished product, because there is no specific benchmark that can say what is right or wrong. The lack of rigidity can be analyzed as being both positive and negative, depending on which stance a person wishes to take.

ADVANTAGES OF FUZZY SYSTEMS

The applications of fuzzy logic systems can be seen in many different facets of business and society. The improvements fuzzy logic has offered to appliances and products have already proved its worth beyond doubt. Fuzzy logic has been applied in so many shapes and forms that defining why it is advantageous would require recognizing every triumph it has had. Products and successes will be discussed later, but for now we will weigh the pros and cons associated with fuzzy logic in general. The following are some of the advantages of fuzzy logic.

Simplicity

Fuzzy logic eliminates the difficulties of mathematical modeling. It allows the designer to describe inputs, rules, and outputs in a natural language. Overall, there are fewer rules required compared to traditional logic. This was shown in the inverted pendulum example discussed earlier in which seven rules versus hundreds or more lines of codes were used. Generally speaking, fuzzy logic systems require up to ten times fewer rules than many conventional systems; also, coding is reduced, and therefore the efficiency and effectiveness of the system can be improved.

Contradiction

One of the most unusual characteristics of programming with fuzzy logic is the ability to include contradictory statements. Rules can be completely contradictory and yet exist side by side without any problems. If traditional logic was given two opposing instructions, the computer would not be able to decide which path to branch on and the problem would be unresolved. Fuzzy logic allows a certain degree of tolerance and compromise. For example, a member in the membership function can belong to two sets. However, the degree of membership will be different. Membership functions allow degrees of membership to many fuzzy sets. Rather than having an item or state belong to only one set (as in traditional logic), the item or state can have a belonging of .65 to one set, .45 to another, and .15 to yet another. The number of sets that an item belongs to can depend on the degree of accuracy and sensitivity. Also, fuzzy logic is a precise problem-solving methodology that gives the designer complete control over its accuracy (by choosing the degrees and number of rules required).

Reducing Development Time and Increasing Flexibility

The analysis phase is reduced because designers can begin work without most of the information required. Functional objectives can be focused on, not having to worry about the underlying mathematical concepts. The ability to evaluate multiple rules and grade multiple input simultaneously reduces the time spent in design. Also, part of the reduction in development time, tools, and applications can be reassessed and redesigned much faster than before. Components of the fuzzy inference process function independently, so systems can be easily modified.

System Autonomy

Fuzzy systems consist of a number of rules that function independently of one another. One rule could be faulty and the others will still compensate for the error. Removing one rule at a time can test the robustness of the system [9].

Using fuzzy systems eliminates the tradeoff between robustness and sensitivity; sensitivity will actually increase as a system becomes more robust. Rules will continue to work even in circumstances when the whole system is completely changed.

Reduced Costs

One of the major reasons businesses take an interest in any product is the cost. The processors that use fuzzy logic can be much smaller and still more powerful than the traditional processors that would be too costly to put into many home appliances.

User-Friendliness

Natural languages and commonly used jargons in many cases provide phrases with which we are familiar. This in turn provides an easy to understand user/system interface, avoiding much of the number crunching and formula solving.

FUZZY LOGIC SHORTCOMINGS

Fuzzy systems, with all the advantages just mentioned, include some disadvantages and shortcomings. Following are some of these shortcomings:

1. A difficult task in fuzzy logic implementation is determining the optimum membership functions. Presently, there is no precise mathematical method of verifying the correctness of a fuzzy system.

2. Fuzzy logic currently is not able to optimize the efficiency of a fuzzy system. Fuzzy logic probably cannot reach the optimum efficiency, say 100 percent; but it can achieve 95 percent efficiency, which is still better than the traditional systems. Modeling and simulation are the ordinary method to verify a system using fuzzy logic, but it has not been sufficient to gain the confidence of mathematicians and control engineers [25].

3. Fuzzy logic can be an obstacle in verifying a system's stability and reliability, especially in a safety-related area. However, using simulation can complement this obstacle. In fine-tuning and improving a fuzzy system, however, there is no substitute for simulation. Where classical control systems demand a lot of work establishing the model in advance before doing the design, fuzzy systems require a large amount of simulation and tuning to optimize their performance and verify their reliability [23].

4. Front-end design becomes increasingly more time consuming when the complexity of a system increases. It can become almost impossible to know if the correct rules are being kept during fine-tuning. Redefining membership functions is a process that has no guidelines or set examples that can be easily followed. As a result, users do not always know if they are improving their systems or moving away from a better solution [3].

5. Fuzzy systems lack learning capabilities and have no memory. This is why hybrid systems (discussed later in this chapter), particularly neuro-fuzzy systems, are becoming popular for certain applications.

6. The term "fuzzy" is generally misunderstood as meaning imprecise or imperfect. Many practitioners believe that fuzzy logic represents some magic solution without concrete mathematical models.

7. Finally, other problems will arise simply because people will try to apply fuzzy logic to situations which are far more suited to traditional reasoning. People will see that fuzzy logic has helped others and thus try to throw a solution at a problem without stopping to think about their needs.

FUZZY LOGIC HYBRIDS

Fuzzy logic can effectively be integrated with other technologies such as expert systems, neural networks, and genetic algorithms. By applying one or more of these techniques in unison, the hybrid system can increase speed, fault tolerance, and overall effectiveness. It is also possible to choose the strongest feature of each application and add it to the integrated system. The integrated system should be stronger than the contributing system. In the following sections we briefly explain the hybrid systems of fuzzy logic, neural networks, ES, and genetic algorithms.

Neural Networks

In the next chapter we will discuss neural networks in detail. Neural networks attempt to bring a learning capability into computer applications. A combination of fuzzy logic and neural networks used in National Semiconductor's Neufuz is a popular example of the integration of these two applications [3]. Input and output data and application parameters are fed into the neural networks that then pass knowledge and data to a fuzzy-rule and membership-function generator. These rules are then verified and optimized before the process moves to an automatic code generator that produces microcontroller assembly code.

Neural networks and fuzzy logic have complementary strengths [17]. Neural networks, saving countless hours of work for the developer, easily handle the front-end processing that sorts fuzzy logic's rules and membership functions. They learn the importance of each rule and, given time (and sometimes some help), will readjust those rules that need to be changed. Neural networks can work on all levels of a fuzzy-based tool, working toward being perfectly self-maintaining. The following are specific advantages that a neural network adds to a neural-fuzzy hybrid: prediction capabilities, selection capabilities, and mechanical subjective analysis [16]. These properties are especially useful in financial analysis, as will be discussed later.

Expert Systems

ES and fuzzy logic make incredibly powerful hybrids. ES add a knowledge base, working memory, and an inference engine to a hybrid.

By using fuzzy logic, ES can make predictions with degrees of certainty, instead of making bold sweeping statements. Several authors underscore the importance of ES that can now learn and adapt to an ever-changing environment [19, 27]. Before hybrids were used, an ES would work well until crashing catastrophically. Now an ES can learn from past experiences but also cope with unforeseen exceptions that would otherwise lead to its demise. Expert traders can now be utilized on stock markets without making an extreme decision that could be very costly.

Genetic Algorithms

Although not as widely accepted, genetic algorithms are becoming more recognized as a form of artificial intelligence that lets machine thought processes evolve. As with natural selection and evolution, GAs reproduce in various recombination, each time hoping to find a new recombinant that will be better adapted than their predecessors. GAs are emerging as a new way to look at problems in their entirety or in large chunks instead of in one piece at a time [11].

John Holland originated the concept of GAs in the 1940s while he was working at MIT. The term *genetic algorithm* applies to a set of adaptive procedures used in a computer system that are based on Darwin's theory of natural selection and survival of the fittest. A GA can put complicated items of information into a simple bit string that represents a solution to the current problem. The GA then refines the solution through an evolutionary process until an acceptable solution is found. The original bit strings are just a "guess at a solution," and the evolutionary process imitates the processes of reproduction and natural selection [6].

GAs can examine complex problems without any assumptions of what the correct answer or solution should be. There is no one best way to start, and the computer does not need vast amounts of variables to be input by the user. It is an interactive process and can adapt quickly to reach an acceptable solution [15]. GAs are already being used in conjunction with neural nets and fuzzy computing systems to solve problems in areas like scheduling, engineering design, and marketing. For example, a docking truck algorithm uses neural net and fuzzy functions in conjunction with a GA to find the best and shortest route for a robot to take to a docking bay around obstacles and between walls [22]. Metropolitan Insurance uses a GA called Evolver from Axcelis to solve insurance financial problems [15].

To begin a discussion of GAs, you should know how a GA is set up and what basic operations are carried out. The first and most basic item is a chromosome.

It is a list of items shown as a binary number that represents a solution to the problem. Each item in the chromosome is called a gene and is one part of the solution. A creator operation starts the GA by developing an initial population of chromosomes that are possible solutions [12].

An evaluator or fitness function rates the chromosomes on their ability to solve the problem and passes the best ones on to a generator. The generator or genetic operator carries out mutations and crossovers on the chromosomes that were passed on. These are recombined with selected mates to create new chromosomes, and a replacement strategy is then carried out to keep the population size constant. Finally, the generation cycle is repeated [12].

GAs cannot be used for every type of optimization problem. A prerequisite to using GAs is that the correct solution must be able to be represented as a bit string. Also, one must note that rules used in one situation may not work in another, even if the two problems are very similar. To overcome this problem, a technique called "breeding" can be used. It is a method of getting the computers to learn how to solve problems for themselves. However, to breed correct solutions there must be reproduction and crossover breeding (crossbreeding) [18].

Reproduction (the breeding cycle) creates a new generation of possible solutions that are "more fit" by selecting answers that have a high weight figured by the fitness function. In crossbreeding, nodes are randomly selected from each of two potential solutions; the nodes are then switched [22].

Mutation occurs in a single chromosome in one of the following two ways: (1) order-based mutation occurs when two genes within the same chromosome switch places; and (2) position-based mutation occurs when one gene is placed in front of another within the same chromosome [12]. The chromosomes are then evaluated by a fitness function that determines the best solution of the population by assigning weights. The solutions with the worst fitness score are eliminated to make room for the new offspring chromosomes, and the chromosomes with the highest or above average fitness scores are allowed to contribute more than one copy of themselves to the offspring chromosomes. The GA then starts the process over with reproduction and crossover, focusing the majority of its activity on the chromosomes that are most closely related to the solutions with the highest fitness scores [22].

There are some precautions to take when setting up or coding a GA problem. There are a few parameters that have a major effect on how fast the optimum solution is found. The first parameter is population size. If you have a large population size, it takes a long time to carry out the process, but there is a wide range of diversity. A population size of ten seems to be an optimal size. As a rule, fewer than ten does not work well, and greater than ten takes a long time with no visible advantages [21].

The other parameters that have a major effect are mutation, crossbreeding, and number of tests or iterations. Mutations should be used only to make sure duplication of members does not occur. Care must be taken to ensure the right amount of crossbreeding. If no crossbreeding is done, no new structures will be created; however, if all crossbreeding is done, good genes will disappear. It has been recommended that approximately 90 percent of the population be crossbred. The number of tests or iterations of the GA needs to be regulated also. The more tests there are, the slower the GA will be in coming to an optimal solution but the more accurate it will be [21].

FUZZY LOGIC APPLICATIONS

Fuzzy logic, in a relatively short period, has established itself as a successful concept. The next few sections provide a listing of some of the successful applications of fuzzy logic.

Microelectronics

Motorola, Intel Corporation, Hitachi, National Semiconductor Corporation, and VLSI Technology are all actively working on their own microprocessors that implement fuzzy logic [14]. Intel and Hitachi made the news in 1992 by launching their fuzzy logic processors' 32-bit controllers. VLSI Technology also made the headlines in the same year when they teamed up with Togai Infralogic to design their new embedded controllers on 32-bit processors. The new controllers can be designed in a 10-bit configuration but can range from 8-bit to 32-bit in performance [13]. The activity in designing these new embedded controllers is the backbone of the appliances and electronic applications in which fuzzy logic has been successfully utilized. Without these new controllers, fuzzy logic would not be as cost effective or as powerful.

Transportation

The underground train in Japan was the breakthrough that stirred a more concerted interest in fuzzy-based control systems. Other systems have mimicked this application on a smaller scale, allowing transportation to be controlled without the need of human drivers. Other areas of transportation include many parts of new automobiles. Anti-lock breaking systems, automatic transmissions, and smart airbags that are released only in potentially harmful conditions are just some examples of the ways in which fuzzy logic has entered the automobile industries.

Government

The military is a natural user of fuzzy logic. As with many new sciences, progress and research can depend heavily on the amount of money a government puts into its own projects. Fuzzy logic could be harnessed in numerous areas of the military from ES to using intelligent missiles. NASA is also a major investor and user of fuzzy-based control systems in various areas of space programs.

Home Appliances

Home appliances have brought fuzzy logic into our homes with many consumers not even knowing that it is there. Washing machines that know what settings to use from soil contents in the water and toasters that will refuse to burn bread are just the tip of the iceberg. Perhaps these applications do not appear to be that clever, but these products would not be able to perform such intricate functions for such low costs without the aid of fuzzy controllers. The following are other applications of fuzzy systems in homes:

air conditioner: prevents overshoot, undershoot, and temperature oscillation and consumes less on–off power

dryer: converts load size, fabric type, and flow of hot air to drying times and conditions

elevator control: reduces waiting time based on passenger traffic

humidifier: adjusts moisture contents to room conditions

microwave oven: sets and tunes cooking conditions

refrigerator: sets defrosting and cooling times based on usage

rice cooker: sets cooking time and method based on steam, temperature, and the amount of rice in the pot

shower system: suppresses variations in water temperature

still camera: finds an object anywhere in the frame and adjusts autofocus

television set: adjusts screen's color and texture for each frame and stabilizes volume based on viewer's location in the room

vacuum cleaner: sets motor-suction condition based on dust quantity and floor type

video camcorder: eliminates hand-held jittering and adjusts autofocus and lighting

Robotics and Appliances

Artificial intelligence has been struggling for years to simulate human walking. Companies have been unable to mimic what appears to be a simple process. Omron Corporation of Japan uses fuzzy technology to drive an eight-motor, two-legged robot. Numerically programmed set patterns have never been able to smooth out the motion of robotic legs. Fuzzy sensors in the biped allow intuitive decisions from approximately twenty commands. The robot can even adjust its gait according to changes in the surface it is walking on. This achievement is all that more remarkable when one realizes that a human leg uses several hundred muscles to produce the same movement [20].

Financial Management

Artificial traders using traditional methods were known to work perfectly before crashing as soon as any extenuating circumstances arose. This was not acceptable, and so people began to shun the idea of an ES of any type managing billions of dollars. The hybrid fuzzy-neural-expert systems can now learn from the past and also react to a continuously changing environment. If the conditions change, the rules change, making the system utilize its superior processing power and yet emulate human responses in times of volatility. Artificial traders incorporate risk assessment, forecasting, and decision support.

The world of finance has also utilized fuzzy logic to do detective work [7]. The London Stock Exchange is poised to implement a fraud-detection system that blends neural networks with fuzzy logic. The networks are used to spot patterns in insider dealing, unveiling all of the techniques used to aid illegal activities. Fuzzy logic helps the system by allowing for contingencies when actions do not follow a perfect pattern but are still highly suspicious. A system called Monitors System can even work by itself, setting its own parameters. The legal sector will be very interested to see how the trials of those caught by the artificial system will be conducted.

Database Management Systems

Despite much cynicism and skepticism, fuzzy logic has already moved into relational DBMS. Fuzzy words stored in databases appear to be useless and unmanageable. It would be quite interesting to be able to make statistical analyses about tall, middle aged, and other data items. Future development in fuzzy logic should make this powerful application a reality.

Systems Development

Hyperlogic Corporation released Rulemaker in April 1995 to add to an existing fuzzy-based tool called CubiCalc. This tool uses statistical analysis, heuristic methods, edge enhancement, data filtering, center emphasis, and user-defined manipulation options. These features make it possible to work with sparse data and other ad hoc situations [1].

Software Development

Byte Dynamics, Inc., markets a CASE tool that creates portable C code for rule-based analysis applications. The graphic capabilities of this tool allow contour planes, surface plots, and three-dimensional simulation modes to be drafted.

MATLAB has been combined with the Fuzzy Logic Toolbox for creating an intuitive software environment that combines easy-to-use fuzzy logic modeling for practical engineering design. This package allows a comparison of fuzzy and traditional methods; an evaluation of fuzzy designs; the use of a fuzzy inference system; the use of a membership function editor; and the use of a rule editor.

Decision Support

FuziWare Incorporated has two tools on the market that enable decision makers to use a decision support aid that can deal with fuzzy inputs. FuziQuote includes a number of capabilities. Decision makers must teach the package about the operating environment, and the tool will then learn to make rapid decisions based on past history and other changing parameters. FuziCalc allows decision makers to manipulate fuzzy inputs and outputs as graphs that are easy to understand and can be related back to a spreadsheet. FuziCalc allows users to run simultaneous what-if analyses on vast amounts of data. FuziCalc can run under a regular Windows environment.

The following are other tools and platforms used for fuzzy system development: Fuldex (TSI Enterprises), Fuzzy Decision Maker (Fuzzy Systems Engineering), MultiFuzz (MSI Corporation), and TILShell (Togai Infralogic).

OUTLOOK FOR FUZZY LOGIC

Before making a forecast of what the future holds for fuzzy logic, it is pertinent to discuss an application that, although it has not been implemented, appears to be a very realistic probability. An article written by Lance Eliot discusses the implications of a recent proposal made by H. Hosmer [5].

There is no question that the information superhighway is expanding almost exponentially, and the number of people using it is almost doubling every year. More than forty million people are using it already in the United States. We are living in the information age, with the industrial age past maturity and into decline. Consequentially, information and data now fly through networks and highways whether you want it or not. Hosmer's proposal predicts that fuzzy logic could be the answer to the rising issue of how to maintain security measures on the information superhighway. Hosmer argues that wherever a continuum is found, fuzzy classes may be appropriate [5]. For example, business-sensitive data like strategic plans and financial data may be a company priority to a higher or lower degree. Employees and customers may have a varying requirement for privacy for their data. Both integrity and availability are measured along one or more continua.

Using the traditional method of classification, security restrictions would have to specify whether someone has access to each category of security clearance, as always. Fuzzy logic, however, could change this by allowing varying degrees of membership to security specifications. Information that was therefore private from particular individuals from day to day could be changed to be accessible as necessary information if circumstances were to change. This could be done without having to work through a bureaucracy that would often prevent important changes from being made.

To clarify this discussion and to give a real-life application that is foreseeable, Eliot's article looks at the health care industry. Here there is private-sensitive data about employees, hospital-privileged information about finance and plans, integrity-sensitive information for accounting and payroll, and, of course, sensitive data about patients [5]. A patient's name would be rated as low for security, whereas medical records would be high security. Rules could determine accessibility, but rules would also allow exceptions to be made in deciding who sees what and when. Patient information could be protected, but in the case of emergencies a health care giver might need to know everything about a patient who needs attention immediately. The health care industry is just an example; the same principles will apply to many industries that will need ever-changing security needs in an ever-changing environment.

Forces Influencing Fuzzy Logic Development

Maytag and Admiral Products, who have been extremely successful with their IntelliSense product used in fuzzy-based washing machines, see certain factors in the near future that have pushed them toward developing smarter products. Energy will become more expensive; therefore, washing machines and dishwashers that can work effectively using less energy will become increasingly more valuable. In the near future, water management will become one of the important considerations in many communities. Already several states have implemented some kind of restrictions on water usage. Water shortages in the western United States will create an even bigger need for more efficient fuzzy-based machines that can make decisions to use water more sparingly without hurting performance. The government is also indirectly helping fuzzy-based product development by pushing water and energy regulations that demand higher standards [4].

The most obvious force acting on the future is money. If fuzzy logic allows a company to install a more powerful processor at a lower cost, it is bound to be accepted. Using fuzzy-based tools in design, development, and redesign can now help companies provide new products more quickly. Motorola has given the name "natural computing" to fuzzy logic, neural networks, GAs, and their integration. Jim Huffman from Motorola adds that these technologies allow us to "deal with the real world in natural ways." The end result that will be visible in the future is that natural computing equates to more cost-effective, high-performing products for every type of user or consumer [8].

Training and Support for Fuzzy Logic

Fuzzy logic development tools are approximately one-fifth as costly as their CASE tool counterparts in today's marketplace. Educating a workforce in the new technology does, however, initially offset some of these advantages. Training and support will naturally rise in both real terms and as a percentage of sales [26].

Payoff in Fuzzy Logic Development

Time and money saved by companies and individuals who utilize fuzzy logic development tools cannot be quantified exactly because each case depends on the user and specific application. If an expert knows exactly what a system needs, then fuzzy-based tools will continue to reduce development time to as little as one-fifth of the traditional cycle. Traditional mathematical models will not become extinct, but fuzzy logic will provide a better working environment when systems are ambiguous and qualitative and a high degree of complexity is involved.

Today, fuzzy logic provides a competitive edge for companies who have already applied many of its capabilities. In the future, fuzzy logic and fuzzy hybrids will become a natural part of business applications and product design. Fuzzy logic has paved the way to a future with intelligent machines.

SUMMARY

This chapter provided a discussion of fuzzy logic systems as one of the growing concepts within the MSS field, commonly used terminology, and the working process of a fuzzy logic system. It also introduced advantages, disadvantages, and popular applications of fuzzy logic systems and reviewed hybrid systems that can benefit from fuzzy logic, including ES, neural networks, and GAs. The chapter concluded with an outlook for the future development of fuzzy logic systems.

REFERENCES

1. "Adapt That Fuzzy System: Hyperlogics Rule Maker Add-On for CubiCalc." *AI Expert* (April 1995): 46.
2. Anderson, Glenn. "Fuzzy Logic: What It Is, What It Does, What It Can Do." *Production* 106 (October 1994): 38.
3. Barron, Janet. "Putting Fuzzy Logic into Focus." *Byte* (April 1993): 111–118.
4. Beatty, Gerry. "Future Shock: Consumers Remain Wary of High Tech Appliance Features." *HFD—The Weekly Home Furnishings Newspaper* 68 (November 28, 1994): 50.
5. Eliot, Lance B. "Data Highway Needs Fuzzy Logic." *AI Expert* (January 1994): 9.
6. Holland, John H. "Genetic Algorithms." *Scientific American* (July 1992): 66–72.
7. Houlder, Vanessa. "Tackling Insider Dealing with Fuzzy Logic." *Financial Times* (September 29, 1994): 16.
8. Huffman, Jim. "Natural Computing Is in Your Future." *Appliance Manufacturer* (February 1994): 10.
9. Kong, Seong-Gon, and Bart Kosko. "Adaptive Fuzzy Systems for Baking up a Truck-and-Track." *IEEE Transaction on Neural Networks* (March 1991): 211–233.
10. Kosko, Bart. *Fuzzy Thinking: The New Science of Fuzzy Logic.* New York: Hyperion Publishing, 1993.
11. Lane, Alex. "Programming with Genes." *AI Expert* (December 1993): 23–27.
12. Lawton, George. "Genetic Algorithms for Schedule Optimization." *AI Expert* (May 1991): 23–27.
13. Lineback, Robert J. "VLSI Technology to Use Fuzzy Logic From Togai Infralogic in ASIC Line." *Electronic News* 38 (July 20, 1992): 134.

14. Rice, Valerie. "You Want Your Coffee How? No Problem for Fuzzy Logic." *Electronic Business* (November 1992): 122–126.
15. Rubkin, Baury. "Applying Principles of Biology to Business Problems." *National Underwriter, Property & Casualty/Risk and Benefits Management Edition* (February 22, 1993): 39–40.
16. Ruggiero, Murray. "How to Build an Artificial Trader." *Futures: Management Commodities & Options* 23 (September 1994): 56.
17. Shandle, Jack. "Fuzzy Logic Is Shoddy; It's Half-Baked Image, Easy to Use Tools, and a Symbolic Relationship with Neural Networks Will Make the Difference." *Electronic Design* (March 21, 1994): 75.
18. Sibigotroth, James M. "Implementing Fuzzy Expert Rules in Hardware." *AI Expert* (April 1992): 25–31.
19. Stein, John. "Expert Systems Enter Gray Area of Gray Matter." *Futures* (August 1991): 16–18.
20. Ven, Sreenivasan. "Clear Grains for Fuzzy Logic." *Innovation & Technology* (December 16, 1993): 15.
21. Wayner, Peter. "Genetic Algorithms." *Byte* (January 1991): 361–364.
22. Wiggins, Ralph. "Docking a Truck: A Genetic Fuzzy Approach." *AI Expert* (May 1992): 28–35.
23. Williams, Tom. "Fuzzy Logic Is Anything but Fuzzy." *Computer Design* (April 1992): 113–127.
24. Williams, Tom. "Fuzzy Logic to Make Rapid Inroads in the Next Five Years." *Computer Design* (July 1993): 43.
25. Williams, Tom. "Fuzzy Logic Simplifies Complex Control Problems." *Computer Design* (March 1, 1991): 90–102.
26. Wong, F. S., P. Z. Wang, T. H. Goh, and B. K. Quek. "Fuzzy Neural Systems for Stock Selection." *Financial Analysts Journal* (January/February 1992): 47–52.
27. Zadeh, Lotfi A. "The Role of Fuzzy Logic in the Management of Uncertainty in Expert Systems." *Fuzzy Sets and Systems* 2 (November 1983): 199–228.
28. Zadeh, Lotfi A. "Yes, No, and Relatively, Part 1." *Chemtech* (June 1987): 340–344.
29. Zadeh, Lotfi A. "Yes, No, and Relatively Part 2." *Chemtech* (July 1987): 406–410.

CHAPTER 10

Neural Networks and Their Business Applications

This chapter provides a detailed discussion of neural networks and compares and contrasts neural computing with digital computing. It discusses the similarities and dissimilarities of neural networks and ES and explains various types of pattern recognition as it is being applied in the real world. The chapter discusses in detail the working fundamentals of a neural network and various learning techniques. The advantages and disadvantages of neural networks and different applications of these systems will be discussed. The chapter concludes with a sample listing of products and services for neural networks design and utilization.

NEURAL COMPUTING: AN OVERVIEW

As we briefly discussed in Chapter 1, neural computing (or neural networks) is one of the new multidisciplinary research fields that has grown because of the study of the brain and its potential for solving poorly structured business problems. Neural networks are capable of performing tasks that conventional computers find difficult. Neural computing technology is also known as connectionism and parallel-distributed processing. These names come from the fact that a neural network connects a number of independent CPUs to perform a task, very similar to the human brain, which uses numerous neurons to perform a task. The computers that we come in contact with in our daily lives are based on the architecture laid down by John Von Neuman.

Similar to ES, neural computing is used for poorly structured problems. Unlike ES, neural computing is not able to explain its solution, because neural computing uses "patterns" versus "rules" used by ES. A neural network uses a large amount of connected microprocessors and software that tackle a problem in a unified rather than a sequential manner. A neural network learns by doing various tasks. Neural networks learn by creating a model based on its input and output.

For example, in a loan application problem the input data are income, assets, number of dependents, job history, and residential status, and the output data are acceptance or rejection of the loan applications. By using many of these loan applications, the neural network establishes a pattern for an application to be approved or rejected [21]. Other areas of applications for neural computing are characteristics of potential oil fields, diagnosing automobile engine problems, and analysis of price and volume patterns in stock trading. Generally speaking, neural computing is suitable in applications where data are fuzzy and uncertainty is involved.

To be precise, a neural network is the complex system of interconnected nerve cells that communicates, processes, and stores information in all animals. Although natural neural networks form the conceptual basis for the current flurry of research into this subcategory of the broad field of artificial intelligence, it is artificial neural networks (ANN) that are the real focus of this attention. Indeed, whereas the natural neural network is comprised of the brain as well as the skeletal nervous system, current research in ANN seems to have completely focused on imitating brain functions [15, 17].

ANN, which we will refer to as simply neural networks, are an attempt to imitate the structure and function of a natural neural network in computer hardware and software. Many authors equate neural networks with "neural computers," on the basis of their apparent belief that special purpose computers (typically multiprocessor-based) are required to implement neural networks. To others, neural networks are a form of a logical information-processing architecture that can be implemented on any computer. For practical, real-world applications, the business requirements will dictate the processing speed that is necessary to accomplish the desired task (such as detecting explosives in airport baggage or detecting the fingerprint of a suspect among millions of criminals' fingerprints stored in a database). This speed or throughput requirement will dictate the processing power needed to drive the network hardware and software. Any computer that can provide the necessary power can be considered a candidate for implementing the neural network. By this description, we can say that massive parallel processor computers would be a reasonable candidate for the implementation of neural computing.

NEURAL COMPUTING VERSUS DIGITAL COMPUTING

For the basis of discussion, neural networks can be said to be a computer with an internal structure that imitates the human brain's interconnected system of neurons (nerve cells). In neural networks, transistor circuits are the hardware analog of neurons, and variable resistors represent the synapses (interfaces) between contiguous neurons [6]. Electric signals received by the transistor circuits are either inhibited or enhanced (depending on the task the neural network is performing) when they are passed on to neighboring circuits. This inhibit/enhance process is performed in a manner that is analogous to the way in which the brain's neurons pass on electrochemical signals.

Neural networks are similar to the human brain in that they do not rigidly follow programmed rules, as the typical digital computer does. Instead, the network builds an information base through an exhaustive series of trial-and-error sessions. As an example, a "trainer" (a programmer in the broadest sense) may input the digital representation of a photographic image for the neural network to identify. The network will "guess" which circuits to "fire" (activate) to identify the photograph and output the correct answer. If the "trainer" determines that the answer is correct, a positive indication will be given to the network (a form of virtual reward) and the pathways that were used to come up with the correct answer will be strengthened by having the resistance turned down. In this manner, the neural network learns from its successes, and this positive feedback further increases the probability that the network will respond correctly the next time the same image is presented [4].

If the network responds incorrectly, as it almost certainly will until its knowledge base is well developed, a negative indication will be given to the network (a form of virtual punishment). This will cause the pathways that were used to come up with the wrong answer to be weakened by having the resistance turned up. This process will decrease the probability that the network will respond with the same wrong answer the next time the same image is presented, thereby increasing the likelihood that the correct answer will be given the next time. In this way, a neural network "learns" from its mistakes (as indicated by feedback from its trainer) and gives more accurate output with each repetition of a task [16, 26].

This dependence on trial-and-error learning for developing the correct output for a given set of inputs is a unique characteristic of neural networks. Virtually all other applications of digital computers involve one form of programming or another in which a human programmer dictates in a step-by-step fashion how the computer is to process the input data. With neural networks, the process is not defined—only the results of the operation are fed back to the network with positive or negative connotations [22]. Indeed, many neural networks are designed to learn from positive and negative feedback stated in terms of degrees of rightness and wrongness ("very nearly correct," "way off," "close, but not exact"). In this way, neural networks can be considered to be black boxes whose inner workings do not need to be understood in order for the trainer to make them work. In fact, the knowledge base of a neural network is stored as variations in the resistance along pathways connecting the input processors to the output processors learned as the results of various trials were fed back to the network [19]. With this approach, the knowledge base is actually stored within the network itself. This is in contrast to the typical information system that is made up of "hard coded" programs and an external database wherein input data are stored exactly as they were input for later retrieval. Table 10.1 provides a concise comparison between digital and neural computers [8].

ES VERSUS NEURAL NETWORKS

As we have said all along, ES are rule-based systems that have proven to be successful where the domain is narrow and the knowledge about the domain is available. In other words, the problems addressed by ES have previously been successfully solved by a human expert. On the other side, neural networks deal with problems that are not rule-based and have not been solved by a human expert, but there are numerous cases available of these kinds of problems. Table 10.2 provides a comparison of rule-based and neural network systems [2, 7].

PATTERN RECOGNITION: AN OVERVIEW

At the present time, neural networks are the most useful products in the analysis and recognition of patterns. Although ongoing and future research may identify additional applications for neural networks, at the present time

Table 10.1
Comparison between Digital and Neural Computing

Digital Computers	Neural Networks
Process digital data that are written in 1's and 0's for mathematical precision	Process analog signals that fluctuate continuously, providing a range from, say, black through all shades of gray to white
Make yes/no decisions using mathematical and logical functions	Make weighted decisions on the basis of fuzzy, incomplete, and contradictory data
Handle data in a rigidly structured sequence so that operations are always under control and results are predictable	Independently formulate methods of processing data, often with surprising results
Find precise answers to any problem, given enough time	Find good, quick--but approximate--answers to highly complex problems
Sort through large databases to find exact matches	Sort through large databases to find close matches
Store information so that specific data can be retrieved easily	Store information so that retrieving any piece of information automatically calls up all related facts

Optical Pattern Recognition

There are three stages in optical pattern recognition: image processing, pattern classification, and scene analysis. Image processing takes many forms (depending on the type of image) but is concerned with sharpening the edges of patterns to make classification easier, quicker, and more accurate [29]. Pattern classification interprets specific items in the processed image such as facial features, letters of the alphabet, numbers, or other characteristics of interest. Many applications of neural networks for optical pattern recognition have been reported, and several are in wide use.

The most successful neural network application to date is in the area of optical character readers (OCR) or scanners [22]. These applications recognize handwritten characters, both printing and script, as well as machine-generated characters. In the military, neural networks have been developed to analyze radar images to detect friendly and unfriendly aircraft. Law enforcement agencies use optical pattern recognition to match fingerprints taken from arrested individuals and found at the crime scene with prints previously recorded to identify criminals [11]. A widely discussed goal is the development of machine or robotic vision systems that could allow moving images to be analyzed and recognized with a high degree of accuracy. This application would be useful in space or in situations that are hazardous, unsafe, or otherwise not suitable for a human.

Sound Pattern Recognition

In order for sound patterns to be recognized by a digital computer, the continuous wave form of the sound must be translated from its analog representation into a digital form that can be analyzed by a computer. Virtually all current applications of sound-pattern recognition are implemented using digital computers that "slice" sounds into their discrete elements [19]. The slow speed typical of these applications is adequate for most uses involving the recognition of human speech because humans speak rather slowly and the information content of their speech is relatively low. New applications of speech recognition utilizing neural networks offer much greater accuracy and throughput [27]. Some researchers hope to achieve even higher performance by utilizing analog computers for their neural networks applications. By eliminating the need to convert the sound to its digital representation, technologists hope to achieve levels of performance comparable to that currently found in some mammals (whales and bats) that use sound as a primary source of information about their environments. This research is currently hampered by the relatively poor performance of current analog computers, which have been virtually ignored in the recent race to maximize the performance of digital devices [2].

Current examples of voice recognition systems are capable of recognizing a very limited vocabulary. Virtually all existing systems are limited to recognizing

Table 10.2
Rule-Based versus Neural Network Systems

Rule-Based Systems	Neural Network Systems
Excellent explanation capability	Little or no explanation capabili
Requires an articulate expert to develop	Requires many examples, but n needed
Many turnkey shells are available	Few turnkey shells available; m customized for your application
Average development time is twelve to eighteen months	Development time is as little as f months
Preferred system when examples are few and an expert is available	Preferred system when examples an expert is not available
Many successful, fielded systems are available for public reference	Few successful, fielded systems a for public reference
Large systems can be unwieldy and difficult to maintain if not carefully developed and designed	Large networks cannot be built too networks can be hierarchically linl complex problems, making them r maintainable
Systems are built through knowledge extraction and rule-based development	Systems are built through training examples
Accepted validation procedures for completed system	Validation of completed system is statistical analysis of performance
Works fine on ordinary digital computers	For all but the smallest networks, b performance comes from use with a assisted or specialized parallel chip

it is most concentrated in the area of pattern recognition. In this co
tern recognition refers to the analysis of the complex processes in
recognizing patterns in input data. In humans, the sense organs i
from the outside world as well as sensations originating within
These data are then transmitted across the skeletal nerve network to
for processing. The field of artificial pattern recognition is involved
design and manufacture of artificial systems that achieve simila
whether utilizing the same methods or not. In particular, the vast m
current interest in the field is in mimicking sight (optical pattern rec
and hearing (sound pattern recognition). In addition, much interest is o
being focused upon the recognition of patterns in data (data pattern
tion), a process that appears to be without an analog in natural systems
probably the most important area as far as business decisions are concer

sounds made by a single individual when spoken at no more than one sound per second [27]. However, the capabilities of these systems are steadily increasing. The physical condition of the speaker as well as the type and volume of background noise further influence the ability of artificial devices to recognize speech. Advances in programming techniques made possible by the neural networks and the massive parallelism usually found in these systems seem to offer researchers a level of performance that was previously unavailable.

Additional Forms of Pattern Recognition

It is widely known that animals possess the ability to recognize patterns in stimuli that enter the brain through media other than sight and sound. Principle among these additional input media in animals are the senses of smell (a form of chemical pattern recognition) and touch (tactile pattern recognition). Anecdotal evidence also suggests that some animals possess the ability to recognize patterns caused by gravity, air pressure, and magnetic fields, as well as various types of polarized and nonpolarized radiation [24]. Although there are few references in the literature to attempts at developing neural networks to exploit these sources of data, there is little reason to doubt that we will be able to do so in the near future.

Recognizing Patterns in Data

Although the study of neural networks got its start in attempts by humans to mimic biological processes, the application of this technology to recognizing patterns in stored data—a capability not well developed in animals—may offer the greatest benefits. As enormous volumes of stored data recording past events become available in computer-readable form, the desire to utilize these data to predict future events becomes virtually unbearable. The potential financial and social rewards that would accrue to those who can anticipate the future have been a key element of mankind's folklore and dreams since the beginning of recorded history. The ability of neural networks to process huge amounts of data in search of patterns without having to be told what to look for makes these devices remarkably well suited to this endeavor. Although some reports of attempts to use neural networks to predict future events can be found in the literature [17, 25], we can expect any real successes that result in financial gain to be kept very quiet.

Some researchers have found that banks that are prone to failure exhibit similar characteristics [25]. Others have found that neural networks can identify patterns that allow credit applications to be processed with lower default rates than conventional techniques [17]. Still other applications of neural networks for financial decision making involve the search for patterns that provide insight into asset valuations and investment decisions [11]. The *Wall Street Journal* and other financial publications frequently entertain their readers with stories about computer experts turned investment advisors, or vice versa, who have utilized neural networks to quickly analyze reams of real-time financial data. Armed with identifiable patterns and calculated risk factors derived from analyzing historical information, these systems are said to identify arbitrage opportunities and investment options in real time. This technology, in the hands of experts, is said to allow split-second investment decisions to be reached and orders placed before humans or slower computers know what is going on.

Recognizing Hidden Patterns

Although much good will certainly come from the use of neural networks in identifying and processing known types of patterns, it is very likely that the discovery of patterns that are so subtle that we neglect to even consider their existence will offer the greatest rewards for mankind. Because neural networks, once constructed, are capable of correlating events whose relationships are very small, "pure research," devoid of predetermined goals, may offer discoveries in areas where we would never think to look. For example, by analyzing the genetic code [24] and identifying patterns in health, behavior, education, social contribution, and a myriad of other factors, insight into the successes and failures of our social systems can be gained. In addition, the ability to utilize conventional statistical analysis to further process and quantify the patterns identified by the neural networks will allow even the most skeptical of researchers to feel comfortable with the results.

The key to the unique ability of neural networks to identify patterns in data without having to be specifically programmed to do so lies in their architecture. Whereas virtually all information systems (including artificial intelligence applications) are based on predefined heuristic processes, neural networks are designed to recognize and identify stochastic processes [10]. A stochastic process is a mechanism of phenomenon that evolves or occurs randomly in time, such as the flow of traffic at a signal-controlled intersection. As compared to heuristic events that are inherently predictable (if you know the rules), the characteristic feature of a stochastic process is its inherent randomness and apparent immunity to predictive rules.

With a stochastic process, at each instant in time there is a random variable that describes the current state of the process—the number of cars waiting at the intersection, for example. A stochastic process is defined by the collection of random variables, one for each distinct instant in time. The most basic example of a stochastic process (and the one most frequently cited in the literature) is the random walk [20]. This is the motion of a particle that at a sequence of times is moved one unit to the right or to the left with probabilities that do not change.

Through the use of neural networks, enormous quantities of data can be analyzed to isolate events or conditions that are correlated in some manner with the particular events under study. Neither causal relationships nor rules need to be established if the neural network is capable of identifying related (hopefully preceding) events. Only a pattern with a certain probability of occurrence is required for some predictive capability to be present. If a legitimate predictive capability can be identified by correlating one or more seemingly random and unpredictable events, the benefits may be enormous. This capability of neural networks to find patterns where none were thought to exist gives them a potential power that is difficult to fully comprehend [6]. It is now easy to see, however, the recent interest being shown by financial markets in neural networks (as well as the scarcity of literature documenting the degree of success being achieved in their use as market prognosticators).

HOW NEURAL NETWORKS WORK: AN OVERVIEW

Typical information systems excel at raw number crunching and often possess the power to store and retrieve large amounts of data in seconds—things humans do poorly. This is the source of their great value to business organizations. It is ironic that these systems perform poorly at tasks at which humans excel—the ability to utilize inductive reasoning and the ability to draw inferences by recognizing subtle patterns. Neural networks attempt to address the shortcomings of conventional information systems by utilizing a unique architecture [20]. They attempt to model and replicate human intuition by simulating the physical processes upon which intuition is based. To accomplish this, neural networks simulate the processes of adaptive learning utilized by biological organisms—on a much smaller scale. A neural network is theoretically capable of giving the proper response (or the best response if more than one response is applicable) to a given problem even when there is no previously defined procedure for solving the problem. In addition, neural networks are capable of doing this even when the input information is noisy or incomplete [11].

Because of this seeming ability to find order within disorder, neural networks are much better suited to support semistructured and unstructured decisions than are conventional systems. They are able to do this because they are modeled after the form and function of the human nervous system. Neural networks possess the ability to learn through repetition—a uniquely biological trait. They do this by mimicking the structure and the basic function of the human brain—the neuron or nerve cell [12]. Artificial neurons serve as the basic functional element of the neural network in much the same way as binary electronic switches serve as the basic elements in digital computers.

A biological neuron is a relatively simple structure that is capable of performing only three basic functions: They can input signals from the environment; they can process the signals; and they can output the signals to another neuron or to a structure that can act on the signal (like a muscle). The input components (called dendrites) receive electrochemical impulses from the output components of other neurons (called axons) or directly from sensory organs. Dendrites are similar to roads and highways connecting various towns (neurons). In the human brain, each neuron may be connected to one thousand or more neurons through a complex network of dendrites and axons. It is in this network of interconnections that the brain achieves its remarkable speed [28].

The central processing unit of the neuron (the nucleus) operates very simply. The neuron's many dendrites (input structures) receive impulses from other contiguous neurons and transfer these impulses to the nucleus. The nucleus collects these impulses, sums them, and then compares the sum to an output threshold called an "action potential." This action potential is the level of stimulation ("activation level") necessary for the neuron to fire or send an impulse through its axon to other neurons to which it is connected. Research on neurons indicates that, as a rule, they are about one thousand times slower than the digital switches in conventional computers. Because neurons are not getting any faster and computer processors are, the already wide speed gap between natural and artificial neurons is getting wider each year.

Even with this speed deficit at the neuron level, the brain is able to resolve difficult pattern recognition problems (such as vision and language) in about one-half of a second. This is in contrast to conventional digital computers that are incapable of resolving even simple pattern recognition tasks. The brain is able to achieve its remarkable speed and processing power because a very large number of inherently slow neurons are linked together into highly complex networks. This network allows many individual neurons to operate (almost) simultaneously on the same task. In reality, the connected neurons earlier in the network (closer to the input) stimulate neurons later in the network (closer to the output) to begin processing the impulse before the earlier neurons have finished. In this way, the operation of the individual neurons in the network is overlapped, not truly simultaneous [10].

How Neural Networks Work: Hardware Aspects

Notwithstanding this minor inaccuracy, both the brain and neural networks are characterized as exhibiting a processing mode referred to as "parallel-distributed processing" (PDP). This term is given to any device or system that subdivides tasks into separable elements for simultaneous completion [15, 26]. Although overlapped processing does not truly represent parallelism in its pure form, this minor distinction is generally overlooked in the literature. Because neural networks are modeled after the structure and function of the brain, it is not surprising that neural networks, too, derive their speed and processing power from the simultaneous functioning of individual neural processors. In most applications, neural networks are implemented using computer hardware based upon parallel processors. This is not because conventional serial computers are functionally incapable of supporting the required processing, but because single threading is too slow. Indeed, some applications of neural networks, such as predicting bank failures and reviewing credit applications, perform adequately with serial processors. Even workstations and PCs have been used successfully for neural networks applications [23].

How Neural Networks Work: Layered Architecture

Because neural networks are constructed in layers (input layer, one or more middle layers, and output layer), very special hardware is needed to really achieve the benefits of this unique architecture [26]. Figure 10.1 illustrates this simple architecture [4].

Figure 10.1
Neural Network Architecture

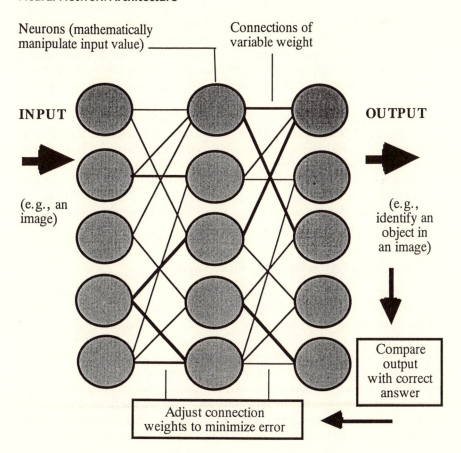

These special-purpose computers are referred to as neurocomputers, as compared to neural network applications being run on conventional computers. In a neurocomputer, there is a front-end processor that captures the input signal, one or more identical middle-layer processors that process the input signal and make inferences, and a back-end processor that formulates the best output based on inferential data. The front-end processor is made up of a matrix of individual processing units, each capable of accepting input information from a sensing device or directly from a digital source such as a database. With applications that are oriented to processing data from the environment in a manner that mimics the sensory processors of animals (vision, sound, etc.), the sensing device would typically capture analog signals. These signals would be digitized and then fed into one of the processors that make up the front-end processor or input layer. In order to increase throughput, a matrix of sensors would be used, each one feeding its digitized signal into a processor in the input layer dedicated to receiving and processing its input.

Each processor in the input layer is, in turn, connected to every processor in the first of the middle layers if more than one middle layer exists (again, each layer is a matrix of individual processing units). If more than one middle layer is required to process the input information, each processor in each level is connected to every processor in the adjacent layer. Multiple middle layers are required if the input information is very ambiguous or very complex or if the number of possible inferences that can be reached is very large. In the literature, the number of processors in each layer and the number of middle layers taken together is a measure of the "robustness" of the neural network. This apparently is considered to be an indication of the inherent power of the system. As with the input layer, each processor in the output layer is connected to every processor in the last of the middle layers (if more than one exist). This architecture makes the neurocomputer more or less symmetrical, although the input layer and the output layer do not need to contain the same number of individual processors (see Figure 10.1).

How Neural Networks Work: Input Layer

An interesting feature of neurocomputers is the structure of the input and the output layers. In the input layer, the number of individual processing units is determined by the number of "pieces" or segments the input signal is to be divided into and the speed with which the network is required to operate. Typically, the more pieces, the quicker the processing. In recognizing individual printed or handwritten characters, twenty-four segments may be sufficient to adequately recognize the character and provide speeds greater than a few characters per second. In attempting to recognize the faces of people exiting a commercial airliner, many more individual processing units in the input layer would be required. The human retina is made up of more than ten thousand sensory cells, for example [29]. This explains our visual acuity (the degree of image resolution). To achieve the same acuity, a neurocomputer would have to have the same number of processing units in its input layer. In a commercial example, the largest number of processing units in the input layer of a neurocomputer was found to be 512 [28]. Although this is a large number and the network is very robust, it pales in comparison to even simple biological networks. Most working networks described in the literature contained sixty-four or fewer processing units in their input layers. This allows input signals to be split into sixty-four individual segments that can be processed in parallel, an adequate number for many applications, but still primitive in comparison to biological systems.

How Neural Networks Work: Middle Layers

The identical middle layers of neurocomputers process signals from the input layer, make inferences concerning the values or characteristics of those signals, and transmit the single best answer (the strongest inference) to the output layer. Inferences are simply based on summing the weights assigned to the signals transmitted from each individual segment of the input layer as these signals pass through each of the middle layers of the network. As the input signals pass through the middle layers, a weight is assigned by each processor in each layer to each signal. These weights accumulate as the signal travels through each of the middle layers of the network. When the signal reaches the output layer, the weights of each of the original signals are compared to values previously stored in a knowledge base. The output layer simply finds the object in the knowledge base that most closely matches the pattern of weights that has been assigned to the input signal.

How Neural Networks Work: Output Layer

The function of the output layer is to match the final values given to the processed signal, which originally entered the neural network via the input layer, to a database or previously stored values. Although it is conceivable that a neural network could output a "not found" condition if the processed signal correlated very weakly with the base of stored values, most networks are designed to output a "best guess." For example, a network that is designed to perform OCR of machine-generated characters may have in its knowledge base the letters *A* through *Z*, lower case *a* through *z*, numerals 0 through 9, and a space. Characters input into the network (even if the image is distorted or blurred) will cause the network to output the character in its knowledge base that most closely resembles the original image. This matching will proceed even if portions of the original character are missing or if the input image is partially masked by "noise" (external data). Neural networks that must produce highly accurate output, such as those that scan handwritten addresses as input or automated letter sorters may be programmed to output an error signal if the network cannot make an inference that is within predetermined confidence levels. Input that cannot be recognized with confidence will require manual intervention to identify the questionable characters in the address. Eventually, unrecognizable addresses get sorted by hand [22].

LEARNING IN NEURAL NETWORKS: AN OVERVIEW

As compared to ES and virtually all other examples of artificial intelligence applications that require knowledge be entered into the system before processing begins, neural networks start out without a knowledge base. Through iterative processes of the neural network, the knowledge base grows as the network is taught correct responses to input signals. Unlike virtually all MSS, neural networks are not provided with quantitative descriptions of objects or patterns to be recognized. Neither are they provided with IF-THEN rules that would allow them to distinguish individual objects from similar objects. Instead, neural networks are presented with repetitive examples that attempt to display variety in approximately the same way that the universe or real objects display variety [16].

For the network to learn to recognize automobiles, images of all automobiles would have to be processed through the network until the network "learned" or "was taught" the correct name for each automobile image. With this learning accomplished, the network could begin to recognize images of automobiles that were distorted or had missing features. After sufficient learning, the network could learn to identify moving vehicles and those viewed at unusual angles.

Through the teaching process, neural networks discover or infer the relationships between various occurrences of inputs by processing the image and progressively developing and refining an internal matrix of weights. These weights are assigned to each attribute of the input image in relation to the degree to which that attribute correlates with the "right" output pattern. In this process, the neural network learns through adaptation, similar to the way biological systems learn. This capacity for adaptive learning is the characteristic that most distinguishes neural networks from ES applications. ES rely on inference that is based on an accurate representation of the domain of the problem. Traditional ES do not have adaptive capability. However, expert networks (a hybrid of neural networks and ES) are considered to be a very promising area of research and development activity [7]. These ES do possess learning capabilities.

Training Neural Networks

Because neural networks are designed to mimic biological processes in function as well as structure, it is not surprising that they are trained by rewarding desired (typically correct or nearly correct) responses and punishing undesired (wrong and not even close) responses. When the system responds with the correct output response to an input pattern, the reward consists of a strengthening of the current matrix of signal weights [20]. This is the key to understanding how neural networks learn to discriminate. It is the weight of the processed signal that is compared to the previously stored weights of right answers that allows the network to select the best (closest fitting) pattern from its knowledge base. This is compared to virtually all other MSS that utilize previously determined IF-THEN rules as their basis for discriminating among the universe of potential right answers. If the network selects the correct response to an input pattern, the weight of the processed signal (actually a matrix of weights corresponding to the number of processing elements in the output layer) goes into the knowledge base with a pointer to the right output pattern. In addition, an inference weight is set to correspond to the frequency at which the particular processed signal points to the particular output pattern is established for future use.

The first time a connection between a processed pattern weight and a (correct) response is input into the knowledge base, the inference strength connecting the pattern and response is set to 100 percent. When this same connection is found to produce a wrong answer, indicating an inability to accurately discriminate, the inference weight is decreased as a form of punishment. This method of increasing the weights of correct answers makes it more likely that a similar response will be produced by similar inputs in the future. When the system responds incorrectly, the punishment entails the adjustment of the inference weight downward so that the system will respond differently when the same input is received again.

Adaptive Learning in Neural Networks

Because the selection of the right output pattern is relative (the best match of options currently in the knowledge base), not absolute, further learning may lead to an even better match. In this way, a response that was right today because it was the best match in the knowledge base may be wrong tomorrow. This would occur if an even better response to the input pattern was learned today and added to the knowledge base. This adaptive learning capability is the feature of neural networks that offers the greatest potential benefit to business decision making. It is evident that a system that is capable of virtually unlimited learning capacity can, in a relatively short time, outpace the discriminating ability of other types of MSS (such as ES) that must be taught through additional programming.

Another feature of the more sophisticated neural networks is the ability to increase the speed of the adaptive learning through the feature of "back propagation" [10]. Using this technique, when a wrong response to an input pattern is given, the network is not only told that the response is incorrect, but the system is also given the right answer. For example, a system designed to identify pictures of automobiles may respond with a "1997 BMW IS" to an input pattern of a "1997 Mercedes Benz 280 C Class." A response of wrong from the system's trainer would weaken the inference weight of that response, reducing the probability of the same incorrect response to the same pattern—this is an inherent feature of all neural networks. In a system with back propagation, the system teacher response to the same incorrect response would be wrong—that is a "1997 Mercedes Benz 280 C Class." By providing both the signal of wrong and the right response, the network is given two valuable pieces of information. In this manner the inference weight of the incorrect answer can be decreased and the inference weight of the correct answer can be increased in a single processing cycle. This approach, reminiscent of how human learning occurs, greatly accelerates the rate of learning and adaptation in neural networks.

Another method of adaptive learning in neural networks is a technique whereby the trainer responds to the system's output not simply with a binary right/wrong response, but rather with a range of responses that identify the degree of rightness or wrongness. Gradations of responses may be simply "right," "very close," "close," "not close," and "way off." In very sophisticated systems, the range of feedback responses could become quite large. In such a system a range of numeric responses would probably be employed [6]. In any case, the more categories of feedback responses, the greater the ability of the neural network to tune its inference weights, resulting in more rapid adaptive learning.

If a human trainer is employed to educate the network, the capability of the network to learn from the fewest repetitions is a definite advantage. Overall, in neural networks as well as in biological systems, the more information that can be gained from a processing cycle, the better. As in all education, the more enriched the learning experience is, the more benefit it provides to the students (learner), whether they be biological or artificial.

Supervised Training

A neural network can be trained using a supervised or unsupervised methodology. In supervised training (most examples given in this chapter refer to this type), an input pattern is explicitly paired with a specific output response. Although many iterations may be required to accomplish this, the learning experience is not complete until the system produces the correct response. For example, the input may be a series of numbers, and the desired output may be the product of the numbers. The objective of the training process would be for the network to discover, through inference, the underlying pattern that forms the relationship between the input and the output patterns [11]. Prior to this training, the network is presumed to have no a priori knowledge of numbers, their relative magnitudes, or mathematical operations. Through repetitive training sessions, the neural network would have to infer that ten was twice the magnitude of five, and that multiplying numbers produces a quantity greater than that achieved by adding them (with a few notable exceptions). The key to this technique is the presence of a trainer capable of providing the correct answer. In this mode, the network only needs to infer the internal rules of relationships that connect the input pattern to the correct output pattern. It should be noted that supervised learning does not require a human trainer. Several successful neural networks utilize computers, videotape players, or other mechanized devices to provide the correct responses to input patterns.

Unsupervised Training

In unsupervised training, the neural network is presented with only the input pattern—no correct output or target pattern exists. The objective of the system is to detect, isolate, and identify patterns in the input. To accomplish this, the neural network must parse through the input information in a repetitive manner, organizing it until a consistent output (not necessarily the right output) is achieved each time the same input pattern is received. This is the equivalent to unstructured decision making. The characteristics of the output may be entirely unpredictable prior to training. It is for the human researcher to determine any value in the network's output. As with any repetitive process, conventional statistical methods may be utilized to determine if the pattern is intrinsic, random, or just noise. Just as with supervised training, the system in an unsupervised training mode discovers recurring patterns in the input information, but it must accomplish this without information about the expected, desirable, or correct output [11].

Although this undirected approach seems inherently inefficient, results that are not expected, intuitively obvious, or even perceived to be possible can be achieved. Using this approach, a neural network could be trained to recognize patterns in financial data that could be shown to have statistically significant predictive capabilities. Identifying patterns in stock market data for investment, speculation, or arbitrage purposes could easily provide the user of a neural network with profound economic advantages. This advantage may be in the form of insights that are not available to others or just plain speed in identifying momentary imbalances that could be exploited through arbitrage transactions. Technical stock market analysis attempts to identify patterns in financial data and capitalize on investment opportunities not available to those who do not use this technique (or whose interpretations of the patterns result in different insights). The use of neural networks for this type of research appears to offer considerable advantages to traditional, manual analytical techniques. The ready availability of enormous volumes of data in computer-readable form, much available online and even in real time (if one is willing to pay for it), would seem to indicate that the use of neural networks in unsupervised training mode could provide insights and advantages well beyond the scope of most people's imagination.

ADVANTAGES AND DISADVANTAGES
OF NEURAL NETWORKS

In addition to the benefits derived from providing inferences and insights not readily available through the use of other techniques and technologies, neural networks have other advantages over alternative MSS [16, 24]. These include the following:

- Avoids explicit programming and detailed IF-THEN rules
- No need for troublesome and expensive experts
- Inherently adaptable—no need to update the system when input changes
- No need to input a predefined knowledge base
- Dynamic system that continues to improve with use
- Able to process erroneous, inconsistent, and incomplete data
- Able to generalize from information context or other clues
- Creates abstractions from diverse data
- Uses common sense to make educated guesses

Similar to other MSS, neural networks are not without their drawbacks. These shortcomings include the following [18, 23]:

- Hard to trace steps taken in process of making inferences (i.e., there is no explanation capability)
- One must monitor output in order to deliver correct results
- Hard to determine reliability and accountability of black box approach
- Many repetitive training steps may be required
- Scarcity of available talent and expertise
- May require special-purpose computers not commercially available
- Certain amount of trust involved

APPLICATIONS OF NEURAL NETWORKS: AN OVERVIEW

Neural networks are theoretically capable of any information processing task we can perform. Currently, however, neural networks have been most effectively applied to three tasks within the broad field of pattern recognition—classification, associative memory, and clustering [18]. Classification involves the assignment of input patterns to predefined groups or classes based upon patterns within the input data itself. Recent applications of neural networks to classification tasks include the following: optical recognition of handwritten and printed characters (this may prove to be a very significant step for automating the source data); target recognition and acquisition of radar and sonar images; grouping financial instruments by risk class (this may be used for capital structure analysis); and identification of plastic explosives in luggage.

Associative memory (also called a content-addressable memory) involves the ability to retrieve a complete pattern from the knowledge base using only an element or subset of the original pattern. Recent applications of neural networks to associative memory tasks include identification of fingerprints based on incomplete images and prediction of movements in financial markets.

Clustering involves the ability to compress or filter input data without losing important information. Recent applications of neural networks to clustering tasks include clustering bonds into homogeneous (but not predefined) risk classes based on financial statements and grouping loan applications into risk classes.

NEURAL NETWORKS IN ACTION

There are numerous real-life applications of neural networks reported in the literature. The following is a list of some of the areas that neural networks have been successfully employed [1, 5, 9, 13, 14]: bankruptcy prediction, credit rating, data validation, financial forecasting, industrial process control, machine diagnostics, material usage optimization, medical field, oil and gas exploration, production and manufacturing scheduling, quality control, risk management, sales forecasting, speech and pattern recognition, stock market, and target marketing.

OUTLOOK FOR NEURAL COMPUTING

With the possession of learning capabilities, neural networks offer remarkable opportunities to explore and enhance our own capabilities. Because they are designed to do the same tasks that we do well, these systems may provide benefits to mankind in a different way than other forms of automation and mechanization. Although neural networks are new and the technology is immature, the potential for exploring our own limitations as humans using these surrogate brains is currently unimaginable. These systems will undoubtedly serve us well in the future as powerful assistants to which we delegate repetitive tasks and mundane jobs. But, their greatest potential benefit to us will probably be in two areas: identifying fundamental patterns in our universe that we have so far overlooked and integrating with ES to form expert networks [7].

In the task of identifying fundamental patterns, the tireless processing of parallel processors will almost certainly identify patterns and relationships in our lives and environment that will provide insight into new ways to improve our lives. A well-designed neural network operating in unsupervised training mode with access to the enormous databases available to us could identify patterns that are, even now, beyond our comprehension. In addition, the integration of the inferential capabilities and speed of neural networks with the user-friendliness of ES could allow us to benefit from the strong features of both technologies. These developments will open up new areas for research and development efforts and allow us to learn more about our own intellectual and perceptive capabilities, as well as provide greater insights about our environment.

SELECTED NEURAL NETWORKS PRODUCTS AND SERVICES

The following are selected examples of products in the neural networks environment. For detailed information, you should contact the vendor of the particular service or product [3].

CAD/Chem Modeling and Optimization System (AI Ware) is a product design tool for chemists. CAD/Chem automatically develops neural network models of formulation data, discovering the underlying relationships between ingredients, processing, and product properties. GAs are used for finding optimal formulations according to current design preferences and constraints expressed with fuzzy logic. Two- and three-dimensional graphics help visualize relationships and sensitivity.

IDIS Predictive Refinement Module (Information Discovery, Inc.) analyzes predictive modes such as neural networks for success and failure and pinpoints where the model works best. The module automatically builds a hit-and-miss database and a critique database for analysis and suggests where to improve the neural predictive model or that a different model should be used on some data segment.

Neural Network Toolbox (MathWorks, Inc.) is a collection of MAT-LAB functions for designing and simulating neural networks. It also includes unsupervised training functions that use associative learning rules for competitive layers, feature map layers, and Hopfield networks. The Toolbox integrates with MAT-LAB, a numeric computing visualization environment, and runs under various platforms.

NeurOn-Line (Gensym Corp.) is a graphic, object-oriented neural network software package capable of online adaptive learning that is integrated with an ES shell.

NeuroSolutions (NeuroDimension, Inc.) is a Windows-based neural network simulation environment that supports static, fixed-point, and trajectory learning through back propagation, recurrent back propagation, and back propagation through time. Because of its object-oriented design, NeuroSolutions provides the flexibility needed to construct a wide range of learning paradigms and network topologies.

Propagator (ARD Corporation) is a neural network development system with a graphic interface. It has three dynamic graphs, up to five layers (32,000 nodes/layer), data scaling, and C/C++ source code generation.

Stock Prophet Version (Future Wave Software) is designed to perform the preprocessing of data for application of neural networks to market timing. It also performs evaluation of neural network indicators for your choice of markets through profitability testing. It can generate larger training files, includes new indicators, and has several other features that make the development of neural network trading systems even easier.

VantagePoint (Mendelsohn Enterprises, Inc.) is a pretrained trading system that uses neural networks to perform synergistic market analysis, combining technical, intermarket, and fundamental data inputs. VantagePoint also gives the strength of the move and forecasts whether the market is about to make a top or bottom.

SUMMARY

This chapter provided a detailed discussion of neural networks (neural computing) as one of the growing applications of artificial intelligence and MSS and compared and contrasted neural computing with digital computing and neural networks with ES. It also explained various types of pattern recognition and the working fundamentals of neural networks, introduced various types of learning in a neural network environment, and presented several advantages and disadvantages of neural networks. The chapter concluded with several applications of neural networks and a selected listing of commercial products and services for neural networks design and implementation.

REFERENCES

1. Azoff, E. Michael. "Extracting Meaning from a Neural Network Solution." *Neurove$ Journal* (January/February 1995): 7–10.
2. Barron, Janet J. "Chips for the Nineties and Beyond." *Byte* (November 1990): 342–350.
3. Berg, Tor D. "Neural Networks Resource Guide." *AI Expert* (June 1995): 35–42.
4. Brady, Herb. "The Neural Computer." *Technology Review* (August/September 1990): 45.
5. Brockett, Patrick L., William W. Cooper, Linda L. Golden, and Utai Pitak Jong. "A Neural Network Method for Obtaining an Early Warning of Insurance Insolvency." *Journal of Risk and Insurance* 61 (September 1994): 402–428.
6. Brunak, Sore, and Benny Lautrup. *Neural Networks—Computers With Intuition.* New York: Times Book, 1984.
7. Caudill, Maureen. "Expert Networks." *Byte* (October 1991): 110.
8. "Computers That Come Awfully Close to Thinking." *Business Week* (June 2, 1986): 93.
9. Enrado, Patty. "Application Watch." *AI Expert* (June 1995): 48.
10. Gabriel, Michael, and John Moore. *Learning and Computational NeuroScience: Foundations of Adaptive Networks.* Cambridge, Mass.: MIT Press, 1990.
11. Hawley, Delvin D., John D. Johnson, and Dijjotam Raina. "Artificial Neuron Systems: A New Tool for Financial Decision Making." *Financial Analysis Journal* (November/December 1990): 63–72.
12. Jubak, Jim. "Think Like a Bee." *Venture* (January 1989): 48–52.
13. Kestelyn, Justin. "Application Watch." *AI Expert* (May 1991): 72.

14. Kestelyn, Justin. "Application Watch." *AI Expert* (February 1991): 71–72.

15. Khanna, Tarun. *Foundations of Neural Networks*. Reading, Mass.: Addison-Wesley, 1990.

16. Kirrane, Diane E. "Machine Learning." *Training and Development Journal* (December 1990): 24–29.

17. Klein, Elizabeth. "Thinking Machines and New Expertise." *Savings Institutions* (February 1992): 37–38.

18. Li, Eldon Y. "Artificial Neural Networks and Their Business Applications." *Information Management* 27 (1994): 303–313.

19. Meiklejohn, Ian. "This Does Not Compute—Yet." *Management Today* (November 1989): 181–184.

20. Pao, Yoh-Han. *Adaptive Pattern Recognition and Neural Networks*. Reading, Mass.: Addison-Wesley, 1989.

21. Rochester, Jack B. "New Business Uses for Neuro Computing." *I/S Analyzer* (February 1990): 1–12.

22. Schantz, Herbert E. "An Overview of Neural OCR Networks." *Journal of Information Systems Management* (Spring 1991): 22–27.

23. "Software Developed for Using Neural Network Technologies in Problem Solving." *Aviation Week and Space Technology* (June 17, 1991): 216.

24. Stein, Richard Marlon. "Real Artificial Life." *Byte* (January 1991): 289–298.

25. Tam, Kav, and Melody Kiang. "Managerial Applications of Neural Networks: The Case of Bank Failure Predictions." *Management Science* (July 1992): 926–927.

26. Touretzky, David S., and Dean Pomerleau. "What's Hidden in the Hidden Layers?" *Byte* (August 1989): 227–233.

27. Waibel, Alex, and John Hampshire. "Building Blocks for Speech." *Byte* (August 1989): 235–245.

28. "What the Brain Builders Have in Mind." *The Economist* (May 2, 1987): 94–96.

29. Wright, David P., and Christopher Scofield L. "Divide and Conquer." *Byte* (April 1991): 207–210.

Glossary

adaptive design A systems design methodology that advocates an evolving process in building a MSS.

algorithmic languages Any standard procedural computer languages such as C, FORTRAN, BASIC, or Pascal used for developing an artificial intelligence application.

artificial intelligence Computer applications that try to mimic human thought behavior for solving problems. They include expert systems, neural networks, patterns recognition, and so forth.

back propagation In neural networks using this technique, when a "wrong" response to an input pattern is given, the network is not only told that the response is incorrect, but the system is also given the "right" answer.

classic life-cycle approach A systems design methodology that follows a series of well-defined steps for the construction of a MSS. The steps include problem definition, feasibility study, systems analysis, systems design, systems implementation, and post-implementation audit.

crisp logic Another name for traditional logic to differentiate it from fuzzy logic. In crisp logic, the three logical operations AND, OR, and NOT return either a 1 or a 0.

crisp set Traditional, classical, or crisp sets have strict membership criteria in which an object is either completely included or excluded from the set. They are mathematical sets with definitive boundary points (e.g., those with a score of 70 are passed; those with a score less than 70 are failed).

critical success factors Those issues that make or break a business. Different organizations, divisions, and individuals have different types of critical success factors. For example, in a financial institution, the interest rate may be considered the critical success factor.

database A collection of a series of integrated files stored in a central location. A database can include only one file.

data flow diagram (DFD) A graphic tool that illustrates the flow of information in a system.

data warehouses Contain read-only snapshots of corporation data that are periodically refreshed. They can be organized and classified in different fashions for effective decision making.

decision support systems (DSS) A computer-based information system consisting of hardware, software, and the human element designed to assist any decision maker at any organizational level. However, the emphasis is on semistructured and unstructured tasks.

desktop conferencing A conferencing type that uses the workstation as the conference interface, it also runs applications shared by the participants. Modern desktop conferencing systems support multiple video windows per workstation.

dialog management Hardware and software used as a component of a MSS that provides user access to the system.

direct (crash) conversion A conversion method that stops the old system and starts the new system right away.

drill-down capability A very important feature of an executive information system (EIS) that allows access to multilayered information on request. For example, at the first layer an EIS may report the performance of a company in eight sales regions. In the next layer, a marketing executive may be interested in the northwest region, the analysis of which can be further broken down.

DSS generators (DSSG) A combination of hardware and software used for development of a MSS. They usually include most of the features and capabilities needed by the MSS. Microsoft Excel is an example.

DSS tools (DSST) Hardware and software used for the development of a MSS. They can be programming languages such as C or a graphic terminal.

economic order quantity (EOQ) An inventory model that minimizes the total cost of inventory by ordering the right amount on certain dates.

electronic data processing A computer-based information system designed for processing structured tasks such as inventory and payroll processing.

electronic meeting systems (EMS) Teleconferencing and other technologies that enable decision makers to meet electronically without leaving their offices.

end-user computing A method for the construction of a MSS by end-users using commercially available software products.

executive information systems (EIS) Computer-based information systems designed to analyze both external and internal data for the key executives with drill-down capabilities. Ease of use and providing information related to the critical success factors are essential.

expert systems (ES) Computer-based information systems designed to solve problems in a narrow field that have been successfully solved by the human expert previously. These systems use heuristics in a given field.

expert systems shells (ESS) Software packages that include most of the features and capabilities needed for the construction of an expert system. First Class is an example.

expert systems tools (EST) Artificial intelligence or high-level programming languages used for the development of an expert system. LISP or C are two examples.

feasibility study Investigation of the desirability of a MSS from four major dimensions: economic, technical, social, and time.

flowchart A graphic tool that illustrates the logic and information flow in the system.

forecasting models Mathematical and statistical models that generate the best possible forecast based on the past data.

fuzzification The process of fuzzifying an element by combining actual values (e.g., the temperature of a liquid) with stored membership functions to produce fuzzy input values.

fuzziness A term that expresses the ambiguity that can be found in the definition of a concept or the meaning of a word or phrase (e.g., usually, most often, or rarely).

fuzzy logic A kind of logic using graded or qualified statements rather than ones that are strictly true or false. The results of fuzzy reasoning are not as definite as those derived by strict logic, but they cover a larger field of discourse.

fuzzy sets Sets that do not have a clearly defined membership but rather allow objects to have grades of membership from 0 to 1.

genetic algorithms (GAs) These apply a set of adaptive procedures used in a computer system that are based on Darwin's theory of natural selection and survival of the fittest. These systems demonstrate self-organization and adaptation on the basis of exposure to the environment.

geographic information systems (GIS) An information system that consists of computer hardware, software, geographic data, and personnel, designed to effectively capture, store, update, manipulate, analyze, and display all forms of geographically referenced information.

geographic information systems objects Include point, line, and area. Points are the intersection of lines on a map (e.g., a customer location, a dealership location, the location of a fast-food restaurant, or the location of an airport). A line is usually a series of points on the map (e.g., a street, a road, or a river). An area is usually a section of the map (e.g., a particular zip code such as the zip code for the southwest region of the city of Portland, or the San Diego Zoo on the San Diego maps).

goal-seeking analysis The user establishes a goal and by manipulation of other variables in the system tries to achieve that goal.

graphical user interface (GUI) An icon-based system with pull-down menus that can be accessed by using a mouse (instead of the keyboard) for easy user/system interface.

group decision support systems (GDSS) Similar to decision support systems. However, by using communications technologies they provide decision-making support for a group of decision makers regardless of their geographic locations.

group support systems (GSS) Computer-based information systems designed to support a group of decision makers making and implementing decisions regardless of their geographic locations. They include GDSS, EMS, and GroupWare.

GroupWare A MSS that supports groups of decision makers engaged in a common decision-making task by providing access to the same shared environment and information. The shared environment may be in the form of a memo, a single file, or an entire database.

hybrid systems A combination of one or more systems into a hybrid for taking full advantage of the strengths of each system. Hybrids of fuzzy logic, genetic algorithms, expert systems, and neural networks are very popular.

hypermedia An extension of hypertext. It combines text, images, sounds, and full-motion video in the same document. The user can access various information by clicking the hypermedia links.

hypertext An approach to data management in which data are stored in networks of nodes connected by links.

intermediary The individual who serves as a liaison between the MSS users and the data-processing personnel.

iterative design A design methodology that advocates an iterative process for the construction of a MSS.

knowledge acquisition Extracting, structuring, and organizing the knowledge from a human expert or experts and representing it in machine-readable forms.

knowledge engineer An individual similar to a programmer or analyst in a decision support system environment. The knowledge engineer must have an extensive computer background, communication skills, and general knowledge about the field.

knowledge engineering environment Used for expert systems development. Includes an elaborate multiwindow, icon, graphic, and blackboard-like environment. It is expensive and requires high-powered personal computers or workstations.

knowledge representation Writing down in some language or communication medium, descriptions, facts, objects, or pictures that correspond to a real-world situation.

management information systems (MIS) Computer-based information systems designed to generate periodic reports for middle management.

managerial designer A designer who is concerned with the managerial issues of a MSS development. These issues include types of data, sources of data, system security, and so forth.

membership The degree of inclusion in a set. Fuzzy sets have values between 0 and 1 that indicate the degree to which an element has membership in the set. At 0, the element has no membership; at 1, it has full membership.

middle-out methodology A design approach that starts with the most immediate problem and then applies both the top-down and bottom-up methodologies for the construction of a MSS.

model A representation of the real-life system. It typically includes a series of variables, relationships, and constraints.

model base A component of a MSS that stores mathematical and statistical models and model-based management systems for the MSS utilization.

multimedia The ability to present and transfer information through more than one medium at a time. This may include voice, data, images, full-motion video, and animation.

neural computing Computer applications that learn by doing various tasks. They try to simulate the function of the human brain.

nonoptimization models Mathematical and statistical models that do not provide the best solution. They only illustrate the outcome of certain actions taken by the decision maker. They include forecasting, decision-tree, and queuing models.

optimization models Mathematical and statistical models that provide the best possible solution by a rigorous analysis of all the variables and constraints imposed on the system. They include linear programming, PERT, and CPM models.

outsourcing Using outside sources and consultants for the construction of a MSS.

parallel conversion A conversion method that advocates running the old and new system simultaneously until the new system is fully operational.

phased-in–phased-out conversion A conversion method that advocates the conversion of one part (phase) of the system at a time.

pilot conversion A conversion method that advocates the introduction of the MSS to a small part of the organization, such as a division or department, before its widespread introduction.

product life cycle Applying the four distinct phases of product life cycle to the construction of a MSS. These include introduction, growth, maturity, and decline.

prototyping Construction of a small-scale system before the large-scale construction of a MSS. They include four different types: illustrative or throwaway, simulated, functional, and evolutionary.

raster (in graphic information systems) Divides the coverage area into grid cell series in either a detailed or thematic basis. A thematic map is a map that displays different quantitative ranges of data by varying colors, textures, symbols, or embedded charts.

real-time computer conferencing A conferencing type that allows a group of users who are either gathered in an electronic meeting room or physically dispersed to interact synchronously through their workstations or terminals.

sensitivity analysis It measures the range or elasticity of a variable by changing other variables in the system.

specific DSS (SDSS) A decision support system (DSS) developed either from DSS tools or DSS generators that solve a specific problem (e.g., a DSS for advertising allocation budget).

specific expert systems (SES) Expert systems developed from either expert system tools or shells to perform a specific task in a given discipline. XCON, XSEL, and XSITE, developed by Digital Equipment Corporation and Carnegie-Mellon University, are examples of SES.

subroutine A series of codes written in a particular language for solving a specific task.

supervised training In neural networks, input pattern is explicitly paired with a specific output response. Although many iterations may be required to accomplish this, the learning experience is not complete until the system produces the correct response.

symbolic languages Languages such as LISP, PROLOG, or some dialect of these languages used for developing artificial intelligence applications. These languages process symbols. They can reach conclusions on a logical level, unlike the algorithmic languages.

technical designer A designer who is concerned with the technical issues of MSS development. These issues include sound user/system interface, comprehensive security measures, timely response, and so forth.

unsupervised training A neural network is presented with only the input pattern; no "correct" output or target pattern exists. The objective of the system is to detect, isolate, and identify patterns in the input data.

user interface A combination of hardware and software used as a component of a MSS that provides a comprehensive and easy-to-use access for the user.

validation In expert systems, construction involves testing the system by subjecting it to examples. There are different types of validation.

vector (in geographic information systems) Stores maps as spatial attribute tables for each type of map element, containing the point and line coordinates.

video teleconferencing A conferencing type that approximates face-to-face meetings. Television sets and cameras are used to transmit live pictures and sounds.

what-if analysis Measures the effect of changing one or more variables over the entire system.

Index

ABOUT THE AUTHOR

HOSSEIN BIDGOLI is Professor of Management Information Systems at California State University-Bakersfield. He is the author of 39 textbooks and dozens of technical articles and papers. He helped set up the first operational PC lab in the United States.

ISBN 1-56720-176-8